NORTH DAKOTA

MINNESOTA

SOUTH DAKOTA

Yellowstone R.

Missouri R.

ING

NEBRASKA

IOWA

Omaha
Council Bluffs

Fort Laramie
Scott's Bluff
Ash Hollow
Plattsmouth

N. Platte R.

Platte R.

Ogallala

S. Platte R.

St. Joseph

Boulder
Denver

KANSAS

Kansas City
Westport

MISSOURI

OLORADO

OKLAHOMA

Santa Fé

TEXAS

MEXICO

THE CALIFORNIA TRAIL

〰〰〰〰〰〰 **Main Trail with starting points**
– – – – – – – **Sublette's cut-off**
–·—·—·—· **Old Spanish Trail**
············· **Hastings' cut-off**
✕╫╫╫╫╫╫╫ **Manly – Bennett Trail through Death Valley**
–·—〰—·—· **Sutter's Fort by way of Walker Pass**

HARD ROAD WEST

GWEN MOFFAT

HARD ROAD WEST
ALONE ON THE CALIFORNIA TRAIL

THE VIKING PRESS   NEW YORK

Copyright © 1981 by Gwen Moffat

All rights reserved

First published in 1981 by The Viking Press

625 Madison Avenue, New York, N.Y. 10022

LIBRARY OF CONGRESS CATALOGING IN PUBLICATION DATA

Moffat, Gwen.

Hard road West.

1. The West–Description and travel–1951–

2. Overland journeys to the Pacific.   3. Moffat, Gwen.

I. Title.

F595.2.M54   917.9′0433   80-54196

ISBN 0-670-36145-3

Printed in the United States of America

Set in Photon Baskerville

CONTENTS

ILLUSTRATIONS

Erosion, Death Valley
Death Valley
Red Rock Canyon at the start of the Mojave Desert

All photographs are by the author. Cameras: Leica and Pentax ME.

MAPS

ACKNOWLEDGEMENTS

THE RESEARCH FOR this book couldn't have been undertaken without assistance from organisations and individual people on both sides of the Atlantic.

From the United States Department of the Interior to the newest seasonal ranger in the National Parks and Monuments, in the Forest Service and the State Parks and Reserves I received much practical help and far more information than I had asked for or expected.

I travelled by Pan Am, who flew me through an arrangement with the U.S. Travel Service, which comes under the Department of Commerce.

The assistance of individual Americans appears in context, with the exception of Malcolm and Janet McWhorter of Palo Alto who welcomed me, a total stranger, when the journey was over, who revived, informed and delighted while introducing me to yet another style of California living: the swinging intellectual life of Stanford.

As for finance: exclusive of air fares, this was raised from my advance on royalties and in loans from friends, one of whom also lent me her Leica. Advice on cameras, photography and processing was given me by Philip Evans, the Welsh photographer, whose patience with a complete tyro was unfailing, and unflinching.

Berghaus supplied the rucksacks and walking boots; for climbing I used a rock boot by Bryn Boots of Llanberis.

A great deal of research involved libraries. Staff of the American, and the British Library, of Gwynedd County and the local libraries in Caernarvon and Bangor were eminently attentive, sympathetic and resourceful.

Lastly there was the support and encouragement of Gollancz and Viking Penguin, in particular that of Livia Gollancz and Richard Barber, support which went way beyond any formal contract.

The book is a team effort then; there were people in front of me and people behind. Now we pass it on to the reader, who is part of it too.

SNOWDONIA   GWEN MOFFAT
1980

INTRODUCTION

THIS WAS THE endurance road: where wheel ruts ended at abandoned wagons and the emigrants continued with their remaining possessions on the backs of oxen and mules, walking through the wilderness. *My* road, the one which bears on my story, was metaphorical: a relationship, and a triangular one. There was my friend, the mountains and me. We had other loves but the relevant one was this sweet passion, not only for steep rock but for everything that went with it – the plants and animals, the sweeping ranges, shared solitude, shared danger.

It ended in a moment: the slip, the fatal fall, annihilation. Her body fought for three days but *she* did not come back, and for three days I raged because I could not give the last gift, the exchange of my life for hers. The morning after she died I woke to the sun shining through the bedroom skylight and, half-conscious, knew a moment of serenity. Later, travelling north to the Isle of Skye, I saw the Howgill Fells above the motorway and knew the same bliss, fleeting but infinitely reassuring. There were only two points of the triangle left but somewhere a third would be found. Meanwhile I would follow her philosophy, which had been that our purpose is to do the job that we have gravitated to. My job was to write and so I would continue writing.

A book was half-finished – a crime novel. In the intervals of managing a climbing hut on Skye I applied myself to the book, and wrote trash. So I went out and found gentians on the river bank; I went with people to the tall cliffs and was pushed into the lead. I discovered that I could still function; I was aware of achievement: in finding a strange flower, surmounting an overhang, in seeing beauty – but there was no feeling. And I could not write.

I returned to Wales and realised that if I didn't start work soon the alternative was regression to rage and self-torture that would end in breakdown.

With hindsight the similarity of life to a river started then. I had to get back in the stream. Once there I would be carried along. I didn't think of it that way. I thought that I must leave Wales and my empty cottage and go to a new country where I would be stimulated to write. I have always written best about strange places. But at my first plunge into the river the current shouldered me aside. I had told my publisher I would write a travel book and I suggested Yugoslavia or Ireland. A mistake; the first wasn't strange to me and the second wasn't wilderness.

The response was negative but I had no reaction and, indeed, it was the locations, not the idea that had been turned down. Within a few days I received a second letter from Livia Gollancz saying that she had a suggestion but it would mean my going to America. She asked me to go to London to discuss it.

I didn't dislike the thought of America but it held no attraction. Had I been asked I might have said I went to London for work and money, in that order, but basically I went because I was now in the river.

Across her desk Livia handed me *The Oregon Trail* by Francis Parkman. One of her directors had read it and, hearing of my proposal to travel, they wondered if I might follow the trail and write a book about it as it was now.

A school atlas was discovered and we found Oregon and the Missouri River. I regarded 2,000 miles of America without enthusiasm. Livia suggested I go to the American Library at London University, do some research and write a synopsis. I realised that my publishers wanted this book and thought I was the person to do it, and that the money involved meant that I could retain my cottage a little longer. The mortgage is always an albatross round an author's neck.

This was December 7, and with the chance of mail being held up over Christmas I must get the synopsis to Livia within two weeks since she wanted to take it to New York at New Year. Between my animal in-tuitiveness and my professional ability there is a welter of emotions. The emotions had been anaesthetised, the animal didn't enter the present situation but Livia, cool, collected, abrasive, threw out a challenge and up came the professional pride, not raring to go, but there.

The next day I spent at the American Library. The work was historical and geographical. I learned where the pioneers went, and why. I went home and found a different kind of book in my local libraries: human, reflective, stories of great endurance. I made another unimportant mistake. I wrote a synopsis full of facts and figures which was promptly thrown back by my agent with the comment that people knew their history. Implicit in the remark was the demand, 'Give us something real, give us passion, give us humanity.' Or that was how I read it, for even while that first synopsis was in the post I had returned compulsively to reading that was now far more than research. To hell with synopses and trying to convince people that I could write a book, to hell with the mortgage; I had found reality plodding westward at two miles an hour in a creaking wagon, in the sound of galloping hooves in the desert night, in dust and stars and a different, terrible sun. The second synopsis was no more than a distillation of this involvement, with a change of direction from the Oregon to the California Trail. Technically the latter made a grand design; it was a steady crescendo: plains, Rocky Mountains, deserts, and then, worn down by the deserts, the overlanders had the climax of the Sierras. I had known mountains for decades but the Great Basin was alien and frightening, for me as it had been for them. I had to go to the deserts.

Much of the California Trail is now followed by a main road, so, in order to see the country as the pioneers saw it, I would make diversions to north and south of my westward line and explore the areas that were still wilderness. I would follow the snow and the spring into the mountains. This would mean the deserts in high summer but if that was the only way to do it then that was how it would be done.

The second synopsis sold, in America as well as London, and the book was commissioned. On a spring morning I stood on the pavement outside the Pan Am building at Victoria, surrounded by my gear, alone, and exulting. For a moment I was utterly abandoned: a curious word that can be used for transcendental happiness and for a state beyond despair. I was exulting in my emptiness, in the knowledge that in the depths of the thing we call a soul, neither dead nor lost, joy lay curled like a sleeping cat.

This is the pioneers' story and, behind their suffering and survival, behind the beauty of the land and the gallantry of its travellers, is my own journey: at first following, then parallel, then fusing. It is a story of how the joy came back.

HARD ROAD WEST

1

FITTING OUT

LEAVING EUROPE FOR the first time is like being shot into space. Three thousand miles out over the Atlantic I looked down and saw shadows where there was no cloud, then noticed that the shadow was fringed with white. Threads of roads appeared as on a developing print and I thought in utter amazement: but people live down there.

The reaction was ridiculous. Americans, I told myself, were the same as us, many with a common ancestry; even the country would be different only in degree. The desert itself one had seen, of a kind, on the dry plateaux of south-east France. There was something of play in this attitude: playing down initial reaction so that I might be the more astonished in the event, but also, and more to the point, keeping a tight rein on myself. I knew my capacity for wonder, and my dislike for logistics, and for a while at least I must forgo the one in order to concentrate on the other. New York was for business.

Less so than I'd anticipated. I met my American agents for the first time and my publishers. Everyone was cordial, welcoming, brimming with vitality. At Viking Penguin I found Richard Barber, who was to be my editor. Young and enthusiastic, he demanded periodical reports, with maps, not for any technical reason but for a share in the fun. He gave me lunch, arranged a mail drop, telephoned me: a friendly voice in my hotel room chatting about the trip. I thought of Fabrice in *The Pursuit of Love*: '*Allons, racontez, madame.*'

I liked New York. I was unprepared for the beauty of its women, for young men on Wall Street who wore three-piece suits and gave directions with exquisite courtesy, for a building glimpsed at a crossing – a cliff and a flaring base of black glass. I saw the city from a skyscraper and I mooned over the Turners in the Frick collection, and on an evening of drizzle and low cloud I drove to La Guardia and boarded a little wet aeroplane for Omaha.

Whereas on the initial flight across the Atlantic I had clamped down on my excitement even at landfall, particularly at landfall, now all my antennae were bristling. I had never flown after dark and even while we were stationary I was thrilled by the sight of another aircraft oozing by on the tarmac, its belly lit up like a cruising shark. And there was the beauty of a city at night with its pattern of roads and motorways, and a river of darkness trimmed with orange, joined by the cobweb of a spangled bridge.

We took off through the clouds and found a gap along which we flew parallel with a sunset band of jade above the smouldering horizon. The ride was bumpy; there was heavy weather in the south with thunderstorms and flooding. It was snowing in the Rockies.

I had been corresponding with a historian in Omaha called Charles Martin. With his wife he met me at the airport and bore me off to a motel, leaving me with the assurance that tomorrow we should buy a car.

The first vehicle I looked at was a Scout International, something between a Land-Rover and a Range-Rover, and fully automatic. It was above my maximum price so we went to look at other vehicles but I kept walking past the Scout and eventually I put down the rear seat and stretched out on the floor. Cater-cornered, my toes just touched the tail-board when it was closed. I could sleep in it comfortably. The garage owner dropped $500 on the price. I stood back and looked at the truck, sand-coloured, solid, powerful – and waiting. This, I thought, is Old Crump, and I bought him.

Their owners invest machines with sex. Ships are always female, so are most of my cars, but Old Crump was male from the start although he was named for an ox, which is neutered. The animal belonged to one of the Forty-Niners who discovered Death Valley and he was one of the steadiest beasts that ever plodded the long road west.

Leaving the garage, the last big hurdle passed and the tiresome paper-work assumed by an expert (Charles was in insurance), I relaxed, the owner of a well-found wagon. 'What do you want to see?' Charles asked. The Missouri, I said.

Apart from a bird's eye view of the East River and the Hudson from the top of the World Trade Center, I had seen no American river and I thought of the Missouri as the first, which was fitting. In the early nineteenth century this waterway marked the edge of civilisation as the white man knew it.

The corridor to the Rockies was the valley of the Platte River which flowed for 600 miles across the plains to join the Missouri near Omaha, which is why most of the overlanders started here or in the vicinity. The Platte was the road west and as early as 1800 trappers were venturing as far as the slopes of the Rockies and bringing back furs, but three decades later there was still no white man's habitation between Oregon and Council Bluffs, between the Sacramento Valley and the Missouri: nearly 2,000 miles of desert, mountain and plain.

That May morning the river was basically the same even though it ran between strengthened banks. Swollen by melting snow it rolled towards the Mississippi – majestic and muddy, deep, wide and silent.

The overlanders crossed at various places, ferried by rafts and boats. At Omaha they assembled at Council Bluffs on the Iowa bank, and we drove to the top of strange knolls that were the only high ground in the great flood plain. The bluffs had the consistency of solidified mud, something with which I was to become familiar in the next six months. In their form they bore witness to the harsh climate, their miniature rounded buttresses scored by dry watercourses which would erode a few more inches with every spring. Here, where the suburbs lapped up the backs of the bluffs, where tulips were showing colour in cherished gardens, I sensed the violence of this land that was so new that the elements could be seen at work, grinding, shattering, pulverising.

I stayed in Omaha for four days. Charles had an extensive library and I took his books back to my room where I read until the print swam. We copied maps and texts, and he showed me every slide that he possessed which might have interest for me. He had been absorbed in the overland trail for decades, had followed the main route and its variants on foot and by car, and nothing pleased him more than to share this lifetime of knowledge with one who, in practice, knew nothing. We drove in a congenial party to see the sights and surveyed the great river, wandered in the restored fort, visited the Mormon cemetery where squirrels and jays played in the pines. A memorial stood to the Mormon dead, a couple bowed above the open grave of a child. I was suddenly embarrassed, a tourist, on the outside peering in, a *voyeuse*. What was I doing here, in a Mormon cemetery?

At two o'clock on a warm afternoon I stood at the intersection outside the Hinky Dink supermarket and studied the traffic system. So might the emigrants have waited, tense and cold, for the signal to move. Behind me Old Crump stood, loaded with all my possessions and two weeks' food, with the map open on the seat. I climbed behind the wheel and eased on to the highway. The journey had begun.

2

NEBRASKA

THE INTERSTATE WAS four lanes wide and the speed limit was only 55 m.p.h. Travel should have been smooth but the steering was so light that every frost-heave in the surface resulted in over-correction. At the garage they'd told me that I was unused to power steering, which was true; now, spinning that butterfly wheel as the miles unrolled, I was tense. Fortunately there was little traffic. I shook down to some extent but I was uneasy.

We passed through mixed farmland where barns were capped by secondary roofed structures astride the ridge that must serve for ventilation. I was curious to know when summer came to this country which, lush and green, was not all that different to an English shire in May. It had turned cool and against the overcast the vegetation and colours of fat cattle – Friesian, Charollais, Aberdeen Angus – were vivid as a primitive painting.

The plains were less flat than I'd expected; they swelled in gentle waves with trees grouped round the farmsteads, but the trees thinned out the farther west I went, and the farming changed. The soil was less fertile, the grass was not so forward and it was less green. There were more cattle and these were all beef herds. Farms had become ranches and each had its corral and, to English eyes, a superfluous number of horses.

The Platte valley went on for hundreds of miles. I had tried to envisage this wide corridor with its river so broad and shallow that the emigrants had said of it that it was a mile wide and an inch deep. I'd thought it would be evocative to travel through such a historic valley, but the pioneers had known an expanse that was virtually without trees and their vistas were far-ranging; now cottonwoods had taken root on the banks and sand-bars. This continuous and attenuated woodland would be good for wildlife but it meant that the only time the modern traveller saw the Platte was at the crossings. There it had a faintly formidable look, the apparent innocence of its shallows belied by the size of dead trees which lay, smoothed and whitened, like stranded dinosaurs.

Some hundreds of miles west of the Missouri the old travellers started to see buffalo so numerous that soon they darkened the plains. All the buffalo were gone now, all the land fenced, and I drove on wondering when, if ever, the fences would end, when I would see high ground.

About 150 miles out I did catch a glimpse of something to the north, something higher than the plains, but I had to drive another hundred miles before I saw a definite range. It was to the south of the road and only about 1,000 feet high but shortly fining down to shapes that were almost conical. I'd driven a long way with nothing to look at but the ground-swell of the high plains. Now the weather deteriorated. I saw the rain approaching from the west in a broad and gauzy curtain. My arms ached from the effort to keep the car straight, so I turned off the interstate at the ramshackle town of Ogallala. It was late and the only place still open was a sporting goods shop. I needed paraffin for my stove and they couldn't help me but they told me where there was a campground. I drove for nine miles across a bleak wet moor, found a track and nosed down it warily to come out on an empty space of gravel overhung by trees.

I ate bread and cheese while the rain lashed the roof and I speculated on the level of the snow-line. The temperature was about 37°F. I rearranged the truck for sleeping by climbing over the back of my seat and shifting the load to the front until there was room to get the sleeping bag across the floor. It was a very wet night, and my feet were cold.

I woke to a grey morning like a bad day in the Scottish Highlands, and to stress the similarity I saw that I was parked on the shore of a wide loch. Birds on the margin I took for ringed plover until I saw that they had two breast bands, which identified them as killdeer.

According to the radio there was a lot of snow ahead of me. I dressed in my cold weather gear and drove back to town, found a farmers' co-operative where I bought paraffin, a five-gallon water container and a cushion. I was having difficulty in seeing over the top of the steering wheel. I had breakfast on the shore of the lake, then trundled westward until I came to the place where the fences ended, at Ash Hollow, and for me the trail became visible and interesting.

It came along a low ridge which ended abruptly at Windlass Hill. A windlass was not used on the descent but they locked the wheels and everyone who was available hauled back on the wagons. There were no brakes. They would have skidded all the way down and in the steepest place the track had eroded until it was a stony gully.

Thinking to give the weather time to improve I drove to the Visitors' Center to see the museum. I was the only customer and, since I had an introduction from Charles, the superintendent showed me round himself. This was good as it meant I could handle things. He hefted an ox yoke and passed it to me. It was immensely heavy and I wondered how anyone could yoke oxen without help. Presumably two old beasts would have stood obediently side by side while the yoke was lowered, a bow fitted under each neck and pinned to the yoke. How was this

accomplished with an untrained animal? The milch cows took the place
of the oxen when the latter died of thirst or strain or tainted water, or
were shot by Indians. How did one get a milch cow under the yoke?

I was thinking of Eliza Ann Brooks whose husband left her in
Michigan when he went to California to the gold mines. Eliza got tired of
waiting so she wrote to him saying she was on her way and then left
Michigan to travel 2,800 miles with a wagon, two teamsters and six
children aged from four to thirteen, the eldest boy being eleven. One
teamster deserted when they reached the Missouri; the second she dismissed when he got too rowdy on July 4th. After that she was often alone
with her family, although sometimes travelling in company with Crow
Indians. They met the father coming east on a mule, out in the desert by
the Humboldt Sink. He hadn't long started, Eliza was near the end of the
journey. Some time after her death (she lived only six years after crossing
America) her husband rebuilt an old ghost town. Perhaps he did it as
some kind of memorial; at some point he must have had her in mind for
he quoted *Proverbs*, 'Where there is no vision, the people perish.'

In the museum's cases there were slim, lethal arrows, hair bridles (the
Indians had no bits, they tied the bridle round the lower jaw of the
pony), and a tepee the poles of which were shortened and abraded from
friction with the ground. These poles were the framework of the travois,
the only vehicular transport the Indians used. The front ends of two
poles were lashed to a horse, the hinder ends trailing. The space between
was bridged, probably by hide, and on this platform were carried the
old, the sick and the young, and all their household goods. Dogs drew
smaller versions of the travois.

The Indians had many dogs. Some tribes ate them, but then so did the
white Americans although they did so as a last resort, when other food
was unavailable.

I walked up Windlass Hill wearing my survival gear and I was still cold.
The temperature was about 33 degrees, in May.

The hill appears innocuous but it assumes a different aspect when you
look down it and imagine the covered wagons approaching this point:
tall, top-heavy, over-loaded. And this was the first of many similar
obstacles. Cringing inside my anorak, I looked westward and saw snow-
covered mountains, not a range but a line, the forerunners of the
Rockies. On that bitter eminence (my gloved hands deep in my pockets,
my shoulders hunched) I looked at them with a feeling of dull resignation, no longer the sophisticated traveller with snow ploughs to clear the
road and helicopters for rescue in the last resort, but one lone wagon-
driver contemplating the mountains that stand across the trail.

I dropped down the back of the ridge away from the full force of the wind – and almost immediately found a pasque flower. Overhead large buzzard-like birds wheeled on two-toned wings. The superintendent had said I'd see turkey vultures.

The country, seemingly devoid of habitation, was broken into dry scrubby ravines with scars and little ragged bluffs high up under the ridges. Although the only deciduous trees were the few cottonwoods in Ash Hollow, up here on the higher ground cedars had taken root in crevices so that the country was reminiscent of the Slovenian Karst but for the dry spikes of yucca and the occasional prickly cactus. And the rock was neither sandstone nor limestone; it resembled badly mixed concrete and crumbled at a touch. Massive plates of it overhung bases scooped concave by the wind. I traced back a line of bird droppings to a hole. A burrowing owl? I worked my way along this lonely slope and for all the company that showed, I was the only denizen of the plains; a happy thought after the traffic of the last ten days.

Climbing back to the crest of the ridge I found myself walking down the ruts of the trail and there I put up a deer. It went romping across the ravine below me and up the other side making an astonishing amount of noise in the dense undergrowth. I was accustomed to red deer trotting delicately through the heather of a Scottish moor.

The ruts were hypnotic. The strange deer brought me back to a reality that was unreal: the line of the Rockies in the west, the alien landscape. About my feet were small white lilies with yellow stamens, and unfamiliar vetches. As I turned back to the truck snow began to fall and I felt closer to the emigrants than to the present. Then I remembered that I was far ahead of the wagon trains; they couldn't start before the grass was a grazing length, so even with an early spring they couldn't have reached this point until the middle of May. But they never had it easy; if the weather was balmy when they reached Ash Hollow they'd be worried about early snow on the Sierras, and if it was hot they suffered from cholera.

Cholera was the scourge, and if there are fewer graves than there were deaths along the trail it is because many victims were buried under it, each team trampling the mound and the wagons rolling over it as they pulled out in the morning. The primary motive was to foil the coyotes, or Indians hard up for scalps. It is unlikely that the practice had any effect in stemming the spread of the cholera bacteria for in their congregating round the water sources everyone was at risk and only those with resistance could have survived.

From Ash Hollow I drove on through thickening snow. There were dipped headlights on the cars. Not wanting to pass a campground in this swirling gloom, I pulled off the road to look at the map, but the verge was waterlogged sand and Old Crump ploughed in and stalled. I was in a place that had a name but consisted of no more than a motel. Behind its lighted windows people looked out at me incuriously. The gear lever slotted nicely into four-wheel drive and I reversed to the road but, once there, couldn't get back to conventional drive. For five minutes I struggled and sweated while the traffic queued to pass. Eventually I blundered into two-wheel drive by accident and continued, fuming. I had meant to practise in private.

We ran out of the snow into clearer weather, but showers drifted across an immensity of space where the air was like crystal and about as cold. Away to the south stood two great bluffs powdered by the snow, Courthouse and Jail Rocks, and beyond them was the distant range, whether the same that I had seen from Windlass Hill or another was immaterial. They were all the Rockies. It was their presence that made me pause at a small town called Bridgeport; thinking that the passes would be blocked I spent the night in an hotel. In the morning there were several inches of snow on the truck and it was still snowing in a desultory fashion but the temperature was above freezing and the roads were slushy. About ten o'clock I drove south to look at Courthouse and Jail Rocks.

They lay five miles south of Bridgeport, seven miles south of the Platte. The clarity of the air is demonstrated by the fact that the emigrants, although familiar with the prairies east of the Missouri, misjudged the distance by anything up to five miles. A contributory element in a wilderness devoid of habitation and trees was the absence of scale. Many who turned aside to visit the bluffs failed to reach them. It could be done speedily on a good horse but that tired the horse for its proper work.

The bluffs were approached by a road that was covered by several inches of untracked snow. I drove fast, aware on the steepest rise, as the tyres strove to grip in a bovine manner, that the surface was gravel, not tar, and then we ran out on a level sweep from which there was no exit except on foot.

A fierce north-easterly was blowing. I dressed in winter gear from balaclava to gaiters. I had glanced at Courthouse as I drove up and dismissed the thought of going to the top. It looked like solidified mud but was a conglomeration of volcanic ash, sand and clay. The rises between ledges would be devoid of holds and the ledges themselves sloped outwards and were deep in the new snow.

So I walked round the rock. Shallow gullies radiated from its base and these were choked by vegetation on which lay about six inches of powder. I slithered into the gullies and climbed out by cutting steps with the ice axe up banks of red mud veneered with slime.

The rocks stand at the end of an ill-defined ridge stretching westward, a ridge which, although still far from the Rockies, marks the transitional region between the peaks and the plains. In reality the plains have been rising all the way across Nebraska; the significance of Courthouse and Jail Rocks is that at this point the rise becomes perceptible.

Eastward of Jail Rock the cultivated plain ran almost to the foot of the bluffs, the pastures and the tilled land holding little snow. Lapped by that strange sea of civilisation, the bluffs looked curiously contrived, as if they remained on sufferance, not from the elements but from man.

I drove on towards a brightness in the west, and out of the flat land rose Chimney Rock. Behind it was the eroded scarp of the Wildcat Hills, and it stood in isolation, a conical and symmetrical mound, crowned by a column like an old tooth with the decayed roots uppermost. The shaft is 150 feet high and there is no record of its having been climbed.

I wasn't tempted to a closer inspection. I'd walked round one bluff today, and contouring a consistently angled slope with one leg higher than the other is an awkward form of progress. Besides, the sun was shining in the west.

I pushed on towards Scott's Bluffs. Old Crump was increasingly in need of a garage. For some time there had been a noise, vaguely familiar, in one of the hub caps, but leaving it unidentified gave me an excuse to approach an expert. I could no longer convince myself that the light steering was a result of my own inexperience and not something radically wrong.

The range of Scott's Bluffs is massive enough to embrace two passes and it was by way of these that nineteenth-century travellers avoided badlands, which, at a lower altitude but wickedly contorted, stretch from the foot of the bluffs to the Platte. Emigrants on the north bank of the river had the advantage here. This was the Mormon Trail although the Mormons never confined themselves to it and in the main, before and after the founding of Salt Lake City in 1847, people stayed south of the river and crossed Scott's Bluffs by way of Robidoux Pass following, in the first instance, an Indian trail.

The first white men to use the pass were a party of trappers led by Robert Stuart travelling east on what came to be known as the Oregon Trail. John Jacob Astor had sent people overland by way of the Missouri and the Yellowstone River to link up with a seaborne group sailing round the Horn in the *Tonquin*. The aim had been to trap, and to trade with the Indians of the Pacific coast but the Indians were hostile and the ship was blown up with her attackers on board. Stuart returned through Robidoux Pass in 1812 carrying the bad news to Astor in St Louis.

In 1850 the other pass, Mitchell, came into use, slightly shortening the route. The modern highway goes over this pass and here the trail is a deep cut in the arid soil, for the ground was so rough that each wagon followed in the track of the one ahead. The dust must have been appalling. The Pony Express crossed Mitchell Pass, then the Overland Mail and the stagecoaches – and finally Old Crump rattling up the gradient where his namesake had plodded 130 years before.

It was late when we came over the pass into the glare of the sun. The bluffs were still snow-covered, the Visitors' Center was closed, I couldn't find the campgrounds marked on the map, and the thing in the hub cap was abominable. We came down the western slope of the pass, looped back under the cliffs to cross the Platte and enter Scottsbluff, a town which was at one time the centre of the open range country, before the fences came.

I found a campground beside the zoo, where the quiet of evening was broken occasionally by curious cries. The site was rough but spacious, scattered with trees, and empty except for two of the motorised caravans the Americans call campers. The lavatories were sparkling, and heated.

Supper took a long time to prepare. The paraffin can had leaked on to the floor and soaked the food cartons. I salvaged most of the food but for a while no meal was free from the taint of paraffin.

I sat on the tailboard watching the moon rise – a large cool moon as quiet as the night. I would see five more moons in America. The thought was marvellous.

I didn't sleep out, anticipating difficulty in drying the sleeping bag if it snowed, but I left the back open and put my feet in the larger of the two rucksacks. There was heavy frost and the morning was bitterly cold. I waited until the sun reached the sleeping bag before I got up.

I was directed to a garage where the foreman found a loose wheel-nut in the hub cap. He was amazingly handsome – the melting pot, I thought – and I asked him to give Old Crump a road test. On his return he put the truck on the ramp and found a broken bolt on a shock absorber. The shocks were not a set anyway. While they fitted a new set I wrote postcards in the customers' lounge and drank pale, frail coffee from a dispenser. The bill for the shock absorbers was $103. I thought it was cheap.

Now Old Crump handled like a powerful lorry: steady as a rock, responsive to the wheel and not making his own unpredictable decision every time we hit an excrescence in the road surface. I drove up to Mitchell Pass singing, and so to the top of the main bluff by a road where the ambience was almost alpine.

Looking back the way I had come, over the shadowy plain where the showers moved so slowly they appeared stationary, I could make out the column of Chimney Rock, while westward and 100 miles away stood a snowy mountain that must be Laramie Peak. In 1834, prior to the building of Fort Laramie, a trapper called Hiram Scott had been taken ill this side of Laramie Peak. His party were returning east before the winter set in and wouldn't stop. But two men were left with him although they wouldn't stay either, and after a while they left him to die and pushed on to overtake their party. But Scott didn't die there. The following season those same companions came west again and found his body under Scott's Bluffs. Weakened by illness, without horse or gun (they were too valuable to leave with a dying man), he had made his way 50 miles to die near the water now called Scott's Spring.

3

DINOSAUR

THAT NIGHT I slept on the Wildcat Hills. This was buffalo country and between here and Laramie River the early travellers might halt to make meat, hunting the buffalo and drying the flesh for the rest of the journey. The skill and courage of such hunters in the days of muzzle-loading guns was high. The horse would be going at a hard gallop and, after the first shot, which may only have wounded the quarry, reloading was a matter of pouring powder down the muzzle and the bullet after it. Three or four bullets were carried in the mouth. The stock was then struck hard on the pommel, but if this failed to seat the bullet there was a chance of the gun exploding when the rider took aim. The risk could be eliminated by the use of a ramrod, carried round the neck on a string, but its use involved another intricate action. The ground was often undermined by the burrows of prairie dogs and, if man and horse escaped injury from a fall, there was the chance of being trampled by the herd or gored by a wounded beast. Whatever the outcome the chase always tired and often exhausted the horse which would have to be rested, leaving the owner without a mount. Few people could afford two saddle horses.

In the morning the sun was brilliant on the Wildcat Hills and I thought of a canyon in Colorado of which I knew little more than the fact of its existence. At some point I had to leave the main trail and go south; this seemed as good a time as any and it would give the snow a chance to recede from the high passes. So I breakfasted and packed the gear, arranged the maps and the cameras, and we came over the Wildcats and rolled down the shimmering roads where nine-tenths of the world was sky.

It was a bare country. The only trees were clumped about the few ranches or planted for shade in the back streets of the odd small town where I looked straight down the wide main street to the continuation of the plain at the other end. Against this the store fronts, the dusty trucks, the one set of traffic lights suspended from a cable above the one intersection, had an air of defiance in a land of elemental exuberance.

I sat on the tailboard eating lunch in a lay-by so spacious that fumes from the occasional truck didn't reach me. I chewed on my meat loaf and rye reflecting that, although the food could be as awful as reputed, space was bigger than they said. The clouds towered. Smears of showers hung in the atmosphere neither progressing nor falling, motionless. It could be intimidating, living on the plains.

A blackbird, an American species with a yellow head, landed on a fence post and cocked an eye for crumbs. I rolled on towards Colorado rejoicing in the difference of this country, revelling in the awareness that the journey was only three days old, and another blackbird flitted across the road – and this one had scarlet wings.

It took me a week to reach my destination. I stayed with a friend at Boulder hoping that I might do some routes on the Front Range but the snow was down to 8,000 feet and everything was in avalanche condition. I managed to get high enough to gloom at the east face of Long's Peak and see what we might have done two months later, and I had fun on some granite pinnacles called the Flatirons above Boulder. I went shopping for gaps in my equipment – maps, a new stove – and, on a hot afternoon, I came to a new kind of country up in the north-west corner of Colorado, where a little dirt road left the main highway and ran out into limitless stretches of sage. Of course they couldn't be limitless but since they were bounded only by the horizon and one had the impression that having reached it one would see the same country ahead as far as the next horizon, for all the difference it made, the view was infinite.

The country looked flat but, once into it, it was a maze of dry gullies of varying depths. To my delight I realised that these were called draws, one of the advantages of a large-scale map. The ground was pale and hard: open flats alternating with a sparse and scrubby woodland of juniper and small conical pinyon pines, dense and symmetrical. Although early evening, it was still too hot for big animals to be out and in seventeen miles I saw nothing other than chipmunks and butterflies except, surprisingly, one cow and her calf, solitary in the scrub. That brought home in a practical fashion the vastness of the land and the poverty of the soil. This was range country. Somewhere in here a whole herd was hidden, and the fact that they were so scattered (I saw two in seventeen miles) must mean a colossal acreage to each cow – fifty acres, sixty? I wondered where they drank; I could see no water in the gullies.

The road surface was quite good and even nursing Old Crump I could have driven faster than the 15 m.p.h. that I favoured but a gentle pace suited my state of mind. I was adjusting to a place without traffic, without people, without habitations.

After an hour I crossed a ridge at about 7,000 feet and came to the boundary of Dinosaur National Monument. The trail descended to a long bench on the edge of which stood Haystack Rock: a grey, lumpy pile from my angle but showing the top of a shadowed wall that hinted at space before it was blocked off by a sunlit rim.

We ran out on a level called Cactus Flat and turned west. At the rear of Haystack I eased up a side-track to a No Camping sign, switched off the engine and climbed out into the still and brilliant evening.

I stretched cramped fingers and reflected that I could be twenty miles from the nearest human being. That was pleasant enough but what made me tense with excitement was a sound, a long rising whisper. I walked a few steps through the pines and came out on the canyon rim.

The river was the focal point, not only for its intrusive and continuous voice but because the plunging cliffs and the sloping talus under them drew the eye down to this mud-coloured riband so far below that the cataracts showed as long diagonals on the surface. The drop was so impressive that I would have put it at 3,000 feet but for the fact that I could distinguish individual trees on the river bank, and that made it nearer a thousand. I might be adjusting to the spirit of the land but not to its scale. I was over-correcting.

I couldn't see what was directly below me; the edge was formed from a shaky sandstone with parallel fissures in it and although these faults could have been there for decades, the ambience was too awe-inspiring to venture beyond them. But I could look outwards. I stood almost at one end of a massive amphitheatre enclosing an elbow of the river, and the opposite horn of this arc was a line of red cliffs and tottering yellow buttresses above steep scree slopes dotted with diminutive trees.

I turned and moved along to Haystack which, from the back, was merely a 200 foot point on the rim, and that only a matter of sloping ledges and incipient walls, but the front of which dropped like a plumb-line for nearly 1,000 feet.

I scrambled round the back of the bluff to see what the canyon looked like to the west. I went carefully, watching for rattlesnakes, alert for the rattle which I'd never heard, hearing only, as I approached the edge again, the soft rush of water rising out of the depths. A group of vultures appeared and circled silently. Their wingspan was nearly that of an eagle, the tip-tilted, two-toned wings giving them an airy semblance of transparency.

From Haystack westward there was a haze in the canyon and out of this rose three gauzy buttresses to form an abrupt escarpment on the south while, northwards, the ground rose less dramatically in long receding folds fading into the distance. Over these inclined planes and precipices the golden beams came streaming to light the river in the bottom and make of it a stretch of riffled mercury.

I slept there on the rim, where no light showed below the horizon and there was no mark of man but my own wagon humped against a multitude of stars.

I'd first heard of the Yampa canyon when I was tracing the journey of a pioneer called William Lewis Manly. He was ten years old when he drove a horse and cart from Vermont to Michigan behind his uncle's wagon. At thirty he was working as a teamster in a train going to California in the Gold Rush year of 1849. This party was late coming up the Platte and at Fort Laramie they were warned that they couldn't expect to reach the Sierras before the first snows. Three years after the Donner Pass earned its name no one was going to risk another early winter on the Sierras, so the owners in the train considered wintering at Salt Lake City. This appalled Manly and his colleagues because it meant they would be discharged but with not enough money to equip themselves to continue across the Great Basin, and they were anxious to reach the gold mines.

The train held together until it had crossed the continental divide at South Pass and had come down to the Green River. Now, the theory was that all water west of the divide flowed to the Pacific, and Manly, seeing a derelict ferry-boat on a sand-bar, with the sublime confidence of the as yet untried explorer, said that from this point they could float down to California.

Seven of them made a mad and heroic attempt. At first they covered about thirty miles a day but when they reached Flaming Gorge the boat was wrecked. They built canoes and lowered them down the rapids, and their progress dropped to four or five miles a day. They lost one canoe and all their guns, and they nearly lost a man except that Manly and another went in and pulled him out.

Finally they met a friendly Indian chief who warned them of a hostile tribe ahead, and an enormous canyon. Whether it was the terrain or the human factor that influenced Manly, prudence asserted itself and, bartering clothes, needles and thread for a couple of Indian ponies, the little band left the river and struck across country to Salt Lake City, thus avoiding not only the hostile tribe but almost certain disaster in the cataracts of the Grand Canyon.

Flaming Gorge had been flooded to form a reservoir, and this was how I came to concentrate on the Yampa, where I'd hoped to find the primaeval atmosphere that Manly had known on the Green. The relevance of the Yampa lay in the fact that at the end of its canyon the river flowed into the Green. It was all the same kind of country.

Dawn was so fresh and wonderful that although I crawled out of the bag with the first rays of the sun, I took ages over breakfast and by the time I approached the edge again I'd missed the morning shadows on the rock. So, not bothering about pictures, I wandered along the rim until I could look back and see what lay below the point of Haystack.

Pink cliffs, stark in the morning light, were crossed by crumbling transverse ledges which, jutting from the wall, presented lines of overhangs, revealed by their shadows. From the summit the wall sloped outwards slightly short of vertical, dropped to a beak and then sloped *inward* so that the lower half of the face, perhaps 400 feet in height, overhung with a gentle but implacable regularity.

There were rabbits on the rim, and chipmunks. I traced alarm calls to the edge where, 30 feet below, a chipmunk had paused on a ledge and threatened me with impunity. An intelligent little animal, I could watch him only by lying on a boulder that sloped the wrong way – down the cliff – and even then I had to hang on. He knew that in such a position I represented no direct danger but I could loosen stones and damage his burrow and he threatened me valiantly: a small golden beast about four inches long with lateral stripes, a tail as long as the body, a sharp mask and snapping eyes. Every time he called the tail jerked in sympathy and he was so concerned that had a hawk descended at that moment he wouldn't have known what hit him. I retreated – and two birds like house martins came jinking along the wall, but their backs were violet and green.

The commonest animals were lizards: fatter than ours, indicating that there was more food for them in this comparatively barren but warmer country.

By the middle of the morning, having gone out without a hat, I was moving from tree to stunted tree, trying to keep in the shade as I made my way back to the car.

Before I took to the road again, I put the cameras in plastic bags, placed them in a zippered case and tucked a blanket round it. The dust was amazing. I trailed a long streamer behind me – and thought of the plight of the emigrants. Every member of a wagon train was exposed to dust through the daylight hours and for several months – yet many of them lived a long time without apparent damage to their lungs. They inhaled it; how did their bodies get rid of it?

If dust was a thinking point, water was a basic commodity. I hadn't washed that morning, reflecting that dirt was of no consequence beside dehydration and my container held enough water to keep me going until I reached the end of the road but not if I washed. Accustomed to camping and climbing in Europe where water is looked on as a con-venience, on the Yampa bench my attitude changed. The presence of water, most particularly its absence, started to influence my plans. Water – and heat – had become a factor in survival.

The ground soaked up moisture like a sponge. Above the bench ran the long ridge of hills which I'd crossed yesterday at their northern ex-tremity. They held a lot of winter snow which must be melting steadily in the heat but the water never reached the road although in places it was close to the surface, judging from the luxuriant vegetation. It occurred to me that, had I been desperate, I might have reached that water by scraping out a hole with the ice axe.

The Yampa, in the bottom of its canyon, meandered in wide loops so that sometimes it was several miles away, and the country was such a tangle of draws and thorny scrub that there was no question of my walking out to the rim. I waited for paths that appeared when the road came close to a southward loop of the river, and then there would be an overlook on the rim.

In its middle reaches the canyon had a different character from that in the vicinity of Haystack. There it had been simply structured: long walls above sloping talus, but here the river's course was so tortuous that, despite its general progress west, it flowed to any point of the compass, even east, in convolutions so exaggerated that there appeared to be a maze of canyons rather than one.

The elements had worked harder here, and they'd had harder rock to deal with. Honey in the sun, sable in the shade, it was smooth, scooped out in overhangs of cataclysmic proportions, scored in parallel grooves down a chubby buttress so that the buttress itself was left like the paw of a pink china cat, claws sheathed. On one side of the canyon the gouged faces streamed black tears, and reefs crested like the spines of dinosaurs basked in the sun while, on my side of the river, shadowed walls dropped sheer into the water. On the bank across from me there were green flats like meadows. This place was called Harding Hole.

It was hot. I sat in the shade of a juniper drinking beer and cooking broccoli by instalments in my tiny pan. Clouds were coming up and I tried – and failed – to envisage walls and river lit by lightning, to imagine thunder trapped down there and trying to get out.

I wandered on to the next point and looked up a crested reef which I'd seen from the last overlook. The reef was several hundred feet high with two faces of straw-coloured rock, and it had no name. The air was thin and dry. Up-river from me two shapes moved down the bank and took to the water. If they were deer they couldn't cross for there was a wall on the other side. I went back to the truck for the binoculars.

The two figures had turned back and they emerged from the water to walk up the bank followed by a gaggle of miniatures. At the edge of a meadow the adults stood up with long necks and flapped their wings. I'd got the scale wrong yet again and had mistaken geese for deer.

Indians lived in the canyon in prehistoric times, and later tribes had farmed and hunted here, but there was only one residence left in Dinosaur: the Mantle Ranch. I camped on the rim about a mile from it. Although it was hidden by trees I could fix its position from the map and in the dark I went out to the edge to see if there were a light. There wasn't.

I sat down above the great gulf but after a moment I moved back. I didn't like sitting on the edge in the dark, but a few steps back and I felt secure. The drop was in shadow and possibly the lack of vision upset my sense of balance – which was interesting since I was sitting down.

There was no moon but a few evening primroses unfolded to glow in the starlight. Later, before I dropped off to sleep, I heard distant sounds which at first I thought were children and then, horribly, *mad* children. I sweated a lot before I guessed that these were coyotes. They ran the gamut of wild calls, howling, yapping, screaming, and then stopped as sharply as they'd started.

On the next day I left the rim. Away to the north the Yampa approached its confluence with the Green while on my level the bench came to an end in deep canyons and ridges slanting down from the south-west. The road descended to Sand Canyon and then a block of land forced it round three sides of a square: up Sand, over a ridge, down another canyon. The surface turned smooth and soft, inches deep in dust, and we came to a little white house dwarfed by cottonwoods. They were the first trees, apart from pinyon and juniper, that I'd come to in two days. It seemed like weeks.

I stopped and got out and stared at the house, which was unoccupied but in good condition. The cottonwoods were shady and there was a running stream. There were birds everywhere, and a flowering lilac was covered with bees and gorgeous butterflies: lemon, sulphur, tortoiseshell, and a huge black and yellow swallowtail. The place was called Chew Ranch and was used as accommodation for official visitors to the monument.

The house had been built where the canyon of Pool Creek was still open, the walls lying back in alternating terraces of maroon and ivory, stippled with pines. Beyond the homestead the road dropped gently and the canyon closed in until the red walls towered above the trees, streaked with old black water-stains and the occasional line of droppings that betrayed a nest.

A sign indicated petroglyphs but led only to sooty modern graffiti. The rock looked as if it had been sliced with cheese wire leaving golden corners so clean and bright that even on the shadowed side of the canyon, even under the trees, they glowed like the eyes of cats, reflecting all the available light.

I drifted past a long slit-cave in the base of a cliff, below tall chimneys choked with boulders, under monstrous overhangs. The sound of the engine was drowned in a wash of birdsong until the walls and the trees stood back and I emerged on the meadows of Echo Park in the bottom of the great canyon.

On the left, across the Green River, stood the 800 foot face of Steamboat Rock – another of those two-dimensional reefs. On the right, at the end of the first meadow, Jenny Lind capped Steamboat: a right-angled cliff whose jutting corner marked the confluence of the Yampa and the Green.

The term 'park' applies more to good grazing than to anything resembling stately grounds. Yet here in Echo Park there was a hint of elegance. It derived from the cottonwoods. With their thick grey bark and delicate foliage they were unlike any English hardwood but they were massive and shapely, and in their spacing and their shade on the deceptive green levels were reminiscent of summer in the Home Counties. But the soil was as hard as laterite and on close inspection was covered with a spare mauve weed. And under the big red wall the Green flowed silently. A continental river, it hinted in its sleek power of the savagery upstream in the canyon of Lodore, of the wild water ahead in Whirlpool Canyon and the gash of Split Mountain. Manly would have landed here because nowhere would have looked so hospitable since he left Brown's Park several days' journey to the north, and by the time he reached Echo he'd need to repair his boats and to rest his men.

Two biologists, Marta and Geoff, were working down there. They gave me coffee and we sat and talked while a pair of Canada geese and their goslings occupied themselves on the river bank. Geoff was the senior of the two; Marta was in her twenties, a strong vital woman with a mind like a laser beam and a great capacity for fun.

We spoke the same language. They were astonished at the abuses in British national parks – such as low-flying aircraft. These were not permitted over American parks and monuments; how could they be wildlife sanctuaries and recreation areas if the Air Force were allowed to train there? But Marta and Geoff suffered from double standards all the same. They washed in the river without soap while rafts of detergent and scum floated past from communities upstream.

Geoff offered cool comfort in regard to rattlesnakes. Since the venom is carried in the bloodstream the worst thing you can do if bitten is to hurry for help. In the back country you should sit still for two or three hours. And do deep breathing, I suggested, wondering from where I might dredge the requisite self-discipline.

It was very hot. Marta said that they got up at five and finished their field work around ten when they would work on their reports in the shade and not go out again until early evening.

When the sun had lost some of its heat we went up the canyon to see the Indian petroglyphs which were of deer and birds and abstract designs pecked in the rock with something that could have been a punch.

That night I slept under a cottonwood and was wakened by geese flying over, to think for a moment that I was in Scotland with the skeins crossing the coast and striking out for their breeding grounds in the high Arctic; then I opened my eyes and saw the top of Steamboat gilded in the dawn and remembered I was in Colorado.

I left Echo Park, drove up the canyons and, crossing the monument boundary, came on a sheepherder's wagon, with two horses drowsing under the trees. I drove slowly, quietly, and heard the thin chimes of sheep bells on the somnolent air.

The headwall of Iron Springs Wash looked as steep as a headwall in the Alps but the road climbed it by graded hairpins and I emerged on a surfaced highway. I relaxed with pleasure. For how many miles had I (and the cameras) endured dust? Fifty, sixty? We were on a ridge. I put my foot down and, as the needle crept along the dial, all the dust, that coated the interior like fur, got up and filled the car with a beige mist.

The road ended in a car park but the ridge continued, traversed by a beaten path that brought me to Harper's Corner. Almost in the centre of the canyon system, at over 7,000 feet, I had an eagle's eye view of Dinosaur. To the east I saw Haystack at the end of the bench, northwards I looked over the canyons of the Green towards Flaming Gorge; the way I was to go, the way Manly had come. Westward was new ground. I looked down Whirlpool Canyon, the sides of which, unlike the pale plunging walls of the Yampa, rose, in steady angled slopes of talus sprinkled with pines, to dark cliffs below the rim. On the horizon were the snow-covered peaks of the Uintas, mountains which hold the distinction of being the only range in the Rockies to run west and east. All the others run north and south.

The ground about the confluence of the Yampa and the Green was as convoluted as any in the middle canyons. Below me, way back in geological time, a cliff had slipped and folded and now reared in graceful arcs to a shorn crest over which I could see the river looping south to round the blade of Steamboat Rock.

I contemplated Echo Park, and Chew: a dream basking among its butterflies and birds in the bottom of the sunlit canyon. A fox called, and now in the late afternoon, the swifts were out, skimming joyfully along the ridge, tilting and planing above vertiginous slopes, the only sound the rush of air across their wings.

Driving back along the crest I turned into an overlook and, finding myself badly parked, put the car in neutral meaning to roll forward as I would with a manual gear change. But the brake wouldn't respond and Old Crump went on rolling with the unfenced lip of the canyon on the left and a snowbank on the right. I spun the wheel and we rushed straight into the snow.

Grille-deep on a gradient, with the manual open on the seat beside me, I went through the complicated procedure to reach four-wheel low and, by alternately engaging reverse and drive, rocked us uphill and clear of the drift.

I was thoughtful as we headed back towards civilisation. I'm not mechanically minded but I could connect power steering and power brakes with engine power; I could also connect all too easily with the roads and the drops we would have to negotiate when we reached the Sierras and I foresaw difficulties – but then I saw that this made a nice balance. The pioneers had top-heavy wagons which couldn't contour slopes without aid; my wagon had a lower centre of gravity and a power-to-weight ratio undreamed of by any nineteenth-century teamster, but there were no husky men to hold us back, or balance us when necessary. Then I remembered Eliza Ann Brooks travelling from Michigan to the Humboldt Sink. Who held her wagon back on the gradients?

In Dinosaur village I found Marta and Geoff. We'd been invited to the traditional party held by the monument staff to welcome the seasonal rangers who started work in May. The permanent staff lived in bungalows that fronted a stretch of rough ground where they'd organised an alfresco supper. I met a young ranger who asked me to call on his mother when I reached Salt Lake City. I met people who knew all about Manly coming down the Green but not what happened to him afterwards. We filled in gaps.

For me it was a strange party: the night sequinned with stars, the glow of the lamps lighting the faces of these people with accents already so familiar I had lost sight of the fact that I didn't speak like them.

A man recounted how his mother-in-law under hypnosis had revealed that in another incarnation she was the daughter of one Liver-Eating Johnson and that, in the 1830s, she had lived in a trading post on the banks of the Green. She had made a sketch of it and with this to guide him the story-teller, after years of searching, had found the site and some trade beads. I looked at the rapt faces and saw the wagons behind them and heard the cattle low. I left on the crest of the wave and, going over to Old Crump, took my sleeping bag and walked through the sage to sleep among the rocks at the edge of the field.

For most people Dinosaur is the quarry, and even I, who thought of museums as a chore and never remembered how much each one had enchanted me when I succumbed to duty, couldn't leave the area without a visit to this one. Next morning I crossed the state line into Utah: 'Big, Breathtaking and Beautiful'.

There were no preliminaries to the quarry, no ballyhoo. I came to a car park beside a building like an enormous lean-to shed and, stupefied with heat, staggered up a ramp and through a door to emerge on a gallery which ran the length of the building.

The roof cut out some of the light but a lot entered at either end for those walls were of glass. Opposite me the quarry wall was shaded and the atmosphere was cool and very quiet as in a cathedral. A few people moved along the gallery or stood and stared. Children nudged their parents with a furtive urgency and whispered. On ledges on the wall little men in helmets and white overalls knelt on mats and worked at the rock as diligently as men restoring icons. A disembodied voice murmured over the speaker system and the words crept out like the ghosts of little animals to be absorbed by the wall, which was covered with gigantic bones: mute and godlike sculptures in bas relief.

There were femurs, tibiae, fibulae, immense curving sections of spines, pelvises. A sand-bar cemetery, I learned, wandering dazed into the nether regions where the models were and coming on a giant crocodile disturbed at a carcass by another monstrous predator. All around, on this sandbank in the Green River, lay the bones and bodies of dead dinosaurs.

A femur was mounted on the gallery. It was over five feet tall. No skull had been found but there were fragments of jaws and now, 30 feet up the wall, perfect, petrified and clawed, I could make out a complete hind limb.

It was awe-inspiring and sad, yet oddly comforting. The dinosaurs bore no relation to the country in which I'd spent the last few days, country on a grand scale which one might have thought a fitting background for these magnificent animals; they had lived long before the Green and the Yampa cut their canyons down through the sandstone plateau. For all the age of the wilderness the dinosaurs were older, and this gave me a strong sense of continuity. The age of reptiles came late in the earth's history, at a time when, up in the trees, waiting for the dinosaurs to die, was a little shrew-like mammal that would evolve into man. The beast from which this femur had come, this bone that I could *touch*, had known my ancestors over a hundred million years ago.

I left the quarry stunned and disorientated, and drove here and there seeking a private place where I could lie down and recover. The campgrounds were frenetic with transistors and it wasn't until early evening that I found a dirt road which led me through a strange high back country. Dune-like formations were clothed with short spare grass, and running parallel with my route was a long crest of rock like the plates on the back of a stegosaurus. Storms rolled round the perimeter of the world and a hot wind filled the car with a lighter dust than that of the Yampa bench. I reckoned I was on limestone.

Shadows lengthened on the dunes and the road dipped to sage flats and cottonwoods on the bank of the Green. The river was broad, silent and scummy. This was Rainbow Park: a strange place, empty but for grasshoppers and frogs, the thunder muttering beyond the rim of the canyon, a dark sky, the river streaming past and reflecting the last of the light.

At ten o'clock I was sitting in the cab writing by torchlight when a truck arrived, shattering the night with its radio. It stopped with its engine running and the headlights turned full on me. I ignored the bad manners and went on writing. They had initiated the situation; a confrontation was their choice. After a few moments the truck was turned inexpertly and it roared away. Rangers would have approached me; an adult would have turned carefully. Youngsters then? Poachers? There was a dead deer on the river bank but too far gone in putrefaction for me to attempt to find out how it had died. We were some 30 miles from the nearest house and no shots would be heard – except by me. I got out the bag and lay on my back beside Old Crump listening to the frogs while my murderer's mind played with murder plots.

In the morning I walked downstream to the start of Split Mountain Canyon until the way was barred by an overhang of loose rock. I considered and rejected a buttress at the entrance to the canyon – about 700 feet of talus and pines interspersed with bedrock. It would be a gruesome ascent with the sun already hot in the depths.

I drove out to the highway, then north, through Vernal and into Wyoming and up the side of the Flaming Gorge, where blue water reminded me of swimming pools in the New York suburbs as we came in to Kennedy. When Manly came through there were bighorns on the ledges above the Green. Now, there are ramps from which motor-boats can be launched. There is water-skiing and fishing where Manly lowered his boat down the cataracts; the visitor may hunt on the banks, bathe in the Swim Areas, drive to a Vista Point or take a self-guided tour of the thin-arch concrete dam 500 feet high that holds back the water for 90 miles and leaves a tide-line some 30 or 40 feet wide and 200 miles long. This was part of a power storage scheme. We have those too; inception of one of the largest pumped storage schemes in Europe had been justified by a spokesman who told us that when the Miss World finals ended on television, everyone switched on their kettles for tea and overloaded the grid. Miss World and tea are part of British culture; I wondered how the electricity authorities had justified the rape of Flaming Gorge to the American public.

4

INTO WYOMING

IN ONE RESPECT the town of Green River reminded me of Fort William in Scotland. As the Fort's urban sprawl is dominated by the bulk of Ben Nevis so Green River's railway yards and factories, its conglomerations of mobile homes, are dominated by the Wyoming badlands. Towers like bland Dolomites appeared to hang above the interstate. Power lines, arc lights and all the garish billboards of the consumer age looked ineffectual and ridiculous against those cliffs. On a hillside was a huge white GR. It must be a hard struggle to preserve a sense of identity in Green River.

I didn't stop. Heading back for the place where I'd left the trail two weeks ago I plodded east at a steady 55 m.p.h. through rain and storms, and somewhere out in the Red Desert I turned off the interstate and, after a long drive where fences barred my way to the interior, came to a dirt road and some abandoned cabins. Half a mile beyond them the track ended at a fence where I turned and stopped.

I didn't work that night; I was close enough to the road for my light to attract attention and now that I'd found my sleeping quarters I had a strong objection to relinquishing them. Sitting in the dark, staring at the occasional headlights passing along the road, I had a sudden feeling of sympathy with the solitary traveller over a century ago, eating his meat raw for fear of his fire attracting hostile Indians.

It was a wet night. In the morning the soil stuck to my boots in cakes and we complemented each other in filthiness, Old Crump's sides splashed and streaked, my jeans muddy to the knees, my nails black and ragged. I couldn't remember when I'd last known warm water.

As I was eating breakfast four pronghorn antelopes approached the other side of the fence and we regarded each other with mutual curiosity. They had no horns so I took them for yearlings. Solid little animals, the size of small deer, they were a rich sand colour with some black on their faces, pale bellies and white rumps. They were animals of the wide and treeless plains, the country that the map (and the pioneers) called desert and which now was overhung by pregnant clouds of rain. My heart sank as it would in Scotland; was I in for a wet summer?

I went back to the interstate and continued east across Wyoming, the country becoming more undulating as I went. I saw a cottonwood and realised it was the first I'd seen for perhaps 100 miles and then I crossed the second ridge of the continental divide (which splits here to enclose the Great Divide Basin) and found myself in wooded country dusted with snow. It was thawing fast; water stood in hollows or came rushing out of the drifted gullies like streams from glacial caverns.

At Laramie I turned north, then north-east, crossing the Laramie Range by Morton's Pass. There were thunder-storms in the west with lightning ripping through clouds the colour of damsons.

The pass was not what one expects of a pass in the Rockies, but a long winding defile above a creek that was surprisingly clear, after the turbid Green, and lined with trees. I came down to a lush country of ranches and farms and I turned and fled back to the hills, climbing high into the range on dirt roads until I could squeeze Old Crump through the tree trunks and blend with the forest.

The place was alive with red squirrels which exploded with such shattering shrieks as I walked under their trees that I had to pause to let my heart adjust while, with nightfall, the coyotes whooped like banshees. After I'd gone to bed I smelled smoke and saw a red eye glowing where people must have picnicked that afternoon and failed to extinguish their fire. I got up and stamped it out and in the morning collected a sackful of cans from the site before the coyotes should get their heads stuck inside.

It was Saturday morning when I descended to the plain, crossed the river and drove east to the Nebraska state line. Twenty-three miles from Scott's Bluffs I turned round and started west on the main trail again. I came to the site of the Grattan Massacre: a mad episode in Fort Laramie's history.

In 1854 a Mormon train was passing up the south bank of the Platte when one of their cows strayed into an Indian village and was killed. The owner reported the incident when he reached the fort but no one was much concerned. She was a lame cow. Only an impetuous young lieutenant called Grattan went out with a cannon and thirty men and, one suspects, with the intention of chastising the Indians as much as reclaiming the cow. His efforts to identify the brave who killed her were frustrated and he fired too soon and too wildly, wounding a chief. Grattan and all his men were surrounded and killed. This happened not long after the Treaty of Horse Creek which was designed to end Indian aggression, but it was followed by the Indian wars.

I looked for the place where the emigrants crossed Laramie River to Fort Laramie but the banks had fallen in. Killdeer were nesting on the shingle and, not wanting to disturb them, I retreated and approached the fort by its main entrance.

It had been restored meticulously but the buildings were late nineteenth century, as they had been in the army's heyday; there was even a poor old horse drooping in the fierce sun, dressed overall in his cavalry harness. There was nothing to show of the old fur-trading post and in this museum of whitewashed walls and green lawns, of gleaming cars and well-scrubbed tourists, I felt out of place. My business was with the creaking wagons, dirt and dust and the slop of ox-hooves on the trail.

For them Fort Laramie was the end of the easy part (discounting the crossing of flooded rivers and the sudden gradients like Ash Hollow). For over 600 miles they had rolled across the plains and now the Rockies rose ahead. The fort was the last outpost before the ranges; here they would restock and recuperate, mend their wagons before the long haul, buy in food. Many of them were farmers, nearly all of them from the flat lands east of the Missouri and as, mile by plodding mile, they approached that long blue barrier streaked with snow, they knew that the section they had completed, for all its risks of cholera, drownings and attacks from marauding Indians, was safe compared with the trials that lay ahead.

That night I camped close to Register Cliff and next morning went to look at the names inscribed on the rock. I saw, because I was looking for it, that of Alva Unthank who died, of cholera or dysentery, and was buried at Glenrock only a few days farther west.

The children died. Women were the heroes of the pioneer trails; they had all their domestic chores to attend to in the onerous conditions of camp life (and May was a terrible month for rain) but, worst of all, they had to keep their children out of mischief that could turn tragic. Young boys would ride on the wagon tongue and some fell under the wheels. Joel Hembree, aged nine, died after his skull was fractured when both wheels passed over him. Another of the same age and after a similar accident had gangrene set in where his leg was crushed, and died as a man tried to amputate it with a butcher's knife. The mothers watched, and buried the bodies beside the trail, or under the trail.

I went up into the hills above Guernsey and had one of those hypnotic walks following the deep ruts the wheels had made in the chalky soil, but eventually rain drove me away and I found another creek high in the Laramies where I settled for the evening, and next day drove on to Casper. Beyond the town red buttes stood on the other side of the river, dark and sombre in the dull morning. It was cool today and I welcomed the drop in temperature. I had wilted in the sudden heat of the plains. Now these were behind me and it was all sage country with only the occasional shanty town of mobile homes and even these were stringing out. The hills were ahead, not just for the evening camp sites, but for hundreds of miles, for weeks.

The trail crossed the Platte for the last time and angled away from the river but my road continued along the right bank to cross some 20 miles upstream and rejoin the trail where it started the long haul up the course of the Sweetwater to South Pass. The ranges closed in: the Rattlesnake Mountains on the right, the Ferris on the left.

A long whale-back appeared: Independence Rock. I parked the car and scrambled up granite cracks where little rabbits got up and raced me to the top, and there I found, beautifully chiselled on the flat summit: 'Milo Ayres. Aged 29. 1849'. I wondered who he was. It was the first time I'd come across the name, but then the only public record of the majority of the emigrants would be a name chiselled in stone.

From here I could see the trail coming in towards the rock and passing away in the direction of Devil's Gate, a cleft on the horizon. Most of the pioneers camped below Independence Rock and, at the height of the season, around the middle of July, the plain would be covered with white-tops. Fortunately they had left the cholera behind in the hot and steamy plains but the increased altitude was a mixed blessing. Sometimes they needed all their winter clothes at this point and many diarists mentioned 'mountain sickness' as they approached South Pass. At only 7,550 feet it's unlikely that they were suffering from altitude for the slow pace of travel (fourteen miles a day was a good average) was the perfect form of acclimatisation – but mountain sickness was a more romantic term for the weariness from which some would be suffering as they approached the continental divide.

There were some who were always active and eager: the type who turned aside to visit landmarks such as Courthouse and Chimney Rocks and, six miles ahead, Devil's Gate. Many of these would be young and all of them on horseback, riding away from the dust and watchful parents for a few hours when sightseeing was only an excuse to flirt and fall in love.

So far as courtship was concerned the migration had advantages for everyone. The young men and women had every opportunity to observe each other's behaviour under the most stringent conditions and the parents had the comfort of knowing that no infatuated son or daughter could leave the tight family enclave during the night for fear of alerting every guard in the camp. Privacy was what they lacked of course, and it must have been difficult to get that even with a minister along to make everything legal. There were no wagons to spare for a newly-married couple and if the wilderness was all around, so were the Indians – or their presence was always suspected. But the emigrants had tents and they were, of all things, innately resourceful. No doubt they managed.

We rolled on towards Devil's Gate and found a dirt road leading to the Campbell Ranch. A smart young woman answered the door and was delighted to give me permission to visit the chasm. I drove across a plank bridge and left Old Crump in a glade where I put up a pronghorn. The Sweetwater flows through the Gate, a clean shallow stream with birds nesting in the banks. I would have called them sand martins at home but here they were bank swallows.

The Devil's Gate is a notch in a thin ridge. The rock looks loose and unpleasant but aesthetically imposing, set as it is between two plains and with walls at least 300 feet high. On the western side a Pony Express station had been sited in 1860 and this was included in the 75-mile section ridden at one time by Bill (Buffalo Bill) Cody. Once he came in to Three Crossings Station about 30 miles west of Devil's Gate to find his relief had been killed by Indians, so he continued for another 85 miles, then turned and retraced his route, covering 322 miles in all.

Cody was fifteen years old at the time of this epic ride. Since weight might make all the difference to survival (and the safety of the mail) a high proportion of Pony Express riders were boys in their teens. Men were employed only if they weighed less than 125 pounds.

They were issued with light rifles but many didn't carry them, preferring to put their trust in a fast horse: Kentucky thoroughbreds on the plains, mustangs in the hills. This made them even more vulnerable to the Indians whose most treasured possession was a good horse.

No allowances were made for *anything*: floods, blizzards, Indians. The riders often slept in the saddle and it was not unknown for two of them to pass without either being aware of it.

What kind of character was this that, knowing the galloping hooves would alert every Indian along the trail, rode alone across the deserts and the mountains for the sake of $60 a month? It isn't all that remarkable that a reckless boy should be happy with a ride in good conditions in good weather but that a youth, after once escaping from hostile Indians, should go back and continue with the job is incredible.

The spirit of the men who manned the stations is equally laudable. They didn't have the glamour of the ride, the terrible thrill of the chase; they were stuck out there in the wilderness, sitting ducks for any Indians who felt like acquiring two or three scalps and some pure-bred horses, and who enjoyed a good bonfire. Only a month after the service was inaugurated all the stations across Nevada were burned by the Paiutes.

There was no sign of the old station at Devil's Gate; if it was not burned by the Indians, its logs would have been used for firewood by successive travellers.

On the wide plain beyond the Gate the emigrant trail kept close to the Sweetwater because everywhere else the water was strongly alkaline, and toxic for their cattle. These dry white basins with a pool in the middle increased the sense of desolation, and the only living things I saw were

small herds of antelope among the sage. It would be a frightening place
in a blizzard. Close by the road is Martin's Cove where a company of
Mormons holed up in October 1856. They were pushing handcarts
because they couldn't afford wagons and they were a family contingent
with a large proportion of children and old people. Pushing a handcart
through a blizzard in the Rockies must be hell, and they couldn't have
carried much in the way of tents and blankets. Caught by the early snows
in Martin's Cove, 77 died before rescue reached them from Salt Lake
City.

Punch-drunk with images I drifted on, Old Crump climbing
effortlessly, and we stopped at an overlook below Split Rock Mountain
where, for a short while, I forgot the emigrants as I traced routes up
what appeared to be good solid granite. Within a few miles I was back
with the pioneers again when, a couple of miles south of the road, the
trail crossed the Sweetwater for the penultimate time (there had been
four crossings since the Platte). A man from an emigrant train was
hanged here.

A murder had been committed for robbery and the man suspected
was the father of four children, which made things awkward, because if
he were hanged what would happen to his family? Some of the train,
perhaps from compassion, perhaps uncertain of the morality of the
proceedings, let alone their legality, were all for postponing punishment
but the council of elderly men prevailed and the problem was solved
when a substitute was found to drive the family wagon. Then they
hanged the suspect.

Within sight of the slope leading up to South Pass I turned north and
came to Lander where, feeling a deep yearning for a bath, I put up at the
first motel I'd entered since leaving Omaha.

I walked into a dark hot room, drew the curtains and slid aside the
window. Fresh air and the roar of water hit me. Immediately below, a
bank dropped to the Popo Agie River: a brown torrent full of melted
snow. The Wind Rivers stood in the background, behind Purina Chow's
cattle feed factory. I made coffee with the motel's equipment and put the
first load of dirty clothes in the wash basin to soak.

Lander was a town of character. It was more compact than Green River,
even though its population was considerably larger, and there was no
scarp of badlands to rob the town of dignity. Its industries (apart from
Purina Chow) were less obvious, it had no interstate with attendant
hoardings and, although it stood on one route to Yellowstone, it was not
the kind of place where tourists stopped. It was a civilised town with the

main street so wide that cars parked diagonally to the kerb. There were meters, but the side streets that led to shady residential areas had so much room to park that meters were superfluous.

I met a reporter called Charlotte Dehnert on the *Wyoming State Journal* and we traded information: an interview from me in exchange for introductions to local people. She laid the framework for the next few days.

She sent me to the museum which was full of curiosities donated by local people, from Victorian fur coats to Indian war bonnets, but the cream of the exhibition was a collection of exquisite patchwork quilts – if not the art form peculiar to America then the one that reached its highest levels there. One quilt had been made on the California Trail with pieces donated by other wagons. How did the maker keep it clean?

Following Charlotte's instructions I drove up Sinks Canyon, the glen that held one of the forks of the Popo Agie. The sink is a limestone cavern into which the river plunges, to emerge half a mile lower down in a deep and sinister pool where water wells upwards in ghastly convolutions. I camped by the river among pink rocks and lupins and a showy yellow composite called balsamroot. These were early spring flowers and the winter was lingering; the first morning I was there they were bowing before heavy sleet, the next they were drifted with snow.

These fluctuations in temperature surprised me but I'd come prepared for mountaineering above the snow-line and, whereas I'd been careful to wear a hat on the roasting plains, my first breakfast in Sinks Canyon was eaten in cord breeches and my eiderdown jacket, and the temperature was only a few degrees above freezing.

However, it was good walking weather and I followed the river upstream to the Popo Agie Falls and explored the forest, coming on swamps and open rocky glades and a colony of marmots, larger than those of the Alps but with the same type of sentinel and the same piercing whistles of alarm. There were pasque flowers, closed like daisies against the dull day, and a tall fritillary with yellow spots on purple that was called a leopard lily. It was very still. A squirrel stripped a pine cone a few feet from me and I could hear every husk fall on the dead needles.

It was a pleasant stroll; but I felt a need to reach some eminence, to find out where I was. Like Manly, who spent a lot of time climbing the hills along the trail, I needed to get high to feel the country.

Next day I drove up Mexican Canyon. Charlotte had contacted a rancher called Facinelli who agreed to let me go on his land, but first I had to find him. I found a ranch house with only an Alsatian and a terrier in charge so I returned down the canyon on a road of bright red dust to the next ranch. Here I found an elderly couple called Gallinger and a beautiful girl who was half Shoshoni. They confirmed that the other ranch was the Facinelli place and asked me to lunch. I chatted with the rancher in the parlour that had a fine old clock on the wall, photographs of the house in the snow, of favourite horses. The girl Terry came to ride the horses, he said, but you could see she came for the Gallingers. Mrs Gallinger was a gardener, a home-maker, a superlative cook. Lunch was her own vegetables frozen last fall, beef from their cattle, home-baked biscuits like rich bread rolls. We drank iced tea and afterwards Mr Gallinger showed me round in his truck, stopping suddenly at a creek to exclaim at two western tanagers: birds the size of a hawfinch but with a scarlet head and a lot of yellow below the black wings and tail. He said he hoped they'd nest.

He left to return to his irrigating and I sauntered along the creek hoping to see a hen tanager because it is only the cocks that are brightly coloured. A long red cliff showed ahead and I scrambled among the rocks at its foot finding a huge nest that had fallen to the ground and that must have accommodated a big raptor, perhaps an eagle.

I'd had the sun in my eyes but when I came back under the cliff I saw some petroglyphs: a strange bird in flight, and a pronghorn. I was studying these when there was a heavy crash in the creek below and a buck plunged up the opposite bank, cleared a fence *uphill* and went up the far slope as if on springs. I saw three male tanagers on the return.

In the west I was constantly surprised at the juxtaposition of hospitality and wild country, although often the two go together – in the Highlands of Scotland for instance, and on the northern Pennines. Wilderness and self-sufficiency are twinned too, and make a satisfying life-style in which common sense is a major factor. There is no room for frills.

The Gallingers produced their own food, broke their own horses and hoped the western tanager would nest. Farther up the canyon Mr Facinelli took one look at Old Crump, waved to the mountain and told me to drive up. Common sense. I wanted to walk on the tops; why waste energy walking the first three miles when I had a vehicle? 'I can do it,' he said, 'I do it every week. Lock your hubs.'

He opened the yard gate for me and almost immediately Old Crump put his nose down like a horse to cross a creek. The other side was equally steep. Mr Facinelli must have thought we spent an inordinate amount of time sitting in the water, but I was reaching four-wheel low in stages, by consulting the manual.

The route was two ruts through the sage that covered a spur between canyons. There were no precipices so it was not a test of courage, rather of Old Crump's power and, to some extent, my strength when it came to the gates. These are different.

You come to a fence and the track continues blandly on the other side.

You fume; someone has removed the gate. But in the ruts are fresh tyre-marks rolling under the fence. You dismiss speculation about very low cars or two wheelbarrows with rubber tyres. Looking closely, you find that a section of the fence is unstable and movable. One end of the section has a post which is attached to the post of the solid fence by two loops of heavy wire. By straining the movable post you can detach the top loop and lift the stake out of the bottom one. You drag the whole contraption aside, drive through, return to close the gap, and the fun starts.

The section is heavy because there is a lot of wire in it and two smaller posts acting as stretchers in the middle. With considerable difficulty you place the lower end of the crucial post in its retaining loop and then you try to bring the top within reach of the second bit of wire. On your first encounter with the contrivance (at the time the most devilishly animate of all American inventions) you do the obvious thing: using one hand to pull the section towards you by the post, you cut the other hand on the barbed wire as you try to increase traction. With your two posts parallel you look around for the third hand to slip the loop over the top – and to see if anyone is watching. I never left a gate open although there were occasions when I would sit down and stare at the sagging post with the same despair with which a climber may sit and stare at a piece of rock knowing rescue will never come and the only way out is up.

There were several of these gates on the lower slopes of the mountain. I wrestled with each one, not so much because I had to get to the top but because I knew there were going to be a lot more of them in the months ahead. In the end I became so accustomed to them that when I returned home I found our own system unnecessary and expensive, even deca-dent.

The gates were a minor problem. I came to the bank of a dry ravine and looked down a slope like the side of a house but the track descended and so did we, climbed the opposite bank, found, after a mile or so, that we were on the lip of the wrong canyon and retreated: across the gulch and up the side of the house (thinking of tractors turning over and that we had no roll bar) while Old Crump purred happily to himself and I was drenched with sweat.

We were about 2,000 feet above the ranch when we hit shattered limestone. It was like climbing a boulder field. Rocks shifted under the wheels and there were loud impacts that sounded like silencers, like shock absorbers, like the sump. I gasped and moaned and Old Crump went on climbing, lurching, but always making progress. I loved him passionately.

The boulder field ran out on a limestone pavement like a Roman road and I got down to take pictures of cloud shadows on a hill called Red

Butte across Mexican Canyon. Far away and below I could see the green
of the ranch, and then I came to the gate that defeated me. Moreover it
was a boundary for there were No Trespassing signs on the other side.
Using this as an excuse (because the gate was so tight I could never have
closed it once opened) I parked and put the kettle on for tea. I had
sweated so much I was dehydrated.

It was a lovely night although I was told later that it froze at the ranch
– a temperature inversion. I was warm in my sleeping bag. The cloud
dropped in the evening until it lay on the top of Red Butte and wisps of it
crept round us but never quite obscured the lights of Lander ten miles
away.

I had found my vantage points; I knew where I was. Next morning,
and now on foot, I saw that the ridge flattened beyond the boundary. On
one side was Mexican Canyon, wild and rocky, but the ridge was grassy
and on the rim of the canyon, about a mile away, three elk were grazing,
like red deer but larger. On the other side of the ridge, beyond a basin
that held a spring, was a canyon even finer than Mexican, broken in the
bottom into crags and forest where there must be a wealth of wildlife. It
was walled by cliffs of a warm colour between pink and dusty gold and
these were interspersed with gullies, steep talus and conifers. There had
to be moose in that canyon, and surely bears.

The rim rose to a point called Bragg Mountain. It may have been
8,000 feet high, which wasn't much in the Rockies, but from its summit I
could see the major peaks of the Wind Rivers. There were deer on top –
I'd crept up on them with the wind in my favour – and chipmunks, the
black and indigo Steller's jay and ravens. From the summit I saw a pool
below my outward route and, descending to it, found it occupied by a
small duck like a cinnamon teal.

There were occasions on this journey when I would have liked
company: when I came to a good cliff and wished for another climber, a
palaeontologist in Dinosaur, a botanist, but most often an ornithologist. I could cope with the showy birds but I was no expert on
duck. Teal should be easy because they are small, but did cinnamon teal
nest so high? One drake that didn't get up on my arrival argued a duck
on the margin.

The l.b.b.s (little brown birds) were impossible. The bird book listed
42 sparrows and 30 flycatchers. Admittedly many could be eliminated
according to habitat and region but you were still stuck with identification that might depend on the precise shade of grey of a flycatcher's chin
or, that fierce stumbling block, young birds of one species resembling
the adults of another. An ornithologist would have solved many
problems.

Long before Old Crump came in sight I had realised that going down was going to be far more hazardous than coming up. Now all the weight was on the front and we dived nose-first into every hole and crevasse in the limestone boulder field until the last shattering bang and we stalled. I got underneath expecting to see at the least a bent track-rod, at the most a sheered sump and oil lubricating the lime, but we'd stopped with a shock absorber on a boulder.

I reversed and engaged the lowest gear. There was a low gear on the two-wheel box which could be engaged manually and used with four-wheel low; I hadn't discovered it on the ascent. Slower than walking we crawled down the mountain, weaving in and out of the rocks, never using the accelerator, but despite the low gear and because of the gradient and the terrain, always using the brakes. These were so hot that when I reached the first gate I couldn't stop until the fender was against the wire. The drums were scorching so I got the stove out and had afternoon tea while the brakes cooled.

Mr Facinelli met me in the yard. He said they never used automatics: 'How would we manage, coming down that hill with a ton of bull in the back?'

I bought a shovel. In Lander I was directed to a dark barn full of intriguing secondhand objects. It looked as if over the last century someone had been buying up the contents of every homestead that came on the market, and its tack room. In a corner I found a long-handled shovel priced at two dollars. Neither the storekeeper nor I thought it was worth $2.00; the handle was probably broken under a sleeve of insulating tape but it didn't bend and if it did break, I'd still have a handle three feet long. So I bought it. It was to become a cherished piece of equipment.

5

SOUTH PASS TO YELLOWSTONE

FROM LANDER THE road to South Pass climbed diagonally over the skirts of the Wind Rivers, traversing the heads of canyons which, although not sensational, were attractive. There was Red Rock Canyon: long slopes of grass and golden balsamroot with high white scars of limestone rimmed by a cornice of crimson sandstone that went on for miles. Homesteads were set in dark fields at the bottom and linked by tracks that were red-raw, as if they'd just been made, but on that kind of soil no road could ever look mellow.

The names spoke of the rock: Limestone Mountain, Iron Mountain, Granite Peak. At Iron Mountain there was an overlook with a view of a mine backed by the Wind Rivers. At one time the forests would have stretched unbroken from the mountains to the road but now only the remnants of the trees fringed the mine as if they were meant to serve a cosmetic purpose. I couldn't decide why the overlook had been sited there: for the mine, for the Wind Rivers, or for a combination of the two?

Mining had founded South Pass City, in 1867, and then the lure was gold. The ghost town stands about ten miles north of South Pass and came as no surprise to me; I had known its own ghost since childhood: in photographs, on the wide screen. It was unreal – all except the hotel, which I took such a dislike to that its source had to be traced. The quaint interior, of small rooms and dark passages, had reminded me of a house in which I'd spent a stormy period of my life. Now, seeing the association, I could dismiss the memory of suffering and was left with the random joy I'd known in that same house, and then the dim little rooms with their great brass bedsteads held an air of conspiracy.

In its heyday South Pass City had seventeen saloons and brothels; now it had one bar. The beer was passable and the proprietor friendly. He had served in Italy during the war and travelled as far as the Brenner Pass but he'd never flown in an aeroplane and would never leave Wyoming again: 'I shall die here.' Like many of his countrymen he diversified. He owned a body shop in Lander (I thought this was a sex shop until I was sent to one when Old Crump needed new brakes); he ran the bar at weekends, did the cooking (he served snacks), sold Indian rugs. Navajo work was best, he said, and the most expensive. You had to examine the work; some of it was less well-made nowadays. The Indians traded on the name.

I asked him about sheep. The numbers were declining, he told me; owners couldn't find good sheepherders. Their range was enormous, but so were the numbers; at one time there would have been as many as fifteen thousand in a band. They returned to the wagon at night where the dogs guarded them from coyotes. Sometimes the sheepherder's wife accompanied him, occasionally the children. I was drowsy with the heat and two questions went unasked. What had these huge flocks eaten in the winter? Surely you couldn't feed hay to fifteen thousand. And what was the system, if any, at lambing time?

The pioneer trail is about eight miles from South Pass City, coming up the course of the Sweetwater, converging with the line of the modern road. At the site of Burnt Ranch (burned three times by Indians), the trail crosses the Sweetwater for the last time and angles up towards the pass. 'Up' is misleading; in the ten miles between the last crossing and the divide the height gain is less than 200 feet. The pass is an expanse of sage 20 miles in width, the mountains at the fringe, and nearer, the eroded buttes, serving only to emphasise the horizontal plane.

The pioneers didn't camp here but went down the other side for about two miles to Pacific Spring. I did sleep on top, having followed a cart track to a place where the pass became obvious: wide certainly, but saddle-shaped. I was at 7,550 feet, among sage that was uniformly low, stark proof of the winds that would howl across this place in the depths of winter. There was no water; there was none between the Sweetwater and Pacific Spring. I washed my vegetables in the collapsible plastic bucket and ate my supper as the sun went down behind the Prospect Mountains. When it had gone birds started to sing in the sage, I switched on the light and, as many of my predecessors had done, wrote up my journal.

The first white women to cross South Pass were Narcissa Whitman and Eliza Spalding: missionaries' wives going out with their husbands to a new mission in Oregon. Narcissa was small and well-made, blonde and blue-eyed. She rode most of the way to Oregon, side-saddle. She was also pregnant.

Spalding had been in love with Narcissa but she had rejected him and married Marcus Whitman. Spalding married Eliza, who was thin, dark and neurotic. The trappers adored Narcissa and came to her for religious tracts, assuring her that they would give up the whisky. The Sioux venerated her and showed off with trials of strength and horsemanship.

The missionary party had four milch cows along with them so they had cream and butter, and Narcissa baked bread in the embers every evening while Marcus cooked the buffalo meat of which she was very fond. She gave tea parties (with a rubber table cloth) to which she invited the leading members of the train. Tom (Broken Hand) Fitzpatrick was their guide, and Narcissa never had to face the horrors that other women were to encounter in the early days along the trail. She had eleven years before her tragedy. In 1847 Cayuse Indians attacked the mission in Oregon and murdered fourteen people, including the Whitmans. The Spaldings escaped.

Narcissa and Eliza were the first white women to cross the pass but not the first women. There were Indian trails here long before Robert Stuart came back from the west coast to report on the hostility of its Indians and the fate of the *Tonquin*. It was because there *were* trails over South Pass that these trappers, wary now about meeting any Indians, crossed the divide some miles to the south, a route which would have taken them across the Red Desert.

The first white men to use the pass were fur traders and trappers with pack trains but it was the passage of wheeled traffic that marked the breakthrough. In 1832 the explorer, Captain Bonneville, took wagons across, four years later the Whitmans had a wagon – but they had to abandon it when they reached the Snake. Five years after that, in 1841, the first true emigrant party came over South Pass with fifteen wagons and four carts. This was the Bidwell–Bartleson party, with whom I was to become involved farther along the trail.

So far as the emigrants were concerned wagons were essential for families and preferable for everyone. Despite Narcissa Whitman's fortitude, few pregnant women would want to emulate her. A wagon carried women, children, sick people, all the household effects and the agricultural equipment. It afforded shade, and you could walk beside it without having to lead a horse.

Pack trains were faster and could go places that wagons couldn't but pack animals had to be unloaded at night, loaded every morning. On the back of a horse you roasted in the sun and froze in rain, sleet or snow. If someone were ill or badly injured there was no way of transporting him, and if he'd been wounded by Indians, it endangered the rest of the party to pitch camp and wait until his condition improved, or he died. Wagons, slow and cumbersome as they were, spelled security.

There was a choice of routes in the vicinity of South Pass. The early trail started a great elbow here, making south-west for 130 miles to Fort Bridger, then north-west for over 200 miles to Fort Hall on the Snake, but if you went due west from South Pass on what was known as Sublette's Cut-off, you could cut across that elbow and save 85 miles. Most people bound for Oregon came to take this route, and many of those who were going to California. The second section of it was dry but they took the risk because 85 miles could save them six days.

I followed them along the first section of Sublette's, finding the water that they found: at the Little Sandy and the Big Sandy. The second creek was lush, with grass and flowers, willows and pines. I stopped for lunch. I wasn't the first to do so recently; there was a lot of litter. There was also, discarded by spring floods, a mouldering sack that contained the remains of what, without close inspection, I assumed was a dog. I was getting my priorities straight and, although disturbed, I could eat my lunch. Only a few miles farther on, the emigrant camps would have been surrounded by putrefying oxen.

It was amazing country. Leaving the Big Sandy I stuck in mud and escaped only in four-wheel drive – but a few yards back from the creek the ground reverted to the caked pale soil of the sage flats, and under Tabernacle Butte, three miles away, the wagons had ground their wheels into sand the colour and consistency of powdered bones.

I slept that night on the Big Sandy, the second encounter with it that day. The streams meandered and so did the roads and often, when I came to a fork, there was nothing to guide me but the sun, the compass and the map.

The grass beside the Big Sandy made an idyllic site. The river slid by without a sound: quite deep, and the low banks were so unstable that one had to be careful when washing. Bare feet could get no grip on slime like submerged clay, and the swift but silent movement of the current close to my face affected balance. I washed ankle-deep in the water with my boots on.

The highway intersects Sublette's Cut-off and at that point the Green River is 45 dry miles to the west. The emigrants cut grass and filled their water containers at the Big Sandy and then they started early in the morning and travelled all that day and most of the next. They rested at night but there was no water for the oxen. Although the hardiest beasts could go one night without water, here they had to survive two days and a night without drinking. The weakest animals succumbed and were abandoned, and now people started to realise that it was not all downhill to the Pacific. It may have been on Sublette's that Manly decided to do anything to avoid more deserts, and when he reached the Green, there was the derelict boat on the sand bar and he had his inspiration to float down to California.

I had difficulty in finding this dry section of Sublette's. Perhaps the authorities wanted to discourage travellers in such inhospitable country. The first road I took ended in a T-junction, and that wasn't right. The second was blocked by a notice saying 'Road Abandoned'. Finally I took the Old Lumen Road that skirted the northern fringe of Sublette's Flat but it went too far north and although I saw herds of antelope and colonies of prairie dogs, it wasn't the cut-off. I returned to the highway, thinking that 45 miles of sage would be dull anyway. Eventually I would go round to the other side of the desert and pick up the trail at the Green River crossing. Now I was going into the mountains, following the snow.

As I travelled north the ranges closed in, the desert ended and I came to the Green some 50 miles upstream of the emigrant crossing. The country changed. There were more trees. There were old log cabins and people were building new houses, also of wood, well-designed, alpine in concept. Some of the barns wouldn't have been incongruous in the Zermatt valley. At the crossing of the Green two men on horses, one a Palomino, the other a grey, were herding a bunch of Herefords across the water. The benches above the river bank were tall as moraines, delicate green from the spring growth of sage. A few lazy fair-weather clouds floated in a vivid sky and the horizon was still the long white range of the Wind Rivers round which I'd described three-quarters of a circle in the past week.

A few miles beyond the Green I came to the crest of a rise and a notice saying it was the Rim. At just on 8,000 feet, this marked the divide between the Colorado river-system and that of the Snake. The first drained to the Gulf of California; the Snake, as the Columbia, would empty into the sea between Oregon and Washington, 1,500 miles to the north.

Beyond the Rim was a constricted valley where the Hoback, a quiet river compared with the Green, flowed past bottom lands that were little more than half a mile wide. In contrast with the high deserts, these flats looked lush, for where there was water there was a thick growth of willows, and there was a lot of water because the fields were irrigated. The channels, dug by the first homesteaders, had the appearance of natural streams.

The river flowed down one side of the little valley, and from its left bank the ground rose to a wooded ridge. On the opposite side a long and regular bench was breached by the mouths of glens that gave access to the Gros Ventre Range. At the mouth of one of these glens was a low ranch house built of logs and this was my first mail drop. The contact had been made through friends of friends and the ranchers were strangers. I was too dirty for social occasions so I passed by, into the jaws of the Hoback Canyon and, finding a creek coming down through willows, bathed, not luxuriously but thoroughly. It was like bathing in a glacier stream.

The Camerons had come to ranching from inclination rather than tradi- tion. Holly Cameron's father was a gynaecologist, Pete had been intended for the Navy; what had drawn them to ranching was the land,

and the unpopular and unpopulated glens of the Gros Ventres where they ran pack trips in the summer.

I dined with them. The meat was elk: not unlike venison but less strong because it wasn't hung. Pete shot a cow elk each fall and they tried to make it last for a year.

That night I slept in their paddock with snipe drumming on the marshes and in the small hours I heard geese and woke to see them beating across the moon.

I had a great admiration for the Camerons; theirs was hard ground to work, and the climate ran to extremes. Despite the fact that a creek flowed down the valley behind the house the water table was low and a few yards back from the banks of the rivers the ground would have been a desert but for irrigation.

In the summer the Camerons' valley was like an oven; in the winter the thermometer could register 50 degrees below zero. Their cockerel lost his comb in the frost; sometimes the fowls lost their toes. The road was ploughed only to their boundary and there Pete kept the school bus which he drove in term time. They skied out to the road-end taking their baby in a carrier on their backs.

The ranch house was 60 years old with low ceilings and small windows so it was dim by day, but that had no importance when people spent most of their time out of doors. It was cool in summer and, they said, cosy in winter. They had electricity, drains, and hot water on tap; the only thing they didn't have was a garden for they fought a losing battle against the chisellers. The meadows were composed of a dry loose soil which was riddled with the burrows of what I had been calling prairie dogs, and what they called chisellers and were technically Richardson's ground squirrels. They ravaged the garden and were more than a match for the dogs who, although evincing wild excitement during irrigation, waiting by a hole that was about to flood, and darting to catch a chiseller when we were riding, lay supine as the plants vanished with a twitch, harvested from below. The chisellers were small and nimble, like earless rabbits, and they chattered.

A pair of red-tailed hawks lived on the hill at the back, but what could one pair do against such hordes? (As in Europe, raptors' numbers had declined, almost certainly due to thin egg-shells as the result of the use of pesticides.) The Camerons didn't kill coyotes, which also preyed on the chisellers, but many people did, poisoning the carcasses of cows.

It was early June and the spring was very late. The Camerons asked me to go on a pack trip into the Gros Ventres but we'd have to wait until the snow melted. Next morning I drove north to try to get into the mountains by a road that went up from Jackson, under the Tetons. I was continually amazed at the vagaries of the weather. At the ranch my washing had dried in an hour in the sun; when I reached Jackson Hole the Tetons were plastered with new snow. Through binoculars I could see the tracks of avalanches.

The Tetons are shapely mountains: a compact range centred on the Grand Teton, a tower that slimmed to a spire as one travelled north. Aesthetically the range was superb, rising suddenly from the headwalls of sloping canyons which themselves rose sharply from the flat plain of Jackson Hole. One didn't deplore the absence of glaciers; had there been any they would have filled the canyons and robbed them of their charm, but it was unfortunate that all the high routes were now overhung by sloping shelves of wet snow. I turned my back on them and started up the valley of the Gros Ventre River.

Past the mouth a landslide had come down in 1925, having started on a ridge 2,000 feet above the valley floor. Debris dammed the river and a lake formed behind it. After two years this natural dam collapsed and the resulting flood swept down on the little village of Kelly drowning six people. Over half a century later a few trees had crept in to colonise the raw ground, and doubtless lichens and mosses were coming back, but from a distance the slide looked as it must have looked on the morning after the catastrophe: a gash a mile in length and half a mile wide where the soil had peeled away taking with it a dense swathe of forest.

Beyond the Lower Slide Lake the Red Hills rose on my left: the colour of bricks baked a little too long. They were cleft by gullies and seamed by rocky spines interspersed with crumbling crimson buttresses across which the strata swooped in every shade of red. The green of the bottom lands lapped the foot of these fiery slopes – and suddenly, as if the paint had given out, the red rock stopped and the next range was pale grey: the same structure, of towers and scarps and buttresses, but now the rock was pearly, almost white.

The wind was strong, gusty and cold. Weather was building up over the grey hills. I drove for some 20 miles up the dirt road above the river, where Indians and trappers had been before me, coming down from Union Pass. There were a few ranches but the land was unfenced: grassland scattered with trees. Eventually there were no more ranches and I took a track above a stream called Soda Creek. Half a mile from the road I parked on a patch of turf. I ate supper as the light was fading; I didn't like the feel of the wind and thought that if I were going to see anything of the country I should do it now.

It was a happy thought. I went quickly up the path while there was still light enough to see movement, and in the shadows was a tall animal which I took for a brindled horse. As it moved away, quietly, fading rather than moving, the gait was nothing like that of a horse, and the shape was wrong. Then a trick of the light showed me the undershot jaw, the small replica moving with an anxious clumsiness at her side; it was a cow moose, moulting, with her calf. I kept walking and she drifted with the same casual lack of fear into a ravine, merging with the trees.

The track rose through pines to come out on a lip where water gleamed against the light. A pair of duck swam away. At the far end sage slopes swelled on the skyline; elsewhere the timber crowded the rocky shore. It was very still and I could smell snow. The moon was up now, a few days off the full, and it was cold. As I went back down the slope there was a heaviness in the air and then an icy breath. I reached the wagon as the first snow came drifting up the creek.

The windows were covered in the morning and all the trees were powdered white. It was still snowing and there was no sound from the birds, only the susurration of the big flakes driving over the sage. The ruts of the track showed smoothly white and, knowing that the ground wouldn't be frozen, I thought I'd better get out while it was still possible.

On the way in I hadn't noticed that one rut was higher than the other, and we crawled out like a crab, Old Crump's rear slewing alarmingly as the tyres failed to find traction on the slime under the snow. The road, when we reached it, was clear but the snow continued to fall and since all the flowers would be covered and the animals sluggish, I decided that this was the moment to visit Yellowstone, utilising a day of bad weather for the drive.

The first impression of Yellowstone, approaching from the south, is of too many trees. They go on for miles: tall regimented trunks that block out all views. The early voyagers must have found them dispiriting. But for most people Yellowstone is geysers and although my goal was the wilderness, I accepted the chore, the inevitability of geysers and, because it was on my way, commenced with Old Faithful.

It was approached by a paved avenue flanked by pines. The Taj Mahal should have been at the end, instead there was a low steaming mound. A thin crowd gathered at a discreet distance and steam started to mount against the grey sky, was scattered in the brisk wind while beneath it, rising to the accompaniment of a growing roar, dense clouds spewed from the cone and a thick white pillar shot into the air, vertical to windward, ragged in its lee. Reaching its zenith after a hundred feet or so it bowed and collapsed. The sound of thousands of gallons of water falling back on wet soil was the sound of an anti-climax.

I moved away to the thermal basin where notices warned me not to leave the boardwalk. I was fascinated to see deer droppings on the lip of the boiling pots. Animals weren't immune; early explorers found the whole skeleton of a bison in one pot. Some of the pools were quite large, blue or green, and all were steaming. Some gave off gentle wisps of vapour, others bubbled and splashed. The overflow ran away across beds of pink and cream and orange algae. Yellow mimulus grew along these channels and a few gentians.

At the side of the basin were grey crusted cones like miniature volcanoes, the largest of which roared without pause, belching steam. The place looked devilish and sounded mad. There was a feeling that the earth's crust was dreadfully thin, that surely we were taking too much for granted; these things had begun at some time, what guarantee was there that a new geyser might not erupt – now, under the boardwalk where one was standing? Would it be quick? I thought of lobsters and trod like Agag, askance in an alien world, and every now and again I was asked to pose as a foreground for a picture. I was in breeches and duvet.

Firehole Lake was up the road. The sun had come out and against the light the basin simmered gently in the pines. Across the way was Fountain Paint Pot where thick white mud plopped obscenely among rose and ivory cones. It was here that an early explorer put his foot through the crust and, a thermometer being lowered into the hole, the mercury shot up to 194°F.

I reached a campground exhausted, to find it cool and quiet – and ordinary. But in the dark, when everyone seemed to have turned in and I was making up my bed, a car came creeping round the site and a voice over a loudspeaker warned us that 'due to the bear problem' all food, utensils and beverage containers must be taken inside the vehicles.

A large camper was parked near me. In the morning the owner came across to chat. The camper was home for him and his wife. They had owned a house in Florida but when you leave a southern coast you must board your windows against the hurricanes and then your place is vandalised. So they sold the house and they had parked the camper in Phoenix, Arizona, for the past eight months; now they were starting their summer travels. He was fond of fly-fishing. I waited for the offer of a trout. 'I always put them back,' he said, 'I don't like to kill anything.' We regarded each other's vehicle with appreciation. I would have revelled in the comfort of a table at which to write, he envied me my mobility. 'You can go anywhere,' he said sadly, shaking his head.

I came to Mammoth Springs, driving below bulges of orange and pearl down which water slid like hot glass in the sun and all the trees were dead, slowly and horribly engulfed in encroaching masses of rock like pale lava. Pastel terraces loomed above the village and held in their strange pale laps water like blue vitriol. I'd had enough. I wanted to walk on grass, to see trees that lived, to hear birds; I needed to get away from reminders that the interior of the earth was molten.

I left the truck at a trail head that said Blacktail Deer Creek and walked over green downland to a valley in the bottom of which was the Yellowstone River, deep and powerful, spanned by a bridge that gave access to Montana. The river was the state line. On the return I saw a moose on the other side of a stream: a bull in velvet. It was a large ungainly beast with a short barrel out of all proportion to the long legs. A second bull stalked out of the trees. The wind was in my favour and they were unaware of me. I kept walking, watching them out of the corner of my eye. After a few moments one great head was raised, then the other. They observed me benignly and then returned to their browsing.

I stayed five days in Yellowstone, alternating long walks with canyons and waterfalls where overlooks were set like eyries on the plunging ochre walls, and crevices in the scree smoked like the vents of volcanoes. The falls were full of flood-water and there were rainbows in the spray; below, the river ran green towards the softer country where I'd seen the moose.

On a high ridge above the Yellowstone Canyon, on the fringe of the grizzly bear country, I disturbed some elk cows about a pool. They moved off reluctantly and I heard grunts and bleating. I sat down to watch. Some stopped while others moved back towards me. They had left new calves in the sage and I retreated carefully before the cows should move away and leave the calves to predators.

There were about 350 grizzlies in the park (a controversial figure but the one the park authorities gave) and most of them were in an area which tourists were discouraged from visiting. If people couldn't be dissuaded they were advised to go armed and on horse-back, advice which might prove at the least amusing if you couldn't stick on the back of a frightened horse. A ranger told me gravely what to do if I met a grizzly when I was on foot. I should curl up in the foetal position, thus protecting the vital organs, with my hands over my neck. On the other hand, he said smoothly, seeing what was in my mind, he would suggest I stand my ground and talk to the bear, which should have the effect of making the animal retreat. I liked this better, preferring a frontal attack to waiting for those great jaws to crunch through my hands into the back of my neck.

It was in the Yellowstone area that the mountain man, Hugh Glass, started his long and curious epic. He had been mauled by a grizzly and left for dead by Jim Bridger and one, Fitzgerald, but he survived to join a party which was then attacked by Arikara Indians, and everyone but Glass was killed. Some Mandan Indians now found him and took him to a fort where he picked up some kit and left the same day, joining a party of four, two of whom were shortly killed by the ubiquitous Arikaras. Glass escaped but without his gun and survived yet again to go after Bridger and Fitzgerald. When he found them he seems to have done nothing more than upbraid Fitzgerald. Ten years later his luck ran out and he and two others were scalped by the Arikaras.

The rangers were eager to know how American parks compared with British, what we did about litter, loose dogs, hunting. I told them that hunting was legal on Exmoor but I understood that the stag wasn't killed; it was caged and carted back to its territory to be chased another day. They thought I was making it up so I didn't tell them about hare coursing. Shooting was legal anywhere, I said.

And poaching, they asked; did we have poaching? Hunting (that is, shooting) is illegal in American parks but with antlers fetching $35 a pound people weren't content with picking them up (itself an offence); moose were being killed for their antlers.

Apart from poaching, tourists in America broke the rules constantly, and usually through stupidity. They would feed the animals, people with cameras would try to get as close as possible to the subject. So they were scratched and bitten by chipmunks and squirrels, gored and mauled by larger animals. Occasionally someone was killed and there would be an outcry about dangerous wild beasts. I listened and sympathised: with the authorities, but even more with the animals.

The campgrounds were anomalies where one revelled in the luxury of hot showers and flush lavatories and every night the rangers broadcast their warnings against bears, like police on Dartmoor telling you to lock your doors because there has been a prison break-out. High Bear Frequency, screamed posters in fluorescent red, and one night, returning from the lavatory without a torch, I caught a whiff of terror as if it were a virus. Every shadow was a grizzly and every tree was a lodgepole pine: unclimbable, with the branches starting 20 feet above the ground.

On the fifth day I left the park reluctantly, going out by way of the Norris thermal basin. A gentle breeze was playing and the steam drifted away so that the colours were revealed in the sunshine: greens and reds and yellows, all a little chalky as if vivid gloss paints had been mixed in a freshly opened can of white. Geysers erupted discreetly in the distance but the subterranean rumblings and burblings as you approached were daunting. They sounded too close, as if whatever was in there was about to emerge, horribly: animate, malicious, scalding. Green pools of crystal clarity shone with a horrid innocence and drained away over courses of pale lavender. One visitor, disregarding warnings (but surely subnormal) had stripped and plunged into one of these pools. When they pulled him out he had third degree burns. Amazingly, he survived.

A vent called Ebony Pot was clogged by rubbish. It emitted soft sounds and wisps of steam, giving the impression of forces working up to a cataclysmic eruption. Perhaps people threw litter down that hole from the subconscious compulsion to seal the vent and stop the escape of a power that was eminently destructive and incomprehensible.

I followed the Madison River west, lunching on its bank where elk grazed under rose-coloured cliffs. Some miles farther on was a notice that mentioned in passing the Nez Percé. I went down to the river and, feeling the cold wind of its passing, withdrew to the sticky warmth of the grey afternoon. Big brown dragonflies rustled in the bulrushes and beyond them and the pewter river I looked back at the pass through which the Nez Percé had gone in their flight to Canada.

Yellowstone was the hunting ground of Indians in prehistoric times. They had quarried the glassy face of Obsidian Cliff and traded the beautiful arrow heads as far east as Ohio; they had known Yellowstone for millennia before the white man came, but it was the Nez Percé, passing through, who monopolised one's sympathy.

Their homeland was in Oregon and Idaho where, in a country of lush meadows and teeming rivers, they fished and hunted and raised fine cattle. Treaties were made with them, and rescinded as gold was found on their land. White stockmen coveted their grazing. In the end Chief Joseph, a Christian convert, repudiated the new religion and died, handing on the struggle for survival to his son, Young Joseph.

In 1877 the Nez Percé were ordered to a reservation. Within a few days of the deadline they swam their herds across the flooded Snake and started their trek, seeking sanctuary with Sitting Bull over 1,000 miles away in Canada. All the way they were harried by the American army but they kept going with their women and children, the wounded, the aged and the sick: fighting, withdrawing, walking to a place where they could live. They killed a few settlers as they went and a handful of tourists in Yellowstone, which had become the first national park.

They were cornered a few miles from the Canadian border and Young Joseph surrendered: 'I am tired of fighting. Our chiefs are killed. . . . It is cold and we have no blankets. The little children are freezing to death. My people, some of them, have run away to the hills. . . . I want to have time to look for my children and see how many I can find. Maybe I shall find them among the dead. Hear me, my chiefs. I am tired; my heart is sick and sad. From where the sun now stands I will fight no more forever.'

He was in his thirties. With his people he was shipped to Kansas and in the heat of the plains many died. From there they were sent to live with strange tribes in Washington. Young Joseph never gave up the struggle to return to his homeland. In 1900 he was allowed to visit his father's grave and he tried to buy a tract of land there but the settlers refused. He died in 1904.

6

TETONS

IN YELLOWSTONE TIME was relative to basic needs and behaviour was controlled by the waxing and waning of the light. I ate when I was hungry, slept when I was tired. The hours passed unnoticed and I felt when I emerged from the park's west entrance that I had been away for an age, a feeling accentuated by the stridency of the outside world where the senses were assaulted by hoardings and fumes and piped music in the stores.

The impact was powerful but momentary; in self-defence one adjusted without delay: to increased and faster traffic, to notices and signs and crossings, to heat. The thermometer rose as the altitude dropped and, as I came south between the foothills of the plateau and the hazy plain of the Snake, I realised that high summer had come to Idaho – and I had scarcely seen the spring.

A week ago I'd left Jackson Hole by the north, now I had looped round and returned from the west by way of the Teton Pass. Cloud shadows were good on the back of the Grand Teton and I stopped to take a picture using a fine old barn for a foreground. The owner was elderly and struggling. He grew potatoes and was suffering from competition with big farms and big machines and too many potatoes. The price went down and the cost of fuel soared. I could have been at home except that he said he'd go out of business when gasoline reached two dollars a gallon. I didn't comment; I no longer told Americans that Britain was paying two dollars six weeks ago. But I did sympathise with the basic problems on this farm that was exposed to the full force of southerly winds which not only removed the soil but the water too. The farmer used sprinklers and when the wind blew, wide swathes of soil were left dry. And a week ago, although it snowed everywhere except here, the temperature dropped to 22 degrees and all his crops were damaged.

I spent the night below the Teton Pass and came up the last rise next morning to a sudden crest that broke to reveal Jackson Hole and the ridges of the Gros Ventres beyond, fading into infinity. They were against the sun but when I came down to the valley and turned to face the Tetons, they were full in its glare with every detail plain and all the colours clear. It was a picture from the lid of a chocolate box: black rock, white snow and blue sky: a vista framed by the leaves of silver birches quivering in the sun.

I went out to watch the Exum mountain guides initiating beginners into the mysteries of climbing technique preparatory to taking them up the Grand Teton. I talked to one, Bill Briggs: middle-aged but so nimble at skipping down rough ground at the end of the afternoon that I didn't realise he limped until we were on the trail. He had been born with an incomplete hip socket which held the ball joint so loosely that gradually the existing bone was worn away. After much study and deliberation he had the joint fused at the angle most advantageous for skiing, and subsequently was the first person to ski down the east face of the Grand Teton. I didn't learn this from him but from his former wife whose telephone number he gave me without saying that he'd been married to her. I found her in an apartment-building like a Swiss chalet on the outskirts of Jackson.

Julie was Canadian: small, neat and attractive; in her flat corduroy cap, *art nouveau* gaiters and white sweater she looked like a fashion plate even after a night out above the snow-line. She had climbed extensively, in Britain, the Alps, Canada and the States, but she had fallen badly some time ago and fractured her back. She worked as a ski instructor in the winter; in the summer she painted in oils, and there she caught the wide play of light that is a feature of the west. She was one of those rare people who have a flair not only for excelling at the things they are naturally good at but for knowing the right moment to bow out of a situation which is deteriorating and won't improve. She had been married three times, was friendly with her former husbands yet cheerful and self-sufficient; and if she was envious of my life-style, it was of that aspect that allowed me to go solo into the mountains, and the feeling was fleeting; within a few weeks she was doing it herself.

At first she was dubious about her ability to climb, to carry loads, even to walk. So I left the thought with her and went off to explore Avalanche Canyon which had several hundred feet of snow climbing beside a waterfall and an interesting descent of a convex slope which I took one look at and turned aside to pull a three-foot length of pine out of some avalanche debris. I kicked steps down the slope but where the angle was at its steepest the steps collapsed and I could do nothing else except glissade, which was fine until my pine splinter, forced through the surface as a brake, cracked with a sound like a pistol shot. The snow was soft and wet so I sat down to increase friction and stopped at the bottom with nice timing just before a boulder.

There were calypso orchids in the lower reaches of the canyon: frail blossoms of rose and cream, always in the shade and so inconspicuous against rotting logs that I went slowly, searching for them, and surprised a dark grey snake who saw me first and was already stealthily uncoiling when I spotted him, and so missed seeing the head.

During my stay in the Tetons I slept anywhere: in controlled sites

Whirlpool Canyon on the Green, through which Manly floated

Camp-site on Box Elder Creek in the Laramie Range

Jail Rock

The Sweetwater coming through Devil's Gate

Evening light on Red Butte from the camp on Bragg Mountain

Storm coming up the Tetons

Yellowstone Falls

Noon break in the Gros Ventres

Green River Crossing at Seedskedee

The Needles in the Wasatch on the Hastings Cut-off

Catherine Lake in the Wasatch

Devil's Castle. My route went up the left skyline
of the left summit beyond the fierce overhang

Silver Island Mountains in the Great Basin

when I was in the national park where no wild camping was allowed, in a glade or a lonely canyon if I still had the energy at the end of the day to drive to the park boundary, or on the floor of Julie's living room. This last was luxury in the context of my journey, for her food was delicious, her bath water always hot, and she taught me to use a washing machine: not an unmixed blessing for in my initial enthusiasm I washed everything, and my most cherished possessions, such as breeches, shrank and started to fall apart.

Even now, in the middle of June, the weather had not quite settled but although clouds might build up dramatically during the afternoon there would be only a few token claps of thunder, some lightning, a splash of rain and then the whole show would move away to another range. One morning I woke to find the bushes sparkling with raindrops and, drinking coffee, was idly moving my head to see the colours change when a large emerald beetle arrived whirring and chirruping and dipped a beak like a needle into the trumpet of a flower. It was a humming-bird. It had a violet throat and looked no larger than those butterflies which sailed through the air, themselves as large as birds.

Julie's apartment was sybaritic but the best camp-sites had delights of a different order. On still nights I might hear the touch of a paw on a dead leaf, or a snuffle that was little more than an indrawn breath, and one morning I woke to a sound on the tailboard and a weight on the sleeping bag so light that second thoughts questioned its existence until it moved. Weight was transferred: up my legs, my trunk, my chest. I raised my head and looked into the eyes of an astonished pine squirrel. He'd come after the food on the front seat.

As the heat increased the mosquitoes became a torment. One evening I sat in the back of the closed truck and swatted them with a newspaper. It was constructive; I wasn't passively enduring them, and while I swatted I wasn't bitten. I slept with a large handkerchief taped over a partially opened window.

Julie joined me for a day in Death Canyon, from the middle reaches of which we looked up at a spectacular headwall. It appeared almost vertical, contoured by a horizontal line that ran right round the head of the canyon. Above it, tall, impending and continuous, was a band of cliff which was called simply The Wall, and the horizontal line was Death Canyon Shelf. I felt a compulsion to walk along it. When we turned to go down two things had happened: Julie was considering how we might do Death Canyon Shelf and spring had come.

In Yellowstone it had been virtually winter still; in Idaho it was already summer. On this day in the Tetons spring came surging up the canyon behind us so that where on the ascent we had remarked each graceful columbine, on the return we couldn't count them.

The flowers rampaged with every colour and shade in the spectrum.

Meadows were a haze of scarlet gilia, glades were blue with lupins, paths ran between pink hedges of the tall geranium we call cranesbill. At lower altitudes there was a gentian five feet high: a ponderous spike of innumerable flowers: four pale green petals, each one most delicately stippled with spots of a colour that defeated designation, sometimes black, sometimes grey, yet reputed to be purple.

Spring overwhelmed us like love and after a few walks we didn't want to come down at night. One morning we packed our gear and walked up Cascade Canyon and came in the late afternoon to the edge of the timber where the snow was melting, and between the drifts were patches of small yellow lilies. There we pitched the tent and lounged in the sun, on one side the snow-covered divide that was our route for tomorrow, on the other, the north ridge of the Grand Teton. It was long after the sun left us that the summit rocks started to turn gold and the birds' songs died. The marmots stopped whistling and I knew for the first time in years the stark silence of nightfall above the snow-line.

We climbed the divide next day to a ridge bare of snow and covered with alpines: moss campion, the most vivid forget-me-nots, deep mauve funnels of a flower called sky pilot. We glissaded into a bowl under gaunt cliffs where all the couloirs ran out in avalanche cones and the lakes showed green patches as the ice melted. It was a long descent down Paintbrush Canyon; our backs were sore from the loads but we were pleased with ourselves and over pints of tea in Julie's dim living room we sprawled in chairs, recovered, hesitated, and plunged into plans for Death Canyon Shelf.

There was a ski lift that terminated at 10,000 feet on Rendezvous Mountain. We took this and were wafted silently and very steeply from the summer heat of Jackson Hole to a gravelly summit where, as soon as we moved away from the tourists, we were on our own. Below us on our right was Granite Canyon which, at around 8,000 feet, split into three forks, the northernmost containing Marion Lake which was to be the site of our first camp. The distance wasn't more than seven miles but there were several divides and although we'd done our best to whittle down the 35-pound loads we'd carried on our first trip, our packs were heavy and the snow was soft. Seven miles was just right for the first day.

We picked our way down snow between the timber and crossed a bowl where every wet patch among the drifts was a riot of alpine buttercups. A rise of a few hundred feet took us round a spur and we dropped down to the south fork of Granite to eat a lazy lunch on the bank of the creek.

Here the wet flats were covered by masses of white marsh marigolds but the divides were all snow which we took at a leisurely pace, occasionally coming on old tracks which might have been human but could have been bear.

When we reached the last divide we saw that the corrie containing Marion Lake was grander than the others and overhung by cliffs, while beyond it isolated mountains stood like Scottish giants but 10,000 feet high. Three miles away we saw the fine corner that marked the start of The Wall above Death Canyon Shelf.

We plunged down steepish snow under a cliff to a stream below a waterfall. There was a bridge and, on the other side, huge boulders where we pitched the tent. We took off our boots, socks and gaiters and spread them on the rocks to dry. We ate, we drank a great deal of lemonade and then played on the largest boulder, water-softened feet cringing from petrified fractured bubbles.

We turned in early and were up at six. We climbed to the frozen lake through the brilliant morning and shortly after eight stepped out on a long ridge to find the Tetons close and very distinct and, even closer, a cluster of rocks called Spearhead which seemed to take us ages to pass. The walking was easy over level snow softening a little in the sun, with buttercups on the gravel and a golden plant called sulphur flower in the crevices of the rocks.

We walked above a valley containing Fox Creek which drains down to Idaho, our goal the pass at its head. There was a small tarn on the saddle with a crescent of emerald water. I was manoeuvring to get a picture of it when Julie, who was ahead, looked back to see a troop of bighorn sheep break away below me.

We trudged up the slope to the start of Death Canyon Shelf. It was about three miles in length and above it The Wall towered like a barricade of yellow Dolomites, unbroken except for terrible loose and vertical gullies, the smooth faces streaked with black and roofed by tremendous overhangs. This continuous rampart varied between 300 and 500 feet and was at its most impressive at either end where it stood in profile above the shelf. The latter must have been well over a hundred yards in width; this didn't detract from the atmosphere but rather enhanced it, making it far more than a topographical feature. It was a specific entity separate from, and yet part of the long bare cliff above and the verdant canyon 1,000 feet below.

It was not a flat shelf but broken into knolls and dells with a steep rise to the foot of The Wall. There was still a lot of snow about (on which were the tracks of moose and deer) but where the way went close to the edge a narrow path ran, sometimes as level as a pavement, and where the ground had been bare for some time, there were clumps of alpine sunflowers.

We moved slowly and when we neared the end of the shelf and started up a rise to Mount Meek Pass, I relished this gentle progress which prolonged so delightfully the moment when we should look down on a new valley. But we emerged on a high plateau and there was another mile to go before we came out suddenly on the lip of a great escarpment above Alaska Basin, a place of scattered conifers and a cluster of little lakes showing as pools in wastes of snow. Our next camp-site was on the far side.

We prospected along the top of the scarp and came to a break and a slope of snow which gave an easy glissade to a level where we could contour above a lip and a waterfall. We had no trouble crossing creeks; if they were too deep or powerful to risk boulder-hopping, we had only to go upstream until we found a snow-bridge.

A short rise brought us over a spur and down to a bowl with a lake in the bottom, its ice broken by navy-blue channels of water. Above the inlet there were some trees on a knoll and there we pitched the tent. At the head of the corrie was the pass we aimed to cross in the morning. In the other direction we looked over the lake and Alaska Basin to the last big wall rising to a flattened cone that added several hundred feet to its height. It was a wild scene of snow and rock and a few trees. The only animals about were marmots, and as we went to bed before it got dark their whistles mingled with my dreams then and in the dawn: part of the night and the mountains and the splendid solitude.

We were at 10,000 feet, and it froze hard overnight. The snow was like iron in the morning and, anxious to be away, I fretted at the inordinate amount of time it took for the water to boil for coffee. But the snow was still hard when we came to the foot of the pass and we cut steps up it happily to come out on a knife-edge below a shattered tower. On the other side a snow field ran down to a basin from which the drainage was into Cascade Canyon, and that was our route of descent. Julie came up and said we were on the wrong pass. A new pass, I said. We dropped down scree, then snow, passing a scooped hollow into which an avalanche had fallen from a couloir on the wall, for this corrie too was delineated by yet another band of cliffs.

On the far side of the declivity we picked up a trail and looked back and saw Hurricane Pass, which we'd been intending to cross, half a mile to the north of our saddle and looking rather dull.

It was a long walk out: ten miles, but all downhill with a drop of nearly 4,000 feet. It had been winter below our pass, at Jenny Lake it was a sweltering summer's day and between, where the trail came out from the trees and crossed hanging meadows, it was like walking through a garden. Again I felt that I had been away for weeks rather than a few days, and now I realised that this disorientation was more a matter of space than of time. We had walked right round the Tetons through that high and lonely wilderness I had come to find and now, as we came into the lower reaches of the canyon and began to meet tourists, we entered a different world. I rose to a higher level of consciousness – or a different one – because who could say that the level you lived at up there, above the snow-line, because it was animal, was lower?

As a human being I was startled to see a mule deer in the shadows with her huge bat ears; was astonished, a little lower, to see Julie's stony face as I turned to her, to hear her hiss: 'Keep walking; there's a moose!' Right beside us, a few feet away, a big bull stood tense, motionless as the tree trunks. I kept walking but stiff as a retreating dog. We were too near civilisation; I could have accepted him 4,000 feet above, not here: a mile from the motor-boats on Jenny Lake.

I went to look at the original cabins of the homesteaders: Mormon Row near Blacktail Butte and, in the north of Jackson Hole, Cunningham's Cabin, the scene of a shooting in 1893. Two men with a string of horses entered the valley from Idaho and found accommodation in the cabin. The following spring men arrived who called themselves law enforcement officers and said they were looking for horse thieves. They were taken to Cunningham's Cabin where, after a short gun battle, the two occupants were killed and the law enforcement officers rode away with the captured horses. At least one historian suggests that the horse thieves may have been the men who claimed to be law officers.

The cabin is well-preserved; set four-square and squat on the wide floor of the valley, with the Tetons in the background, it looks neat and cosy; only the story makes it shocking.

I drove up to Togwotee Pass for the view of the Tetons that makes the most sensational approach to Jackson Hole. It was a hot afternoon with big purple clouds coming up under a milky ceiling. On top there were shattered cliffs without shadows and when I turned for the descent the sunlight had gone and I thought I should see no mountains; but suddenly they burst into view, compact and symmetrical, rising from either end of the range to culminate in the splendid spire of the Grand. I didn't stop but went slowly, losing them as the forest closed in; then it opened out again to reveal them a little closer, a little higher, and so all down the road. And on this lowering evening, with bad weather building up, they were two-dimensional, like the Cuillins of Skye with a warm front coming in from the Atlantic, and the air was sticky with humidity.

I visited an art gallery in Jackson and was approached by the director, a compatriot who divided his time between Jackson and Arizona: a bluff, genial man blooming when he heard the accent. I was bewitched by the pictures.

'How do they get the *light*?'

'It's easy here,' he said airily, 'the light is so magnificent' – as if I hadn't noticed – 'it's in Britain that painters have difficulty.'

I conceded that the light of an offshore island was different; it had to
be because of all that sea: softer and yet investing white with a stunning
brilliance (remembering the lime-washed cottages in the Hebrides) but
what was it that accounted for the clarity of the American west? The
aridity of the land, the lack of atmospheric pollution? Did each continent have its own peculiar air so that if you were set down in the centre of
a large land mass you might identify it as Asia or Australia or Africa?

One evening looking for the buffalo and finding myself out on the
Yellowstone road I thought I might return to the thermal basins – and
then I thought how far it was to drive to Yellowstone and only for a
whim, and I was tired. I was satiated with colour, with violence, with
beauty. I turned and drove south again in an agony of indecision. At a
place called the Oxbow Bend where the Snake comes out of Jackson
Lake, Mount Moran was reflected in the water: in silver and grey and
pastel greens.

I drew into a lay-by and switched on the radio. A weather forecast
might focus my mind.

With the first bars I knew it didn't matter what I did or where I went; I
had only to go with the stream. It was the *Larghetto* from Beethoven's
second symphony. The sweet rhythm of the strings stole out across the
water to brush the tips of the pines and merge with the bulk of Mount
Moran. I drove home in peace. Home was where I slept.

The buffalo eluded me. They ranged over Jackson Hole and I searched
for them in vain. On my last evening I took a dirt road across Antelope
Flats and came out on the bank of the Snake. A storm was coming up
from the south but as yet the mountains were full in the sun. I watched
the shadows advance across the sloping snow fields and the cloud drop
to be shredded by granite peaks. White rain-curtains drifted along the
crests and in the west the sky turned lemon above the plains of Idaho.

A man came along with some small boys in a car. The bison were on
the road, he said. I packed up my tea things and by the time I reached the
highway it was empty. It was dusk now and I dawdled down the road
across a wide meadow and saw them approaching: the massive hump,
the slim hindquarters, unmistakable.

An old bull was in the lead. I was struck by the dainty forelegs under
the shaggy hair and remembered the impossibly slender legs of the Bulls
of Lascaux and knew that the Stone Age artists made no mistake. The
whole herd was there: cows, yearlings, little red calves like domestic
calves.

A car skidded to a halt and a fat man leapt out with a camera. There
was scarcely any light left but he had a flash. He walked towards the
buffalo exclaiming: 'Ain't that sump'n?' His wife sat stonily in the car.

From behind the wheel of Old Crump I watched with academic interest. More cars came speeding up the road and the fat man waved them down hysterically. I warmed to him a little. The buffalo stalked across the road as if they owned it. A young bull stopped and regarded Old Crump, his horns red in a lurid sunset. Not long ago his kind darkened the plains and when they stampeded the ground shook. They faded into the night, amiable but still magnificent.

7

AT INTERVALS I had returned to the Cameron place at Bondurant ostensibly to pick up my mail but mainly because I was fascinated by the life of a working ranch. On my second visit Pete asked me if I could ride a horse. I said I could sit on a quiet one and next morning was mounted on a big grey gelding called Breeches. I appreciated the comfort of the western saddle but realised immediately that dropping the reins, or hooking them over my arm, could spell disaster. They were, of course, the single reins of the west.

The Camerons were moving cattle. Everyone helped. There were the two hired hands and Pete, and Holly on a nimble little horse which could leap into a canter from a standing start and turn on a sixpence. Spurs were the secret, she said, but she wasn't wearing spurs.

One didn't rise to the trot, but sat down and was jogged unmercifully. Pete said my stirrups were too short so I lengthened them and then I seemed to be all legs. I shortened them again and finally put them midway and just sat, which was what I was meant to do. I was captivated when my horse responded to the rein laid against his neck although there appeared to be something of a time lag between command and consummation. The others turned like centaurs, with high hands.

We moved at the pace of the walking cows, Pete going ahead to open gates, the rest of us fanned in the rear like sheepdogs nudging a flock of sheep. I had been worried about chisellers' burrows but Breeches had large feet which he planted like plates across the entrances and never stumbled except at streams, and there it was incidental to a slide and a plunge and one was prepared.

I had wondered, seeing such numbers of them, if horses were not a luxury; they travelled only a little faster than a man on foot. Now I saw their advantages. That slight difference in pace was critical, and how could a walking man spring after stragglers from the herd? Innumerable head of cattle were lost to the emigrants, for instance, because their horses were too tired to follow strays, or had even run off with the cows. And then there were creeks; a horse was essential when it came to water. It was surprising, too, how much advantage the extra height gave, particularly among willows or tall sage. The British think of willows as trees, but in America there is a species any height between a bilberry and a blackthorn, and invariably just too tall to see over when on foot.

Pete initiated me into the mysteries of irrigation. On the bench that was an ancient bank of the river he had a field of alfalfa. It looked flat but it had incipient gradients and these were contoured by parallel ditches which he had dug himself, laying them out with the aid of a spirit level. There were about 150 feet between channels fed from a water-course which came down the valley behind the house, itself supplied from the creek. The water in the main channel was controlled by wooden gates.

The ground between the ditches was irrigated by portable dams which could be moved into position by a man or dragged behind a horse. The dam was merely a piece of heavy plastic, about six feet square, with an oversize hem at one edge through which was slotted a plank long enough to project a foot or so at either end. The plank was placed across a ditch so that the ends rested on each bank. The loose plastic was pulled back against the current, weighted with clods and stones, and the resulting pool overflowed to flood the dry ground.

Down in the meadows where the ditches had not been dug with the help of a spirit level, the channels didn't contour and the water was less controllable; if sluggish, it wasted time in taking too long to fill behind the dam; when too fast it took the plastic with it as it filled the pool.

I found the dams light and easy to move at first but they grew heavier as the heat built up in the afternoons. One became somnolent, grasping at any straw for an excuse to straighten the back: redwinged blackbirds patrolling the margin of the flood for worms, the trumpeting of cranes from the willow thickets – or I would stroll over to the bridge below the house and sit and watch the little dust-coloured garter snakes that lived in the planks. Although it was a far cry from lush Indiana, the place had an air if not the appearance of Gene Stratton-Porter; one half expected a child in a sun-bonnet to materialise, coming barefoot across the meadow with a pitcher of lemonade.

While waiting for the pack trip I went into the Wyoming Range. Old logging roads contoured slopes where aspens replaced felled conifers and in one place a brook crossed the track and the mud was a shimmering mosaic of tiny blue butterflies that had come down to drink. From these high tracks there were views of the Gros Ventres where we were to ride, but at 15 miles distance there was no detail, only a jumbled horizon and muted shades: greens, greys, pale browns that could have been rock or scree or just scorched grass. As I came down to the road-end the light revealed three buttresses across a canyon. Built of earth they fanned smoothly downwards while gullies between them, funnel-shaped, fanned upwards in reverse. The flaring ravines filled with shadow as the sun declined and locked the triangles in an exquisite natural geometry.

We assembled at the ranch on a Sunday morning, the firstcomers being a couple from the east, Sally and John. I arrived to find them mounted and circling the corral, getting the feel of their horses before a preliminary ride. I was given a plump little animal called Mizzou and we ambled over the meadows to the Hoback which we crossed belly-deep with a great thundering of water and a lot of spray. From the far bank we went straight up the hill, raising a couple of sandhill cranes which flew past us with loud calls and so slowly that we could see their red pates. It was steep at the top and we had to lead the horses. On the crest we tied them to trees and dropped down out of the wind to have lunch.

We talked. John had ridden before but Sally had never been on the back of a horse until this morning. American women amazed me. Sally wasn't young and, although lithe and strong, the plunge into the river had been daunting, the climb to the ridge steep – and everyone knew it was sinful to grasp the horn. But they were revelling in the experience and were asking so many questions that I could be thoroughly lazy: leaning back and staring at a curiously shaped snowfield on the Wyoming Range, wondering if the blue butterflies were still forming their fragile pattern round the moose prints where the brook crossed the trail. . . . It occurred to me that one of the subtle attractions of a pack trip, for people who are accustomed to making weighty decisions, is the abdication of all responsibility.

We were accommodated a mile up the road at Game Hill, the ranch that belonged to Holly's parents: a spacious place with a big living room and an old wooden porch. There were a couple of log cabins for sleeping and some tepees, and another cabin with flush lavatories and showers. At dinner we were joined by a small ebullient woman in her sixties, Virginia, who was coming along for the ride. She had once owned and run the Jackson newspaper but now she concentrated on her ranch, and flying. At one time she had flown commercially. I'd seen these little private aircraft at Jackson Hole; they buzzed like venturesome insects past the Teton precipices and over the canyons that must be a welter of down-draughts. It was Virginia who, pottering along the east face of the Grand, looked down to see Bill Briggs' ski tracks descending the summit snowfield and took an incredible picture that I'd seen at Julie's place. (The snow is steep but *en face* it looks like a wall.)

We left next morning, our gear in duffel bags on a pack horse, our personal possessions – cameras, binoculars, cups – in our saddle bags. We had two pack animals: a colt who had never carried anything before except in training, and a large mule called Chester. At the head of the line Pete led the colt while Virginia came last leading Chester – but only for a few hundred yards. Then he was turned loose. He should have followed at the same calm pace as the rest of us, but where we halted on command to give the horses a blow, Chester halted at his own discretion and trotted to catch up, threatening to scramble all the eggs and rattling like a loose canteen. He carried the kitchen: two zinc containers packed with food and implements.

We left the Hoback valley by the glen that ran eastward to Doubletop, a peak of nearly 12,000 feet. It was about ten miles away as the hawk flew but closer to eighteen by the narrow earthy trails which we followed. As we rose, the Wyoming Range was slowly revealed behind us, becoming that much grander with every halt. The air grew cooler and there were more flowers. At the lower altitude it had been quite arid with sage and a few pronghorns – which I associated with semi-desert country. Where the valley opened out to high grazing land we came on one or two herds of Herefords ('Over-grazing', Virginia remarked severely, observing the thin pasture), and two men on horseback deviated to speak to Pete. Apart from ourselves they were the last people we were to see for days.

At the end of the afternoon we came to a long green meadow surrounded by pines. A creek ran down it and at the bottom it had been dammed by beavers so that the water backed up to form a swamp where there were spotted sandpipers. Pete led us, lagging now for we'd come fifteen miles and the horses were fat, down the meadow to the fringe of the trees. I slid off, holding to the horn for support like a sailor grabbing an arm as he steps on the jetty. Mizzou drooped like a dead flower.

We unsaddled while Pete went out to place the picket pins. There was plenty to do about the camp and we were glad to do it. We weren't tired; merely tired of being in one position. Wood was collected for the fire: cones, brash and logs; water drawn from the creek, which wasn't clean because the beavers' dam had slowed it down and the horses were wallowing upstream but none of us was the kind to bother about a few bugs and a bit of silt. The fire was lit, Holly started cooking and Pete came back from the horses.

We were sipping drinks when there was an implosive thud perhaps half a mile away, without warning or echo. A tree falling, Pete said. Once Julie and I had been hurrying through the forest as a wind was rising and there was a splintering crack. It was a trunk snapping, and we'd been ready for it, but when a tree falls on a still evening one has a sense of intrusion, as if a certain privacy had been invaded.

From our camp-site we looked straight up the meadow to Doubletop, a corner of its rimrock projecting towards us in a prow, the two wings flaring back at right angles. The rock looked like limestone, friable but scenic.

Supper arrived. We were ravenous as wolves. We'd had smoked oysters with the drinks, now, after a home-made soup, we had elk marinated in a *teriyaki* sauce. At each meal Holly baked fresh rolls in an oven above the fire.

Before the light faded some of us strolled down to the dam where the beaver was swimming quietly about its pool. I was unprepared for the size of the animal, or for its alarm signal. When it became aware of us it hit the water with a slap of its tail, a noise that resounded across the marsh and sent the sandpipers scurrying up the creek, then it dived.

With dusk the deer came out in the meadow, followed by a moose which startled one of the picketed horses to such an extent that he couldn't get over his fright and had to be moved away because the whinnying got on our nerves. One might have wondered if he'd seen a bear but for the fact that the bitch had shown no interest. Pete took a dog on pack trips to give warning of 'growlies' in the camp. Sis was so similar to a Welsh collie that she would have looked at home behind a flock of sheep on Snowdon but here, in Wyoming, her job was bears.

There was a hunters' camp just below the meadow, complete with folding camp-beds tied to a tree, picnic tables, cylinders of bottled gas. Pete could remember when the Gros Ventres swarmed with elk; now they were decimated. In the fall every draw in some areas was 'an aluminium town'. There was a hope that the region would be designated a wilderness area and then hunting might be allowed only under the auspices of a guide. Such a system should result in fewer animals being killed, fewer dying of wounds, and the conservation of breeding stock. I thought of the threats to Scottish wilderness areas and wished the subject hadn't been raised.

We spent two nights in this place, and next morning the pack animals were left behind while we rode out from the top of the meadow and through the forest to an area of minor ridges which we contoured when we could and sometimes took direct, the horses scrambling up tilted bedrock with a great clatter and flying of sparks.

Quite suddenly we came out of the forest to a thin scatter of pines. Until now the rise from the Hoback, despite the intimate detail of sharp rises and steep drops, had been generally gradual: now the mountains reared above us like a breaking wave. There was a splendid confusion of rock: slabby red walls that looked like sandstone; granite intrusions, rather broken with a lot of vegetation; and then the yellow limestone of Doubletop's prow, bristling with overhangs.

There were two corries, on different levels, with a cliff between them. Down the cliff came a long waterfall and in the lower corrie was a marsh and a shallow lake. An old path led past a mine entrance to a platform and the remains of a cabin, all so wild and overgrown that if Pete hadn't told us the story I might have missed the signs of human occupation. As recently as the 1950s a miner lived here but he was killed when his horse fell down a cliff. I'd remarked on the steadiness of our animals when they traversed steep slopes and Pete had pointed out that these were mountain horses, born and bred to the terrain. Perhaps the miner should have had a different horse.

After lunch we were left to our own devices and I climbed the cliff by a rake and went up the ridge opposite Doubletop for photographs and alpines. We were living at an altitude between 7,000 and 8,000 feet. Below that the spring flowers were over; here they were in their prime. In the meadows the flowers reached to our horses' bellies, sometimes to our knees. There were constant surprises, from the familiar name attached to an alien flower – or animal – to a new name for a familiar specimen. Their bluebell is a borage, the primrose no primula but an *evening* primrose; the American robin is a thrush with a rufous breast. One came to the conclusion that the pioneers were homesick and, feeling that they would never see a bluebell or a robin again (and how poignant that must have been) they transferred the names to a flower with blue bells and the first bird they saw with a red breast. On the other hand one was startled to find that bear berry was kinnikinnick, that a chickadee was a tit, that the golden-crowned kinglet was a firecrest.

The variety of flowers increased until one abandoned all attempts to identify them and even lost sight of which were the English, which the American names. Our boots were coloured with pollen, and the scents, of dust and resin, sweat, leather and a hundred different flowers, were overwhelming.

Two deer passed as we ate our supper that night, and the sky clouded over leaving a gap through which light streamed between the forests and the sable clouds to paint the rimrock gold. Pete and Holly told us gravely that this was the finest view in the country, and we as gravely agreed with them.

The nights were warm, but shortly before the dawn it grew bitterly cold and no one moved until the sun reached us. Everything looked pale and uninviting until that moment, from the dark trees and the colourless meadow to the cold prow of Doubletop. One withdrew to the warmth of the sleeping bag and waited for the sun to rise.

On the third morning we rode out of the meadow and over a divide into a parallel glen with another waterfall. We continued crossing the grain of the land, with strange mountains rising on our right, which changed shape as we travelled. They were big biscuit-coloured bulks which were mostly scree but with the bones of bedrock showing through and, occasionally, on the summit ridges, the hint of a cliff dropping away on the other side.

Mizzou lagged. There was constant skirmishing as Chester the mule tried to jump the line, squeezing into gaps and then slowing down so that the line strung out. Temper showed. If Chester tried to pass Holly's horse it turned and snarled at him like a dog. There were a lot of flies. When we crossed creeks and draws we stayed well clear of the horse in front.

But I was getting the feel of things; on the first day I had allowed Mizzou to descend hills in long diagonals like a frightened novice descending a snow-slope, now I'd persuade him to take a more direct line. If I let him take his own course it became a caricature, as if he were bored. One had to remain alert. We went through a lot of timber, often leaving the trail to circumvent obstacles. There was a constant risk of low branches knocking us backwards, of a knee crushed against a trunk. John, dropping behind, had some difficulty holding his horse when he mounted again; he came galloping downhill through the forest, leaping fallen trees and providing a splendid *divertissement*.

At the end of one afternoon we trailed down a sloping irregular meadow to Jack Pine Beaver Ponds. The beavers had gone and a trickle of water escaped through a breach in their dam. The camp-site faced north and lost the sun early, the light mounting a massive hill where two old snow-drifts were all that remained on a slope that was otherwise all scree. The sky was eggshell blue with a few high clouds. After supper people drifted away leaving me to write and Pete lying on his back by the fire, smoking, his hat over his eyes, the dog at his feet watching something in the reeds by the pond.

That night I slept beside a boulder at the top of a slope from which I could look over the camp to the big scree mountain. It was difficult to sleep. I watched the stars for an hour or so until I realised that the sky was lightening in the east, a frieze of pines silhouetted against the pallor. After a while the glow started to pulsate as if the sky were breathing, and I thought the trees moved. There was the faintest rustle but the grasses beside my head, themselves silhouetted, were immobile. All this time water was talking on two notes, as if there were two voices, the trickle and the drop. Just before the light reached me a single fir tree flamed with silver fire, and then its branches were outlined against the moon which rose majestically and floated clear.

The trees had stopped moving. Above me the rock gleamed roughly as it must have gleamed for centuries. There was a little turfy ledge, crescent-shaped, where I had spread my bag. I wouldn't be the first person to have slept in this place.

Next day we continued westward, over a divide and down the West Shoal Creek. We lunched on its bank where the water was cold and clear and there were fringed gentians in the grass. That afternoon we had to open the trail as we came back over Deer Ridge, chopping up fallen trees and dragging them aside. In the course of conversation Virginia remarked casually that she had a lot of land and no money. I asked if she felt like a custodian and she acquiesced with surprise, as if that were the only relationship one could have with land. She had discovered that one of her ancestors was a Mormon woman who had pushed a handcart over the Rockies. Perhaps it was the Mormon folk memory that had to do with the ethics of holding land in trust rather than owning it.

We came to the top of the last ridge and looked down at the valley of the Hoback. The ground was suddenly dry and we were raising a cloud of dust. Small white lilies bloomed in the arid soil and the red-tailed hawks were quartering the slopes. We dropped down the hill easily, slumped in our saddles: travellers coming home.

8

WIND RIVERS

OLD CRUMP'S BRAKES had become noisy and ineffectual. When I came to leave the ranch I stopped at a garage recommended by Pete and asked them to fit new shoes. They couldn't do it until Monday and this was Friday. I had a weekend to fill. I decided to go into the Wind Rivers.

In the early evening I followed a road above the dark waters of Frémont Lake. In the south-west there was a milkiness over the plains. That, I was pleased to think, marked humidity above the Great Salt Lake. Actually the lake was nearly 200 miles away and it was more likely that the haze was smoke from a forest fire in the Salt River Range; all the same, by the time you were this far west, whether emigrant or modern traveller, the thought of the deserts loomed large in the mind. It may have been this thought that prompted me to turn aside to prolong, if only for a weekend, the delights and advantages of a country that sparkled with lakes and creeks and cascades, a land where the sun was still friendly.

Two miles short of the road-end I left the highway and eased along a track into a glade surrounded by trees. That night I had wild onions with my supper; and since I'd done some shopping I had fresh salad, pineapple and milk so the drop from the luxury of Holly's cooking was not so sharp as might have been expected. It would be different tomorrow night when everything had to be carried on my own back rather than a mule's.

There was a heavy frost. As I ate breakfast in my survival gear a squirrel came down a pine – and suddenly went mad. It raced round the trunk in ascending and descending spirals so fast I was certain I saw head and tail simultaneously but it was a wide trunk so I concluded that this was a red blur of squirrel like a light trail on a night photograph. In fact it was three squirrels.

I drove to the road-end and set off, rejoicing in a load I could scarcely feel. I had no tent, stove or axe. I had food, a jersey, waterproofs, sleeping bag, camera and the mat I slept on. That was a luxury but it weighed less than four ounces.

The path rose gently through timber to emerge on an undulating tableland where the granite spires of the Wind Rivers stood to the north-east about ten miles away.

I like to get the structure of a range clear in my mind; at the best it gives an idea of the country, at the worst it could mean survival. All ranges are different but all have a system, which is based on the drainage. The Tetons are a compact group approached on the east by short sharp canyons. Dinosaur and Yellowstone are plateaux intersected by one or two immense gorges. The Gros Ventres are a chain with access by way of long and gentle glens. And what of the Wind Rivers? I looked at the map (two and a half inches to the mile, so a restricted area) and I looked at the ground between me and the main divide. The map showed that the drainage was roughly north-east to south-west. Looking out over that ten-mile stretch of country all I could see was a glorious jumble of granite with lakes like jewels on my own level, and in the middle distance gaunt precipices intersecting so that I had no idea where or how they might end their plunge – except in one place where, in the bottom of a gash like a sabre-cut, was a glimpse of water with the dark sheen of jet. It could have been Gorge Lake and may well have been Suicide. I was to encounter convoluted topography in the Sierras but nowhere was I to find such titanic and glaciated disorder as prevailed in the Wind Rivers. To have come here before the trails were made would have been a great adventure.

The men who had that experience were members of Frémont's first expedition. When Frémont came to the Wind Rivers he was a young lieutenant in the army's Bureau of Topographical Engineers, a post that meant he was a government explorer. In 1842, the year of the first expedition that he led, the frontier was still on the Missouri and although a few emigrant wagons went to Oregon that year there was as yet no established trail, and two years were to pass before Elisha Stevens led the first wagon train to California. But Americans were pushing west; there were British in Oregon and Mexicans in California. It was politic to encourage settlement beyond the Sierras before another nation staked its claim. Frémont was sent out to survey and map the country between the Missouri and South Pass.

Most of the party were voyagers – mountain men. Among them, acting as guide, was Kit Carson whom Frémont met on the river boat when Carson was returning to the mountains after enrolling his daughter in a St Louis convent school.

From South Pass Frémont saw the Wind Rivers. He was twenty-nine years old and he decided then that the culminating point of this expedition should be the ascent of the highest peak in the range. So they headed north-west, skirting the high ground until they reached a lake where a base camp was set up and, with the pick of his men, including the map-maker, Preuss, Frémont rode away to the mountain.

They travelled north to Island Lake: 16 miles on the map but that should be doubled for the distance on the ground, and they travelled at

16 miles a day, which was good going without trails. (I travelled at 17 miles a day with trails.) Before Island Lake Frémont had split the party again, which was taking a risk since he knew that at any time the Blackfeet might be coming south to raid the Crows and Shoshonis and he could find himself in the middle, but he thought he could climb his peak and be back in a day, so they left the mules and all their equipment, including bedding, and made a dash for the summit.

The place where Frémont left the mules was somewhere in the area that I was making for this July day. I came in from the west and at some point I had to strike the line of his northern route, when I would turn and follow him. From his report he had a rough trip, but he was a pioneer. I had advantages; I had a map and in the morning I crossed the tableland that would have been pleasant walking even without trails. In the afternoon I started to descend a series of switchbacks, and at the same time the trail wound round the margins of lakes, down draws where a gorgeous crimson primula bloomed in the scree; it zigzagged through scraps of forest and at last plunged into the tortuous and tormented valley where Frémont left his mules.

Suddenly I realised that I was on my own, except for a compass. I had walked off the edge of the map. It looked as if the trail crossed a river. There was a powerful waterfall which had scoured out a deep pool at the downstream end of which was a fallen tree that formed a bridge. I wasn't worried about falling in – the water wasn't fast at that point – but immersion would ruin the camera and all the film I'd taken. Forest and small cliffs obscured the country but my objective was Lester Pass and this was on the map. So I took a bearing and decided that if I followed up the near bank of the river eventually I'd be reunited with the trail.

Now I was on the kind of terrain where Frémont had trouble, and small wonder; it was a matter of feeling the way instinctively round bluffs, over crests, through swamps, trying to think ahead over the next ridge or round the corner – and you could seldom see more than a few yards ahead. Occasionally I'd come on a deer path which might help me for a while; once or twice I saw rudimentary cairns, merely a stone or two – the type that people place when lost to guide them if they have to retreat. No trail was ever beaten here. At intervals I glimpsed a high col to the east flanked by a sweeping buttress; now and again I heard water falling. The col demarcated the valley, the water was the river; I clung to the sound of water and progress was slow. With something as grand as an 11,000 foot pass ahead it was frustrating to creep step by step round a thorny shrub on a slope that wasn't steep enough to give me a climb and yet too steep to take in my stride.

After a mile or so I rejoined the trail and followed it smartly, climbing through thinning timber until I came out on a lake cupped in granite, with a frieze of pines against the bare mountains. Frémont would have come past here.

It was an hour before sunset. I stripped and spread my clothes to dry. The explorers had done a lot of tumbling too: in streams, down rocks. I had the same problems – but where mosquitoes were concerned, I now had a potent repellent made by the Cutter laboratories. I pitied Frémont. The evening sun was very bright, the trout were jumping, and the mosquitoes homed in on me in such numbers that, unwilling to cover myself with repellent while my breeches dried, I had to sweat it out in waterproof trousers. There was a new problem: changing a film without trapping a mosquito inside the camera.

There were no clouds, and no sunset colours, but the big buttressed band of rock that formed the skyline was gilded momentarily, then the light waned and the shadows in the great gullies lost their depth, until the mountain assumed the cold and neutral aspect of twilit rock.

It was a good night. Nothing disturbed me. I would have liked to waken in the small hours to see the stars reflected in the water but I didn't wake until the dawn and then it was grumpily. There had been a frost and the sleeping bag was soaked. I dressed in my damp clothes and breakfasted from a wedge of bread, some slimy cheese and a cup of weak lemonade. I was aware that all the mountains, the pines and the rocky shore were reversed in water as still as a pond; I itemised the details so that I wouldn't forget, would be able to recall the image when I needed it. Now, stiff-legged against damp corduroy, belching and shivering, I started uphill for the pass.

After a few strides I found my rhythm and I didn't slow down until I was kicking steps up the snow below the pass and the exertion reminded me that I was at 11,000 feet.

Frémont suffered on this section. Carson had led off at a terrific pace from the mule camp and by the time they reached 10,000 feet everyone was suffering. Frémont taxed Carson with going too fast and they thought they were suffering from 'mountain sickness'. But they were fit, young, hard, and they'd taken nine weeks rising slowly from the Missouri valley. Even though they were acclimatised, they were going too fast.

From Lester Pass I looked back to the lake where I had bivouacked and saw that it was one of a string set like dark sapphires in the bottle-green forests amongst rocks that looked like a pearly pavement and were in fact as contorted as a lava field.

I explored the pass: a wide saddle bare of snow, with a tarn among the stones, and the peaks on the other side. In the middle of July spring had only just reached this altitude and, since it wouldn't be long before the first snows came, the flowers had to put on a spurt to complete their life cycle. So they were showy and of them all it was the alpine sunflower that was the most dazzling. America has many yellow composites; this one is so short as to appear stemless and the disc as well as the ray is yellow. Each flower is about three inches in diameter and their blooming gave the impression that a god had scattered coins across the pass.

There was white columbine; among the alpine cushion plants – the sky pilot, moss campion, golden whitlow grass – this tall and fragile woodland flower bowed in the breeze at 11,000 feet.

I crossed the saddle and came down past tarns at different levels to a lake called Little Seneca where the trail for Island Lake and Indian Pass climbed a depression on the right. If Frémont went the easiest way he took that route. Island Lake was a mile or two to the north-east and there, without food or blankets, his party of climbers spent the night. They did have a fire and Preuss stayed awake, rotating in order to keep warm. It had been the middle of August. I'd had frost a month earlier.

Next day, crossing a snowfield, Preuss slipped and fell 200 feet but escaped with bruising and shock. Suffering from hunger, and with Frémont ill, they retreated to Island Lake. The fittest man went back to the last camp and brought up the mules, food and bedding. In the morning they started again, riding until it was no longer possible then, leaving the mules, they scrambled up what is known as Woodrow Wilson Peak. It wasn't the highest in the Winds but at well over 13,000 feet it was a rare achievement. They had no alpenstocks and no crampons, they carried no rope and the only concession to aid occurred when Preuss and others, hesitating before what appears to have been a smooth and exposed slab, found a timely handhold in a ramrod which someone extended from the other side.

I walked from Little Seneca to Seneca Lake through a pleasure ground of fine cliffs, perched boulders and *roches moutonnées*. Beside Seneca I started to meet people: fishermen, back-packers, walkers out for the day. I came on a bird like a large grouse with three chicks, and there were chipmunks whose lack of timidity suggested that they were accustomed to being fed. In parks and wilderness areas the numbers of chipmunks always increased in popular places.

It was ten miles from Seneca to the car park. The flowers were good, the bird life scanty. Although generally descending, there were un-dulations in the path. I'd done nearly 30 miles and my feet were tender. The temperature was perfect; I had worn breeches in case it should turn cold but it hadn't; conversely I was never uncomfortably warm. In the afternoon I reached the high tableland and saw the sky black to the south, over the Green River, and heard thunder rolling round the hills. A spatter of rain came to nothing. I tramped on. Six miles to go and all downhill and my feet were sore. I tried to use gravity for propulsion but the gradient wasn't steep enough. I met more people, some asking me the way. It grew hot as I lost height, then clouds would shadow the sun and it was cool.

I slept in the glade where the squirrel family lived, the ones that chased each other round the tree trunk. There was a muted sunset; I was too tired to leave my glade to photograph it.

While I worked in the garage office – writing letters, answering the telephone, doing my accounts – the mechanics ground down the brake drums where rivets had scored grooves, fitted new shoes (I thought of shoeing the oxen before the deserts), aligned the brakes so that they pulled less to the left than before, but they couldn't get them perfect. That was all right, I assured the concerned proprietor, I'd got used to the pull; I'd compensate a little less. They did a rough service, wired up the silencer that was hanging by one shaky bracket, and charged me $74. All the way across the States I was to find garage owners and staff, in large towns as well as small villages, uniformly obliging, competent and cheap.

I bought a new ice-box: a hard one; people would sit on the polystyrene type. We – they – had gone through two in two months. I re-stocked with ice, milk, fresh fruit and vegetables. I drew money, bought film and sent exposed film to Kodak with a new return address: Verdi, Nevada. It had a romantic ring; before it were the deserts, afterwards, the Sierras. There was one mail drop between the ranch and Verdi, Nevada; this was in Salt Lake City. I expected to reach it within a week.

So there we were: Old Crump fettled, we'd taken on petrol, water and food. I needed a bath but no doubt I'd find some place where I could get down to the Green River. We drove west out of Pinedale and after 11 miles came to a T-junction and a tiny place called Daniel where one road (the one I knew) went north to the Tetons, and the other south to Utah.

We turned south. The Green River Rendezvous was held at Daniel and I stopped for a picture but there were too many shacks and power poles in the way. It was at the Green River Rendezvous that Jim Bridger met Marcus Whitman, the missionary who was also a doctor, and asked him if he could remove an arrow-head. Bridger had been shot three years previously. Two arrows had lodged; one was pulled out, the other had to be cut and the head left in his back. It was made of iron, was three inches long, not only barbed but hooked at the point. It had struck bone, and a cartilaginous substance had formed round it. Whitman ex-tracted the head in public and the trappers were so impressed that a number of them came forward to have *their* arrow-heads removed, all without anaesthetic.

9

GREEN RIVER TO THE WEBER

A STORM GATHERED across the valley of the Green, the sun's rays picking out bands of cream shale with a lurid light, and then I came to the river: a wide and gentle stream with a low scarp on its far bank above a belt of cottonwoods. The storm moved eastwards but clouds remained with big shadows over the land, and the sunlight between them bringing up the colour in foliage, in the baked yellow clay of the bluffs, in the river, which was blue, not green.

I had expected to find something remarkable at Names Hill without defining what it should be; a collection of cars perhaps, an information centre giving some kind of commentary on the fact that this was where the overlanders came down from Sublette's Cut-off to sweet water – although the river was a mixed blessing. They would have been travelling for most of two days, resting at night with the oxen in the yokes, and when they saw the river their first thought would have been that at last the animals could slake their thirst; their second, the level of the water.

In the early 1840s there was no ferry; if the river was low they forded, if it was high they had to wait and, for those going to California, every day lost would be a day nearer the early snowfalls in the high Sierras. So there would be a point at which they pushed across too soon, and people and animals were drowned. To look at the river now, deceptively smooth and slow-running, one couldn't imagine it in spate – until I remembered the brown flood-waters pouring past Steamboat Rock.

The people arrived at Names Hill after the bulk of the winter snows had melted but if the early summer were wet in the huge catchment area of the Green, the river would be high and they would have to wait at the crossing, or go in and risk everything. Men would swim their horses across but the women and children would stay in the wagons. And if a wagon were caught by the current and turned over . . . the children would have gone down quickly, the women would have floated for a while, buoyed up by their skirts; doubtless very few could swim. Many people must have stood on the east bank, morning after morning, studying the river, calculating whether to take the risk or the one at the other end – deep water or deep snow?

There was an historic marker beside the road and a few car tracks showed that people had stopped recently. Between road and river there was a decrepit café and a dump of rusted cars. The café was closed. I walked up the empty road and looked across the river. It was beautiful but I was disturbed. A strong woman would have stood on the other side and known she could influence her husband either way – but that woman would have prayed for guidance, so why should I feel disturbed? Because when you have small children you must have a hell of a lot of faith when you know that last season a wagon turned over in the middle of the river. It's difficult to have faith when the danger is literally in front of you. It's like having the self-control to stand your ground and deflect a grizzly by talking to it.

After the crossing the emigrants followed the river south for a few miles and then struck west again making for the spurs that terminate the Salt River Range. They would have had some uphill work crossing the spurs, but the week's travelling involved would have been preferable to that section of Sublette's prior to the Green. The Salt River Range had forested ridges; there was wood for fuel, and convenient springs.

I followed the Green south and, at the Fontenelle Creek, took a dirt road west, over a rise and down into the basin of the creek. The bottom land was strung with ranches but on the arid ground there were oil wells. I had been passing these all the way from Daniel: the little nodding-donkey structures that were amusing rather than obtrusive; the land they stood on looked good for little else but oil. Even the scenery was, like the curate's egg, good only in parts.

Eight miles up the Fontenelle, when I must be on the line of the trail again, I drew off the road and stopped beside a willow thicket. I hadn't noticed that a bank above us marked the line of an irrigation ditch. The water was sluggish, the thicket damp, and the mosquitoes flocked in, whining. Repellent had little effect. I didn't mind eating mosquitoes but to have them crawling round the eyes made me think of ophthalmia and hideous tropical diseases. There was a morning on the pack trip when I'd woken with one arm a raised rash of bites; I must have flung it outside the sleeping bag in the night. I envisaged waking here, by the irrigation ditch, with that kind of rash round my eyes, and that was enough: I packed up and drove down the road to the rising ground at the start of the basin. I found a track leading to a sage-covered moor. A mile from the road I stopped, got out and sniffed. There was a slight breeze and no mosquitoes. A big jackrabbit got up and lolloped through the sage. This place would do.

I woke with the sunrise, a sombre flare that promised heat. I looked at the bare uplands and the ridges in the west. How hot it must have been for the emigrants. Many preferred to walk rather than endure the jolting of the unsprung wagons. They rested an hour at midday but in the after-noon, when heat is at its most oppressive, they trudged on – although the women couldn't walk if there were small children in the wagon. They had to be kept out of mischief, and worse. Falling under the wheels, for instance.

I drove back to the highway, followed it for a few miles and turned left for the Fontenelle Dam which held back a sullen black lake that looked as artificial as it was, its hard outline relieved by no trees – an intrusion in the vast yellow plain. I saw two pronghorn with big kids that reminded me how far advanced the summer was; when I'd first seen pronghorn the young hadn't been born.

I came to the Seedskedee Wildlife Reserve where the wide river flowed between a low bank on my side and eroded bluffs on the other. There were shingle beaches (and a solitary deer drinking on the other side), stands of cottonwoods, and huge herons perched in a dead tree. There was also a lot of litter and the decomposing carcasses of a cow and a deer. Spent cartridges were everywhere and notices saying: 'National Wildlife Reserve. Unauthorised entry prohibited. Public Hunting Area. Public Fishing Area'.

Leopard frogs were in the grass: olive with dark spots. I followed the shade round a willow tree, writing letters. A sudden patter made me jump and I looked into the eyes of a chipmunk at my elbow.

Upstream from where I was sitting there was a break in the scarp on the other side. I reckoned that was where the Big Sandy came in: that river which I had camped beside after I crossed South Pass. The emigrants who didn't take Sublette's Cut-off followed the Big Sandy to the Green and crossed at this point. I found it curious that I should so often come on the trail and apparently by chance. I must be on the site of the old Lombard Ferry. Before it was established, there would have been the fording and the waiting and the agonising indecision that the others had known upriver at Names Hill.

From this crossing they had continued south-west. I went down to the interstate and followed it west to pick up the trail 20 miles away at Granger.

Distances seemed long today and I was driving into the sun. Enormous billboards advertised Little America coming up but, when I passed, it seemed to be no more than a motel. The traffic was hypnotic: four lanes of glitter and steel boring steadily across a continent. I drove as if in a dream until I turned off for Granger: a huddle of old frame houses on unpaved streets cheek-by-jowl with railroad tracks. There was a narrow bridge over Black's Fork. This was where the trail crossed, and now the trail itself became a dirt road leading out into the sage.

There were no cars, no ranches. The only living things were the antelope. Somewhere out to the right was the railroad, some six or seven miles to the left, the interstate, but this was a no-man's-land where the only water would be alkaline.

From four miles away I saw sharp needles of rock on the horizon: Church Butte, a fine formation like a miniature mountain range. A little way beyond it was Black's Fork which had been flowing to the north of me in a wide curve. The emigrants didn't stop at Church Butte, pushing on to the water to camp, but I saw I was coming to ranches and that would mean fenced land. It was evening now and soon I would be on the interstate again; I started looking around for a place to sleep.

I crossed the creek by a bridge – they would have camped there, I thought; I pitied them the mosquitoes. *I* had five gallons of water for myself, and no thirsty oxen. I came to a stretch of miniature badlands: gullies, ridges, small pinnacles of eroding clay. The surface was baked so hard that when we left the road and drove into the mouth of a depression the tyres made no mark. I turned round and cut the engine. It was still and quiet and warm, and there were no mosquitoes.

I lowered the tailboard and put the kettle on for tea. Although I'd done no walking today I was dehydrated. I never used the air conditioner because of the need to acclimatise; there would be times when I'd have to go out in the heat, perhaps for long periods, and there was always the possibility of emergencies when one would have to walk in the sun. It was the same principle as going without gloves for as long as you could in winter so that when you had to work without them, climbing in the rain for example, the hands were harder, you were harder yourself. So it was no air conditioner, which resulted in dehydration, alleviated by much drinking.

By nine o'clock the sun had gone and there was a warm light breeze. Far to the south the Uinta Mountains held the last of the light in their snows. A couple of miles away I saw other lights, yellow and red, moving silently and infinitely slowly: the interstate. One light, more brilliant, remained immobile. I focused the binoculars. 'Little America' it read. I thought of motels and a big soft bed, of television and the noise of air conditioners. Suppose one were rich and could afford good hotels, the best service, the richest food? But I could no longer sleep in a soft bed (I'd discovered that at the ranch), rich food didn't agree with me, and the most efficient service wouldn't integrate with my working methods. Luxury is subjective: a mind content. Money would command service; it couldn't command the breeze on my face and the line of the Uintas against the stars. I lived in luxury.

In the morning I scrambled about the badlands and once, in surprise, found myself looking down on Old Crump: tiny, stolid, patient. He was just a little darker than the baked earth; odd that my choice of vehicle (but I'd had little choice) should have been the same colour as the desert.

The badlands had more caves and holes in them than is found even in limestone. They were scooped and rounded like Hepworth sculptures.

On the crests and in the gullies holds crumbled under my feet and necessitated rapid movement. In the depressions there were dry courses where the mud had baked in lozenges, and patches of sand each laced with a web of channels. Nothing grew, nothing moved, not even a snake. There was no food for snakes.

I drove on and crossed the interstate, following a minor road lined with broken glass and cans, old cars and the bodies of dead animals. I didn't stop until I reached Fort Bridger.

Jim Bridger saw the bottom dropping out of the fur trade. The last great rendezvous was held in 1839, two years later Bidwell and Bartleson crossed the Rockies and the deserts to reach California. Bridger foresaw the great migration and on the banks of Black's Fork, he built two adobe structures that were more of a trading post than a fortification. He chose his site well; there was plenty of water and grass and it was in the country of the Snakes who were friendly Indians. But the main reason that he settled there was that in the days before Sublette's Cut-off became popular the main trail came through here, and it was halfway between Fort Laramie and Fort Hall. He bought thin worn cattle from the emigrants, put them out on the meadows to fatten and regain their strength, and sold them the following year as the next wave came through, making a tidy profit.

The fort had the neat, restored appearance of Fort Laramie but it was smaller, more intimate. In the museum Bridger's face stared out from his photograph: lean, hard, old but still powerful, and without illusions. There was a gallery of portraits. Brigham Young had a prim mouth, Red Cloud – what was Red Cloud doing here? He was the war chief of the Sioux, a plains Indian. He had a superb face: a good forehead above hooded eyes, a strong nose, a wide straight mouth with indented lines from the nostrils to the corners of the lips. 'We must act with vindictive earnestness against the Sioux,' General Sherman had said, 'even to their extermination, men, women and children.' Red Cloud looked as if he had a good smile once, before he knew what extermination meant.

There were army exhibits, military information. The infantry marched 15 to 40 miles a day, carrying a blanket, rifle, shirt, socks, and food for two or three days. Wagons followed with the heavier supplies. The Indians had greater respect for the infantry than for the cavalry for whom they were more than a match on their nimble ponies. I recalled the agility of our mountain-bred horses in the Gros Ventres; a big plains-bred animal would have been useless there – and the Pony Express used mustangs in the Rockies. The Pony Express riders came through Fort Bridger following the Oregon Trail, but at this point they forked left to follow the Californians across the deserts to Sacramento.

Until 1846, however, everyone turned north-west from the fort, those bound for Oregon and California alike, making for the Snake in present-day Idaho, coming down to the river at Fort Hall. It was 210 miles to Fort Hall. Then they followed the Snake downstream for 40 miles to where the Raft River came in. From there the Oregonians continued down the Snake but the Californians followed the Raft south-west until they could strike out for the headwaters of the Humboldt. By taking this huge loop to the north they avoided crossing the Great Salt Lake Desert.

In 1846 a man called Lansford Hastings appeared on the scene: a young man with great ambitions. At that time California was still under Mexican rule but Hastings, like Bridger, foresaw the coming of the emigrants. Bidwell and Bartleson reached the west coast by the overland route in 1841 – a small party who had to abandon their wagons – but in 1845 260 people reached Sutter's Fort with the first wagons to be taken all the way across the Sierras. In the same year 2,500 emigrants went to Oregon. Hastings hoped that if he could persuade the trains of 1846 to go to California with himself leading them he might spearhead a revolution against the Mexicans.

At the start of the year he was on the west coast but in the early spring he came east with a pack train, and he made a new route across the Great Basin. It was recognised that if trains could go directly west from Fort Bridger the great detour to the Snake would be eliminated. But Hastings came east without wagons and now he was trying to persuade wagon owners to reverse his route. With a large number of people he succeeded.

First there was a pack train without women or children and led by Bryant and Hudspeth, the latter having come east with Hastings. Of the people who took the new route, Bryant and Hudspeth left the fort first and wove a devious line through the Wasatch Range to reach the Great Salt Lake in six days. No one could follow them; everyone else had wagons.

The second group numbered about 60 wagons. It was called the Harlan train and it was accompanied for most of the time by Hastings himself. The third was a small company which included a wagon owned by three Swiss and two Germans, all bachelors. One of the Swiss, Heinrich Lienhard, kept a journal. Last came the Reed–Donner train which numbered 23 wagons.

It was the Wasatch, the last range of the Rockies, that now blocked the trail. The Hastings Cut-off struck south-west from Fort Bridger but I travelled the interstate west to the Bear River and then followed it upstream looking for the place where Lienhard had crossed. The Harlan train and the Donners took a more southerly route.

The Lienhard variant was a pair of ruts climbing a depression called

Stagecoach Hollow. In about two miles we came out on a plateau where the sage was so high it hid the ruts and I'd think I was coming to a dead-end until I came over a crest and saw the trail ahead. A scarf of dust rose behind us and the wind, snatching at it, drove it through the car like clouds of wholemeal flour. The heat was terrific.

This upland, devoid of any kind of habitation, was surrounded by low hills where a few cedars had rooted, but otherwise the only trees were groups of aspens in gullies, showing that there was water close to the surface even if I couldn't see it.

I came down to Coyote Creek which ran in a bed so shallow I had to peer to see its line, but after a while the channel deepened. On the right a succession of spiky towers climbed the slope. These, the Needles, were made of puddingstone with rounded pebbles stuck in the friable rock like raisins in gritty dough.

The trail came down to the creek and a stretch of grass. My guts were being tiresome. At Green River I'd filled the container with water from a tap under an oil bench in a garage. I was assured it was potable; now I had doubts. Green River water, I thought glumly, and camped under the Needles where I might attend to my problem in decent privacy. Besides, it was a good site. The others had camped here.

Next morning I found a bridge across the creek. It was built of railway sleepers and the first of these stood proud about twelve inches above the eroded bank. The drop to the stream was ten feet. If Old Crump canted as he rose to that sleeper we could be thrown in the creek.

There was some timber lying around and I made a ramp that Old Crump promptly chewed up, then stalled. I made a proper job of the next ramp and wondered, as I eased him across, whether the bridge itself would hold. It did, but it was an awkward moment. The emigrants would have forded the creek, cutting back the banks. They had time to do it; they camped for two nights in this place. On the first morning one of the Swiss boys went out to try to shoot an antelope, meaning to rejoin the company farther along the trail but at the last moment they'd stayed in camp to mend a wagon. By the second morning this man hadn't come in and they broke camp, going over a low divide and descending to the gorge of Echo Canyon, the first major obstruction on the Hastings Cut-off. In its lower reaches they had to cross the river several times and were forced to cut their way through dense thickets of willow. After three days the missing man returned. He'd been all that time without food for, although he'd shot an antelope and a badger, he had lost his knife and had no way of taking meat from the carcasses. At night the coyotes wouldn't leave him alone. They'd surrounded him, forcing him to get up and walk, when they followed him like a pack of dogs. It must have been an unnerving experience, wondering if he would find the others before he grew too weak to withstand an attack.

A few miles below the point where Lienhard's company entered Echo Canyon the other trains came in from the south, and after about 20 miles they came to the Weber River. The bottom of Echo Canyon was rough, but in the next two days, on the Weber, they were forced to cross that river sixteen times in as many miles.

In one place the river widens to form a delightful little valley where a village called Henefer is served by a minor road. I took this because it was on the site of Henefer that the Reed–Donner train started to run into trouble. Up to this point they were making good time but when they reached the Henefer Valley there was a note from Hastings stuck in a sage bush telling them not to follow the others through the canyons but to go south over the mountains.

Hastings hadn't intended that the wagons should follow the river but when the leading company came to Henefer he was in the rear straightening out the route and taking Lienhard up Stagecoach Hollow. He'd meant the emigrants to reverse his own route over the mountains, the way he'd taken with the pack train.

He caught up with the Harlan train in the canyons, saw the trouble they were having, and returned to warn people not to follow. Lienhard's company, after scouting the line Hastings urged them to take, rejected it and followed down the Weber. The Donners compromised. In the note Hastings left for them he said that if they would send a messenger after him, he would come back and guide them over the mountains. They sent three men. The rest of them camped in the pleasant valley.

There were two Donner brothers. George, the elder, was head of the train, though the man who was better suited for the leadership, but who was not popular because people thought him arrogant, was James Reed. At forty-six he wasn't young but he had unflagging energy. It was he and two others who took the best horses and rode to overtake Hastings. They didn't go through the canyons but above them, and that couldn't have been easy going for they made only ten miles on the first day. Reed noted that one canyon was 'impassable although 60 waggons passed through'. They overtook Hastings at the Great Salt Lake, having ridden about 50 miles the second day. The horses gave out and Reed returned on a borrowed mount, accompanied by Hastings. They returned by the way over the mountains although Hastings went only as far as the top of a high pass and from there he pointed out the line the Donners should follow. Reed descended, blazing the trees as he went, and arrived back at the encampment five days after he'd left it.

The Donner train turned south-west out of the Weber Valley. Their route, which the Mormons were to take the following year, is now followed by a minor road and it was this that I drove along on that hot summer's afternoon.

There were wooded hills ahead. Sunflowers lined the verges. We crossed a divide called Hogback Summit and dipped. The descent wasn't steep but the banks of the depression came down so sharply that William Clayton, a Mormon, said that it was 'exceedingly dangerous to wagons being mostly on the side hill over large cobblestones, causing the wagons to slide very badly'. The Donners had to cut a road down the slope; and at the bottom, where it was roughest, they turned up a side ravine. Their ruts are still visible.

The road and the trail ran out in East Canyon. Bryant (the man who left Fort Bridger with the pack train) came down the dangerous ravine with his mules and turned right at the bottom, returning to the Weber at a point between two of its canyons. The Donners turned left, forcing their way through dense stands of willows and probably crossing the creek many times. The Mormons were to cross it thirteen times. Little Emigration Canyon, the way out of this wilderness, proved to be the crux, because the willows were replaced by mature forest through which they had to force a way for between 2,000 and 3,000 feet to the summit of Big Mountain Pass. It was from here that Hastings had pointed out the route to Reed. It took the Donners fifteen days to travel 36 miles.

The present road climbs the side of Little Emigration Canyon. Hastings, earlier in the year, had gone straight down with his pack train, Reed had ridden down, the wagons went straight up. They felled trees in the August heat, dragged them aside, prised out boulders. It took them four days to reach the pass, the distance on the map being four miles.

The other side is steep in its top section and heavily wooded all the way down, but from the summit they would have seen, between the clefts of the timbered peaks, a faint gleam like mist and, beyond that, a range of grey mountains. They were looking across the Great Salt Lake to the first of the desert ranges.

Since the Donner train passed, and the Mormons after them, the trees have not come back and the ruts can be seen driving straight for the summit of Big Mountain Pass and down the other side. At the bottom of the western slope the trail is a green swathe through hardwoods. Pale geraniums glow in the shadows, and humming birds and gorgeous butterflies appear suddenly, flicking through the sun shafts. They must have hated every foot of it.

They came out of this canyon and into another, overgrown with willows, but now the walls of the last dreadful glen opened out and there was the wide and level desert beyond. And at the mouth of the canyon they found the way so choked by rocks and vegetation that they had to retreat. They went up the canyon, up a depression to one side and over yet another pass to descend Emigration Canyon. This narrowed at the exit until it became impassable and they took the wagons, one at a time, over the slopes above the narrows, doubling the teams for each passage.

They emerged from the Wasatch demoralised, their teams worn down, blaming Reed for the route by which he'd taken them. But he had listened to Hastings – and the company had held a discussion before deciding which way they should take. Reed was a scapegoat.

The night after I left Henefer I slept on Little Mountain, the last pass that the Donners crossed in their escape from the Wasatch. In the morning I returned to Henefer. As I went I explored those sections of the trail which I could reach on foot through the dense timber. In the afternoon I came to the upper Weber canyon.

Its entrance was guarded by a gateway of castellated rock and in the bottom there was room only for the river, the railroad and the interstate. There was no minor road so I had to keep to the interstate for a mile or two until I could slip down an exit road that brought me to a row of houses under the Devil's Slide, a landslip of warm brown rock above the river where Lienhard camped. The banks were wooded, and big trees shaded the houses and the bit of street in front of them. The canyon had widened just enough to accommodate this tiny community where sprinklers played among the petunias and on a porch two old men sat and eyed me curiously. It was a strange place to find squeezed between the slide and the tremendous rock walls, a few yards from the unceasing traffic and the bridge that carried the Union Pacific across the Weber. There was no room left for the ghosts, indeed it was I who felt like a ghost, passing under the cottonwoods in that quiet street.

And once back in the line of traffic, when I was looking ahead for the next canyon, the road ran out in a broad fertile valley full of farms and scattered villages. Astonished, I slipped away from the interstate to drive through the villages, and the meadows with their dairy cattle, even a herd of Jerseys. The life-size effigy of a horse stood in a front garden, glossy and black as china. In place of gnomes, I thought. The rich land continued through Littleton, Milton, Peterson; my road dived under the interstate to a place called Mountain Green and I stopped at a real-estate office to inquire about a campground.

The women in the office looked smart and fresh and I felt very rough. I was in boots and stained jeans, my shirt was ripped, I could no longer comb my hair which was like a nest bound together with sweat and dust and Cutter's cream. They had to know what I was doing, where I was from, where I was going – and the youngest woman's face was alight with longing.

They directed me to a campground at Ogden and I went back to the interstate and entered the bad canyon.

It's possible that for the emigrants this was the most difficult, if not the most dangerous obstacle on the journey. The river was a torrent pitted with deep holes and full of wave-washed boulders. There must have been stretches that were a little less rough, but still deep, because sometimes the wagons were floating and held back by every man who was available to keep them from being wrecked on a submerged rock. Where it was possible they shifted the boulders but often there wasn't enough room to manoeuvre and they would have to unyoke all the oxen except the wheelers.

One of the worst problems would have been to keep out of the way of the wagons, for in the narrowest places the river ran between rock walls and there would have been many occasions when they had to get from the front to the back quickly, and vice versa.

The drivers must have had a bad time. There were no reins; oxen were driven by a man walking alongside, controlling them with his voice and the whip. Walking down the Weber would have been impossible; presumably the driver scrambled ahead through the water as nimbly as he could. How they got through without anyone being killed is a mystery. Even when they'd passed a bad stretch, and the men were returning for the next wagon, they were in danger of slipping on the submerged boulders and being carried away by the torrent.

Lienhard's wagon and three others kept to the bottom of the canyon all the way, leaving the water for the bank only when the people in front had found room to make some semblance of a road. They had felled trees and excavated boulders but then, unlike Lienhard, who was to return to the water when things became rough on the bank again, the Harlan company had traversed the slopes of the canyon: going high, making a trail only the width of a wagon, sometimes going even higher and taking to the convex slopes above the cliffs. They used ropes but these couldn't take the whole weight of a wagon and team as the former slid sideways on sloping ledges above the drop: '. . . while hoisting a yoke of oxen and a wagon up Weber Mountain, the rope broke near the windlass. As many men as could surround the wagon were helping all they could by lifting at the wheels and sides. The footing was untenable and, before the rope could be tied to anything, the men found they must abandon the wagon and oxen to destruction, or be dragged to death themselves. The faithful beasts seemed to comprehend their danger, and held their ground for a few seconds, and were then hurled over a precipice at least 75 feet high, and crushed in a tangled mass with the wagon on the rocks at the bottom of the canyon.'[*]

The Harlan train progressed a mile on the good days, half a mile on the others. The difficulties lasted for five miles and then suddenly they were clear of the canyon, and beyond a wide white stretch of water the desert ranges stood, remote and tantalising, like mountains in a dream — and all the rest of the land was flat.

[*] W. W. Allen and R. B. Avery: *The California Gold Book.*

10

WEST FROM THE WASATCH

SALT LAKE CITY had a cosy air despite the hard light and streets that were wider than the norm even for the States. Traffic was slow and there wasn't much of it. There were no crowds. There were fountains in the main thoroughfare and racks of clothing on the sidewalks. It was a world away from the slightly tarnished elegance of New York. Salt Lake City was old-fashioned, a trifle vulgar but endearing, like Brighton or Llandudno.

I had spent the night in a campground between road and railway where my sleep was threaded with the clank of slow freight trains and the rush of traffic under brilliant lights. The site was owned by Mormons and the white wash-basins were flecked with gold. The manageress lived in Arizona in the winter but brought her husband here in the summer because he had emphysema and a heart that couldn't take air conditioning. She mothered me, giving me detergent and ice and a copy of Isabella Bird's *A Lady's Life in the Rocky Mountains* because Isabella was just like me, she explained. To be bracketed with that hard-riding, hard-living Victorian was a startling compliment.

The manageress had been raised at Green River. She owned a tract of land in the hills above Bondurant, Wyoming, where she was going to build a house. She must have been well over sixty but her sense of adventure was still strong.

Salt Lake City, I'd been told, was losing its qualities of serenity and industry; people were moving in, destroying what they sought. There was a notable difference about Utah. In the Wasatch 'No Trespassing' warnings proliferated. Historical markers on the Donner route – which was also the Mormon Trail – were defaced. I wondered if there were a connection between the two. That the Mormons termed everyone else Gentiles implied a parallel with the Jews, and ever since their founder was murdered they had been periodically objects of hostility. Until they reached Utah they had been hounded across the States. I didn't know enough about them to say whether this was because of their religion or polygamy or because they were successful at most things they undertook that mattered, such as business and agriculture.

They were opportunists. After they settled on the site of Salt Lake City, organised trains were sent along the California Trail to salvage the discarded possessions which the emigrants threw out to lighten the load of the wagons.

Their industry was remarkable. Within two hours of their arrival in
the desert they were ploughing, within four hours the first irrigation
ditches were dug. Eight days later the corn was coming up.

As the city was established and flourished, and new townships sprang
up across the desert, hostility to the Mormons deepened. There was a
new factor. As the Gentile emigrants came to the Great Basin they were
faced with 700 miles of desert and mountains, yet here were the
Mormons with their irrigated fields, their crops and cattle, their new
towns and security. There was a lot of trading – emigrants buying fresh
food and staples, replacing their worn cattle – but when there was
resentment it was violent.

In 1857 a party of emigrants came through and camped at a place
called Mountain Meadows. They had given their oxen the names of
Mormon saints and cursed them obscenely. They were attacked by
Indians but no Mormons would come to their rescue – that is, not until a
Major John Lee offered the services of his militiamen to escort the
emigrants to safety if the men would give up their arms. They agreed,
put the small children in one wagon as they were ordered and, with men,
women and older children walking, they moved off, each man walking
beside a militiaman. Hardly had they got going when an order was
given: 'Halt! Do your duty!' Each militiaman turned and shot the
emigrant beside him. Some refused but no emigrants were saved. The
Indians had been waiting, and now they came out of hiding. The
wounded men, all the women and all children over the age of seven were
killed. It was the wagon-load of small children who were saved – they
were thought to be too young to bear witness.

Brigham Young was shocked and horrified. The sect was condemned
by the rest of the United States and all Mormons who had settled
elsewhere were recalled to Salt Lake City for their own safety. Brigham
Young had as hard a job controlling his raw men as the Indian chiefs
their braves, or colonels their junior officers on the plains. The
Mountain Meadows Massacre was only one of a string of tragedies; at
the time it was seen in isolation, and it was to do irretrievable harm to
the Mormons politically and morally. It was to become Banquo's ghost.

I remembered it when I saw the desecrated plaques and the 'No
Trespassing' notices but when I drove round the suburbs of the city by
the Great Salt Lake the old blood feuds faded before the present reality
of a land that had been a desert and now was fertile: a plain lush with
crops and sparkling with moisture. Under the fierce sun the sprinklers
whispered above green lawns and vivid splashes of flowers, and gutters
down all the wide streets overflowed with water.

I met the homely Mormon widow operating my mail drop whose son
was working at Dinosaur and who wanted to visit him. Could she get

down that dirt road to Echo Park where he was now on duty? He said she couldn't. I pointed out that only children were apt to get possessive, to treat parents like imprudent offspring riding hell-bent for trouble. Children, coping more or less successfully with the outside world, but appalled at its dangers, have grave doubts concerning their parents' ability to survive in like circumstances.

I went to a sports shop and gravitated to a small woman in her sixties in a T-shirt and shorts that revealed good hard legs. Her movements were neat, quick and economical. She was a climber and cross-country skier and was now introducing her grandchildren to these and associated activities.

I drove up Little Cottonwood Canyon and came to a forested basin under the headwall and went into camp. It rained all the next day and on the Monday I trotted over a little ridge and two 11,000 foot peaks enjoying myself and looking at the flowers. Indian paintbrush in cream and shades of flame surged up the hillsides in tongues of fire and now, towards the end of the growing season, strange and beautiful thistles were making their appearance.

The Wasatch were pleasant, the flowers pretty, but I needed to feel rock. Looking around for a route where I would have to use my hands, I settled for a traverse of the Devil's Castle which formed the most sensational section of the headwall.

It was the only mountain in the vicinity that sported any rock worth mentioning. There was plenty of granite in the mouth of the canyon but a road as well and I like remote places. Cliffs were tucked away in the back country but they demanded a rope and a companion and, worst of all, logistics.

The approach to the Devil's Castle was by way of a wide ridge where there were chisellers in the sand and chipmunks on the scree – surprised to see me, which argued that this line was used by few people. Then I came to a funny little crest of rock about a mile long and with so many contorted pines on it that I spent as much time climbing trees as rock: trying not to use my hands, because once you get resin on them it can be removed only by scraping away the first layer of skin on a stone.

This curious ridge ended abruptly and I looked across a gap at the Devil's Castle. On the right a fine wall dropped to the scree – that is, fine scenically. It was split by a chasm where capstones, arches, every piece of rock that wasn't a part of the mountain, and often that as well, were perched so precariously that I would have preferred to tackle the snow-filled couloir without an axe than attempt a rock climb there.

The north ridge of the Castle faced me. It was vertical where it wasn't overhanging and it was difficult to see how the overhangs stayed there. The most feasible route for anyone supposed to be having fun was on the eastern side. The upper face steepened in its last hundred feet or so, making it concave, and its right margin was obscured by a buttress. There had to be a fault in that corner, possibly wide enough to accommodate one's body or, if thin, then at an easy angle. A steep and narrow crack couldn't be climbed on this rock; one would have to trust holds, and no holds were trustworthy.

I moved into the gap, traversed under a nose through a kind of postern and paused. Immediately under the summit was a system of ledges separated by short sharp rises. I sighed. On the right was the easy-angled chimney that I'd promised myself. I started up it, straddling, picking out each hold in advance (for only from below could I see if it was cracked all round, or just part-way), pressing on them gently with my feet and as far to the back of them as possible even if they were merely toe holds — which was ridiculous, for how could one distribute the weight over something an inch square? I didn't use handholds as such, merely touching the walls with enough friction to keep me in balance. This was why it had to be an easy-angled fault: because I could pull on nothing; it was all footwork. The sweat streamed off me.

The pitch was about a hundred feet; it felt like five hundred. As soon as I could I broke out to the ledges, working my way to the summit by sloping lines. The angle relented a little as I approached the top. This aspect had been foreshortened when viewed from the gap; I'd misjudged the angle but in my favour. On the summit ridge the rock was more stable because people coming up the other end of the mountain would have traversed to the point where I emerged, and then retreated. Descending the chimney would be hard; from the top one couldn't tell which of the bad holds were the least bad.

The mountain had two tops: one of pink rock, one of black. These peaks were higher than those of the northern Wasatch — higher and more bare. Their crests rose above the timber and the rock was multi-coloured: grey in the bottom where the granite was, shades of red above. From Devil's Castle I looked down Little Cottonwood Canyon and felt my guts contract, and then my mind. I wanted to stay on familiar ground, and tomorrow I would be in unknown territory. I'd stretched the legs on Devil's Castle; tomorrow the mind would have to work. The thought of the deserts had always frightened me.

The Great Basin extends westward from the Rockies to the Sierras, not one enormous desert but a land of innumerable mountain ranges separated by valleys so flat that they are level plains, but without water: a succession of deserts. Until the late 1820s no white man had crossed this basin; it was inhabited by Paiute Indians who were nomadic and subsisted by hunting small game, by gathering roots and berries. Then the

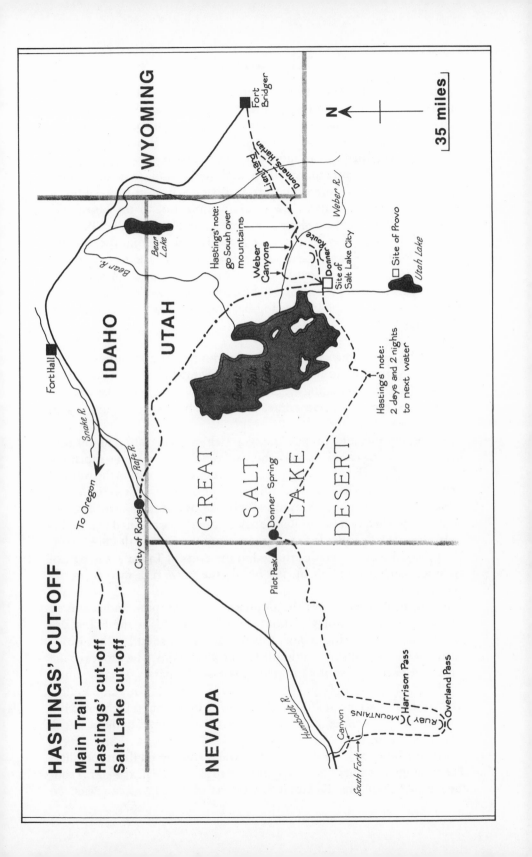

HASTINGS' CUT-OFF

Main Trail ———
Hastings' cut-off ‐‐‐‐
Salt Lake cut-off –·–·–

|‐‐‐ 35 miles ‐‐‐|

N

WYOMING

Fort Bridger

IDAHO

UTAH

NEVADA

Fort Hall

To Oregon

Snake R.

Raft R.

City of Rocks

Bean Lake

Bear R.

Litherland
Donner's, Harlan

Hastings' note: go South over mountains

Weber Canyons

Weber R.

Donner Route

Site of Salt Lake City

Site of Provo

Utah Lake

Great Salt Lake

GREAT

SALT

LAKE

DESERT

Donner Spring

Pilot Peak

Hastings' note: 2 days and 2 nights to next water

Humboldt R.

South Fork

Canyon

(RUBY) MOUNTAINS

Harrison Pass

Overland Pass

trapper, Jedediah Smith, who had gone west by the Old Spanish Trail
that skirted the basin on the south, returned east by a route that took
him over the central mass of the Sierras and straight through the deserts.
His exact line was unknown, and by the time people needed to know,
he had been scalped by Comanches on the Cimarron.

But where one white man had crossed the Great Basin others would
follow. Trappers explored the northern fringes from the Snake to the
Humboldt. Joseph Walker led an expedition west to the Humboldt
Sink, and at the foot of the Sierras he turned south to the Walker Pass. He
returned the same way. The first *emigrant* train to attempt the crossing
was that of Bidwell and Bartleson in 1841 but they went north of the
Wasatch, north of the Great Salt Lake. Frémont's was the first expedition to cross the plain where Salt Lake City stands and to strike due west.
He was closely followed by Hastings leading the migration over his cut-
off in 1846.

Salt Lake City with its suburbs and neighbouring communities forms a
linear conurbation along the foot of the Wasatch. I started across the
Great Basin on a morning when the lake was a molten mass of light
while, back the way I had come, the Wasatch drooped like hot grey
ghosts above the towns.

The emigrants of '46 left the Wasatch in very different moods.
Lienhard, having raced through the last Weber canyon in one morning,
was blithe as a lark as his wagon rolled along 'a fine road' in the wake of
the Harlan train. The Donners, on the other hand, hadn't dared to rest
for a single day when they eventually broke out of their own forested
hell; they pushed on fast but Reed broke an axle-tree and had to send his
teamsters back 15 miles for timber. South of the Great Salt Lake a consumptive called Luke Halloran died in the arms of Tamsen, the wife of
George Donner, and was buried beside the grave of a man from the
Harlan party.

Range succeeded range: the Oquirrhs, raw and pink and scattered
with cedars, then a valley without a river, followed by the Stansbury
ridge. There were springs a day's travel apart as far as Skull Valley, which
lay between the Stansburys and the Cedar Mountains. The ranges of the
basin ran north and south and people crossed by passes or went round
the long and seemingly interminable ends and here, in Skull Valley,
where the salt flats lay wet like shallow meres, the Donners came on what
was obviously intended as a notice board, with torn shreds of paper
ripped off by birds.

Tamsen Donner went down on her knees and pieced them together.
The message was stark: two days and two nights to the next water. From
the Cedar Mountains the Great Salt Desert stretched to Pilot Peak: 60

miles as the crow flew, over 80 by the trail – but they didn't know the mileage.

From here Frémont on his third expedition had the wit and the resources to send Carson and three others ahead on the best horses with orders to light a fire when they found water. The emigrants had the advantage of knowing that the water existed but they thought it couldn't be more than 50 miles away, probably nearer 40, because Hastings said it would take two days and two nights. That was probably the time he took with his pack train.

They set out across the plain where the vegetation grew sparse and then thinned to the odd clump with yellow sand drifted in a long tail on the lee side. The horizontal lines of the desert seemed to increase distance with their vast monotony, and out of them rose small groups of mountains as stylised as backdrops in a photographer's studio.

Salt flats appeared of a deadly whiteness that was appallingly natural and totally alien. The mountains were red and black and looked as if they had been roasted. There were cirques and horseshoes, towers on arêtes and peaks of clustered pinnacles. Drowsiness loomed and faded as we trudged through the sun and one thought of a gay scramble along those ridges, losing sight of the fact that the summit ridge would be unattainable. The temperature in the shade was 115 degrees.

They crossed one desert, then a range with a gap that was just high enough to hide, until the last moment, a second desert which lay between them and Pilot Peak, still ten miles away. On this grim stretch the oxen lay down and died. They unyoked the survivors and drove them on to the water, returning later for the wagons. James Reed, walking through the night with his wife and four exhausted children, stopped, wrapped them in a blanket and shawls and ordered the dogs to huddle about them. September nights are cold in the desert.

It took the Donner train six days to cross the 80-mile desert. On the day they left Skull Valley, Bryant (who had left Fort Bridger at about the same time) reached the Sacramento Valley nearly 1,000 miles to the west.

None of the wagons fared well. Even the ebullient Lienhard had a bad time crossing the last desert to the spring. That spring. I had no idea where it was in relation to the ground; I didn't know its name, but I knew it was under Pilot Peak, on the east side of the mountain. I drew off the road to look at the maps.

I had stopped at the Bonneville Salt Flats and looked beyond them to the Silver Island Range. The trail crossed the Silver Islands so I was in the right place. From here they were backdrop peaks, their true size indicated only by the shadows of a few clouds on their slopes. The range appeared to float on the salt, its extremities slightly curved as though girdled by an inland sea, and reflected, so that one wondered if eventually the salt did change to water – but none was marked on the map. It was a mirage, suggesting that this brittle crust was an illusion, along with the smothering heat and the burned rock. Out there a desert island floated on a cool deep sea. The same mirage would have tormented the emigrants.

A dirt road ran north under Pilot Peak, emerging eventually close to the state line with Idaho. I went into the town of Wendover to make inquiries. In the Post Office the clerks talked about ruts on a ranch over 20 miles away, but the road had been washed out, they said, and the old people who could have helped me were dead.

Wendover's café was hot despite its air conditioning, although not as hot as the street. I was waited on by attentive Mexicans, trailed by their beautiful children. I needed lots of coffee to keep me awake; I'd driven only 100 miles today and I no longer felt the heat as heat, only the symptoms. The worst was drowsiness, the next, lack of concentration. When I left the truck I had to remind myself to put my hat on. The sun was so brilliant that dark glasses gave little protection. I saw why people wore hats with wide brims.

I drove out of town as shadows started to fill the hollows and the desert became withdrawn and mysterious. There was a promise in the air but I did not yet know that the promise was that of the precious moment when the sun goes down.

From the summit of a low pass I looked out to Pilot Peak. Stretching for miles below its eastern flank was a valley that was a plain of salt. The air was dry and so clear that I could distinguish some poplars which, if they marked the ranch for which I was bound, were 20 miles away. The road was of gravel, deep in places but never deep enough to necessitate four-wheel drive.

The poplars *were* almost 20 miles distant: on the site of an abandoned house. It took us an hour to reach them, drifting through the desert to the cool and measured cadences of a Mozart piano concerto. Beyond the old homestead there were silos, barns, fields of corn and alfalfa. I turned into the ranch road as a lorry approached driven by a young Mexican. His passenger was an exquisite girl who looked about fifteen. They'd been married six months, he told me proudly, throwing her into agonies of embarrassment. She clutched a large plastic basket of laundry. I wondered if they could be going all the way to town to do their washing.

The Mexican had worked here for five years. He was a trusting soul, laughing all the time while the big black eyes of the girl watched us warily. (A lot of country people thought I worked for the government.) He pointed out the trees round the spring, the ruts, the place where a man had walked right across the salt and back in three hours. The surface looked good for walking, so the sink would be about six miles wide at that place.

The ranch appeared to be run by Mexicans; probably they worked better than whites in extremes of heat and solitude. Water came from wells; there was a pump beating by the mobile homes where I turned round. There were some horses and the odd sheep in the corrals, and I could see the backs of cattle in the scrub. The Mexicans waved as I drove by. Across a field the owner's cabin nestled by the spring. Only the silos and the mobile homes of the workers spoiled the effect.

The Donner spring wouldn't have looked out of place in an English garden. It was a pond, a little scummy, fringed by rushes and sunflowers with watercress where the spring itself must be, and a fine old willow-tree on the bank. Two ducks floated on the water. When Lienhard reached here wagons were parked so close that his oxen couldn't get to the water and had to slake their thirst at the run-off, which took them two hours, and probably saved them from the fate that overtook a dog which jumped in when he reached the water, drank all he could, emerged and dropped dead.

On the other side of the salt the gap in the Silver Islands was obvious, the place where all of them – Frémont, Hastings, Lienhard, the Donners – stopped and looked and saw yet another desert to cross. The ruts that approached the spring had an air of implacability, of permanence.

On the night that the greater part of the trains gathered at the spring (but the Donners were only halfway through the Wasatch), the young people sang and danced, and a girl called Lucinda became excited and threw a log at a boy called Alfred whom she'd married on the journey but who had abandoned her after the wedding night. Lucinda was always being ejected from wagons. She had started out as a servant to the Hoppe family, who were in the same company as Lienhard, had left them for the Harlan wagon, then went back and forth between the two as each one threw her out. Men, said Lienhard, could not measure up to her amorous needs: 'She was a strong, two-legged animal.' She was a survivor too. Chivvied from pillar to post as she was, she never joined the Donners. She reached California and married a William Thompson in 1847.

The Donners reached the spring under Pilot Peak and stayed there a week. When they moved off, on September 15, they had rested those cattle which had survived the first desert crossing, but they were now three weeks behind the rest of the migration, and they had abandoned four wagons on the salt flats. Reed had one ox left. He borrowed two, and with one of his cows he had a scratch team to pull a wagon which was unusually large but was probably the lightest he owned. Of the four wagons abandoned in the salt, two were his.

From the spring they moved south to turn the end of Pilot Peak and cross Silver Zone Pass. At that point I left them for a time. I went north from Donner Spring towards the Salt Lake cut-off and the main trail that was coming down from the Snake in Idaho.

I drove some 12 miles up the valley – or rather, north; when drainage is into a sink then all ways out of a valley must be upstream – and I parked on a track in the sage. The prevailing wind in the desert was west. Every evening I stopped facing the sun, knowing that this way I would have shelter for cooking on the tailboard.

The flats in the south were silver. The fringe of vegetation round the spring caught the last rays of light coming over Pilot Peak and glowed like April grass. I drank Lapsang Souchong and lemon. The sun sank. The wind dropped to a breeze, to a zephyr. Nothing stirred in the desert, nothing called. The stars began to reveal themselves. The sage was dark and the ground pale. After a while a pale patch moved.

I watched it out of the corner of my eye, and it was certainly moving, circling me: long-legged, silent. I talked softly to it and it kept on its course, undisturbed, neither advancing nor retreating, merely keeping its distance. As it went to windward I caught a strong whiff of fox.

I was up before six. Sunrise was in two phases. First a muted red that faded and then came up in glowing pinks and scarlets and golds until the sun burst above the horizon like a bomb. Pilot Peak smouldered momentarily before the colour was gone and the rock was its own dull dusty brown.

I drove north to Lucin, and the salt flats looked endless and wet, as if the tide had not long gone out. They might have been continuous, winding in and out of the ranges in a serpentine design. I passed a house for sale; its view was of a stranded country. Fifty-one miles from Wendover I came to Lucin, a railroad crossing with two or three houses dwarfed by cottonwoods and a notice referring to the road by which I'd come: 'Dry Area. Do Not Travel Without Water'. A man passed in a truck and said 'Hi'.

I came to a surfaced road and turned north-east, north for Idaho and east for the Great Salt Lake. At the end of the road were the Raft River Mountains: a rounded range of grey gravel with a scatter of vegetation and a few conifers. The roads were almost empty of traffic and even on the highway the local people waved. Old Crump, like an interesting dog, was my passport.

I stopped at a spring under the inevitable willow. A truck driver was there before me. He filled my water container, holding it under the spurting tap with one hand. I smiled dreamily and wondered how this trip would have gone had I been 20 years younger. He had been in the

Navy in the Far East, now he hauled phosphates across the desert. His ambition was to ride a horse from Idaho to northern California. It seemed a modest ambition. Idaho was nice once, he told me, before people spoiled it, and then he asked if he could get his outfit over the dirt road from Lucin to Wendover. No, I said promptly. It was over 70 feet long.

He slept in a bunk behind the cab, which was all right so long as the air conditioner was working. It wasn't now and he suffered. He was a large burly fellow in a pink vest, a little too heavy. He said I would enjoy my work more than he did his. He sounded envious.

Dragon-flies clattered in the willow leaves, Jedediah Smith came this way on his return from the Sierras; Walker came past; Bidwell in 1841. The Bidwell train still had its wagons at this point; the ruts coming in from the plain and the Great Salt Lake could have been theirs. They had no maps. They knew only that if you went west from the lake you would come to the Humboldt; but knowledge of the Great Basin was so scanty that it was thought two rivers emerged from the lake to flow west to the Pacific. As the Bidwell party moved round the northern shores of the lake they soon realised that this was a sink; rivers flowed into it but none emerged. There was no great river to lead them to the Pacific.

It took them nearly a month to reach the Humboldt. On the way they abandoned their wagons, and the occupants walked or rode, driving the oxen, packing on the horses and mules. There were 31 men in the party and one woman, Nancy, the wife of Benjamin Kelsey. Once their wagon had been left behind, she rode, carrying her baby. She was eighteen years old.

Another woman who came north of the Great Salt Lake was Sarah Royce, travelling with her husband and two-year-old daughter Mary. They reached Salt Lake City in August 1849 and rested their cattle for eleven days before starting out with three single men, two of whom were mounted. The newcomers had little food so the family would have shared their rations. Perhaps they thought that this was a fair price to pay for a little added protection. The Indians were said to be troublesome that year along the Humboldt.

It is possible that they had a light wagon, certainly they had six oxen; they plodded steadily across the deserts to reach the Humboldt Sink in thirty-three days, making an average of 19 miles a day. How isolated they must have looked: one wagon and two horsemen, moving at two miles an hour in a world of greys and blinding whites where every vestige of colour had been drained by the heat. The land was like a cadaver. Slowly they inched their way west, camped at the spring with the willow and moved on next day, trending slightly northwards to join the main California Trail some 50 miles away at the City of Rocks.

11

CITY OF ROCKS TO THE RUBIES

THE LAND IMPROVED as I crossed into Idaho. Working round the back of the Raft River Range I came to good farmland with fine houses, Lombardy poplars and evocative names: Elba, Almo, Malta. It was at Malta, 20 miles from the Snake, that I intercepted the main trail as it came up the Raft River making for the Humboldt 160 miles to the south-west.

Many overlanders preferred this route. Despite the extra mileage, its going was so good that when Harlan came to the Humboldt after taking Hastings' Cut-off he found himself five days behind a train which had been behind *him* at South Pass but had taken the route through Fort Hall.

The main trail had good water all the way: the Bear River, the Portneuf, the Snake, the Raft. It was poignant to see the smiling country, lush farmland now, lush wilderness then, and to remember the heart-breaking labour in the forests and the roaring canyons of the Wasatch, the interminable trudge through glaring days and icy nights across the Salt Lake Desert towards Pilot Peak. Here we went from creek to creek, from spring to spring, and there was grass and game and trees and, at the headwaters of Cassia Creek, the camp at the City of Rocks.

It was a sultry afternoon and I was sleepy. I failed to notice when we left the ranchland: at the edge of cultivation in the west, the wilderness massed its forces on the boundary, and that was often no more than a fence. In the frontier region lay the casualties: abandoned cabins and sagging barns in wastes of scrawny vegetation.

Slowly I became aware of granite on hillsides and thought of it as slabs nestling in sage until a glance behind me revealed a neck at the back of an outcrop and I realised that these were not only crags but pinnacles. We came up a dusty track where, in a depression on our right, there must be water, for the place was a jungle of shrubs and aspens. Above the trees rose massive walls and spires of granite each one isolated from its neighbour, the colour of pale doves and rough as sand.

I could see no plan; trees and towers were a cluttered maze, and the rocks were too big for the place. Disproportionate, they had the look of climbers' boulder problems but the trees betrayed the scale. Some of the walls must be a couple of hundred feet high.

From a brow on the road I looked back. Shadows were lengthening on a ridge of dull green hills, and against this and a sky the colour of bruised plums the faces of the spires were livid in the sun. The storm passed with the day, the sun sank, turning the walls of the city gold, and when they were cold and grey a flock of small clouds caught the last pink light on their fleecy backs.

I was listening to a Schubert symphony when I became aware of the calls of frightened birds. In the top of a dead tree the branches of which were too fragile to support a cat, a cat sat upright, its ears silhouetted against the sky, its shoulders hunched. It turned its head and screeched at the birds, which all fell silent as if someone had thrown a switch. Schubert's music played on. The acoustics were superb. The cat turned and screeched at Schubert.

No cat can turn its head in a half-circle. I realised that it must be an owl, but not quite a long-eared owl; the ears were set differently, and it was much larger. I looked it up and identified it as the great horned owl, aptly nicknamed the cat owl.

The radio played on. Carefully, a little ponderously, the owl turned to face the noise, but the twigs were flimsy. It lurched, shifting its feet, then spread great wings and floated across the embers of the sky to drift through the aisles of the shadowed city where even the rattlesnakes must flinch as they felt that presence pass between them and the stars.

In the early morning, with the clouds gone and the sky the colour of flax, I climbed one of the outcrops at the back of the depression and looked down the slope. Now I could see that the place had a design. Reef followed reef and were roughly similar in shape seen end-on, with rounded backs and reared fronts: half-dome formations lumbering in single file diagonally down the slope like a section of a titanic army. The spires were another section: skirmishers. Of the half-domes I had the feeling that they might move, but imperceptibly. One dawn there would be a vacant space in the line; or the full complement remain, but one of them a few yards from where it was yesterday. They had nothing to do with man or with nature; they were associated with the dinosaurs: primaeval and grand and legendary. I could not believe that the dinosaurs had lived. I could not believe that these monoliths were inanimate.

I wandered entranced about their feet, coming on rock suddenly as I pushed through trees – lovely rock, fretted and laced and sculpted with holds. Or I'd look down a glade and see one reared above the foliage, petrified in an attitude of astonishment. And they were different from different angles. A tower was a phallus as I approached; at right angles it became an oval disc balanced on a plinth of similar proportions with a waist between: an hour-glass a hundred feet high.

Among the trees they were all mystery; out on the sage they were endearing, gilded with lichen, and a beautiful texture under the hands. In their upper reaches there were holes and tunnels, slits and slots and letter boxes, and nearly all of these with the sky showing through when seen at the right angle, but there was no instability. This was granite, not clay. Even mushrooms balanced on fragile stalks looked as if climbers might rope down from them. There were beaks and noses and prows, and one frail formation that once, a few billion years ago, must have been obstructed when molten and flowed sideways. All that remained was an attenuated pennant at right angles to the tip of a hundred-foot spire.

I had worked downhill without being aware of it, pushing through woods where gold and scarlet columbine hung out their lamps in the dappled gloom. Unheeding, I left the shade and followed my feet past outcrops that stood in sage interspersed with cacti, cerise and lemon, where little lizards went scuttering through the sand. I came to myself a mile and a half below the truck. I felt lethargic and a mucus had formed on my lips. As I started walking up the road I saw shadows in the dust and looked up to see the vultures circling. I slowed my pace and breathed deeply, conserving energy. A pick-up passed, covering me with dust. I felt no resentment. I had stopped thinking. I trudged on, my legs moving, my mind ticking over at half-throttle. I knew what had happened, accepted it, and let my body do the surviving. It was practised in that, but in cold, not heat. I was discovering that the effects and reactions were similar.

I came to Old Crump, full in the sun. I unlocked the door carefully so that I shouldn't burn my hands, started the engine and pulled across the road to the shade of some aspens. I went round the back, mixed a pint of lemonade and started to drink. After a while I thought: so that's how heat exhaustion feels – and realised yet again how tough the emigrants were. Or did they, as they trudged for day after day through the heat of high summer, lapse into that state below full consciousness where I'd been for the last half-hour? No doubt, as with altitude, one would acclimatise in time.

Bidwell missed the City of Rocks, crossing the deserts farther south, but the following year Joseph Chiles, who had been with him, returned to the east, and the year after that came west for the second time, leading his own party of emigrants. At Fort Laramie he met Joseph Walker whom he engaged for $300 to guide the train to California. Chiles seems to have been feckless. First they took along heavy machinery for a sawmill, which monopolised space that would have been better utilised for food. Then he had intended to shoot buffalo but by the time he stopped to hunt and dry meat for the journey he was beyond the buffalos' range.

When they reached Fort Hall Walker refused to continue without more food so Chiles bought four head of cattle at the fort and split the train, himself and the young men continuing on horse-back, living off the land and trying to reach California by rounding the northern end of the Sierras. Walker took the wagons, the families and the food by way of the City of Rocks to the Humboldt.

The following year Elisha Stevens camped here with 46 emigrants, and from the granite city they went creaking over the low divide and down into the next valley.

I followed, descending to a broad strath where there must have been a river although the only signs of water were trees and a verdant smudge round a ranch, whether occupied or not I couldn't tell. The bones of the land ran from north to south and, where my road kept south, the emigrants had diverged westward, using the valleys for a while then crossing the divides between.

It was lonely country. A location marked on the map might turn out to be little more than a store and a petrol pump, sometimes not even that, merely a bridge and a ranch. Long before I reached the cross-roads that I'd come to yesterday, driving up from the south, I saw Pilot Peak ahead: a beacon for every traveller within 80 miles. I had come up its eastern flank; I would return down the west side.

There was to be no return that night. I was back in the desert and it was too hot. My mind started to collapse and, recognising the symptom, I turned off the road and drove along a faint track.

I saw a scattering of junipers in one place, and their shade would have been heavenly, but I dared not leave the track. The surface looked like baked mud and when I got down it disintegrated under my weight to a deep dust like flour. Where there seemed to be some bedrock under a bank I parked, facing the sun and a brisk hot wind. It was four o'clock.

I drank a lot, ate some supper and lay in the shade of the tailboard doing nothing more than glance at my watch to see how long I had to wait before the sun went down. After a while I bestirred myself to climb behind the wheel and work the truck into a position where the passenger seat was shaded and where, with every door and window open, I could get a little more air than close to the earth under the tailboard. The effort involved in this got some life flowing again, and I saw that the sun wasn't far above the horizon (although, like a wounded dragon, breathing fire) so I knew that soon I would be safe. Under the tailboard I'd felt that my blood was pooling, that shortly my brain would be starved of oxygen.

It was a salutary lesson. I had been active in the heat for too long that morning, I'd thought I'd recovered, but then I'd stopped in an exposed place too early, when the ground and the air were at their hottest. The effects were cumulative and only the awareness of what was happening, of what would happen, made me heave myself into the driver's seat and turn the car.

The sun went down and I revived quickly. Coyotes began to sing. The dry sage rustled, probably with jackrabbits. I walked up the bank and looked at Pilot Peak. The sunset I disregarded. My whole body rejoiced, not in the cool – it wasn't cool – but in the absence of heat.

All night the coyotes called, or so it seemed. I slept on the bank to catch any breeze, with Pilot Peak above and Old Crump below, gleaming faintly in the light of the Milky Way. I got up before the dawn and was drinking coffee in the sunrise – which was beautiful but I watched it warily, calculating that once the sun came up, I'd have no more than half an hour before I should be driving, however slowly, with the roof shading my head and all the windows open.

The shadows were still long as we came down a road alive with jackrabbits, the young ones losing their nerve at the approach of the truck and haring up the tarmac until they realised I'd slowed down and they could swerve into the sage. They were like caricatures: down in front with huge hind legs, but the outline balanced to some extent by long and flaring ears.

The town of Montello was closed and blind to the sun. I looked at my watch: 7.15. But I'd crossed the line into Nevada and we were now on Mountain Time so here it was 6.15.

I was on one of those stretches of desert between ranges. Twelve miles to the east were the Silver Zone Mountains, the pass clearly visible over which the Hasting Cut-off came from the other side of Pilot Peak. The Donners were now far behind, and the first snow fell on the day they left the spring this side of the Great Salt Lake Desert. They made only five miles that day before they were forced to camp.

After Silver Zone Pass the emigrants had about 25 miles of desert before the next range, the Pequops. This was on the Bidwell party's route, and it was here that they abandoned the last of their wagons. They climbed the Pequops and saw ahead the next desert and another range of mountains beyond. . . .

By ten o'clock I had taken on food and fuel in the town of Wells and was rolling south under the Ruby Mountains, relishing the breeze, seeing, all along the range, ranches at the feet of canyons which, funnels in their upper reaches, fined down to narrows full of trees. There were old snow-drifts on the mountains and, out on the flats, a lake called Snow Water with waders on its shore. The Hastings Cut-off had angled across the valley and we were on it, following it down the skirts of the mountains on one of those crazy detours that could have been avoided if Hastings had gone due west from Wells to Elko, not much more than 50 miles distant. The detour was nearly three times as long. There were springs and grass certainly, but the days were passing, the fall was coming – and the Donners were way behind, following his trail blindly.

There were three passes over the Ruby Mountains: Secret Pass that could be used by pack animals but not by wagons, Harrison Pass where Frémont and Bidwell crossed, and Overland, the only feasible route for wagons and the one which Hastings used.

At midday I came to a marsh which must have stretched for 15 miles and filled the Ruby Valley. It was a wildlife refuge: a network of reedy channels broadening to meres and traversed by dirt roads on embankments that must have been artificial, although the sole indication of it was their regularity.

I had driven only a few yards past the boundary when I saw a humpy black bird with a curlew's bill and a white face. It was feeding on mud. I stopped and gaped. Another appeared, then a pair of snowy egrets. I looked round for someone to share this with but there was no one else on the marsh. The black apparitions were white-faced ibis.

I didn't leave the car but crept along the glaring dikes, stopping when I saw something interesting, switching off the engine, listening to a multitude of calls. Above a sea of reeds the scarlet heads of a pair of sandhill cranes turned to watch me, big electric-blue dragon-flies rose, mating, from the verges, like coupled gliders. There were butterflies – a very large tortoise-shell I hadn't seen before – and a family of Harris' hawks, tired of hunting, settled on a dry knoll, red-shouldered but similar to small golden eagles. There were coots, and family after family of ducks (but no drakes so I didn't try to identify them). Terns were diving and then, amazingly, *black* terns. Acre upon acre of bulrushes and reeds made a watery sanctuary for a thousand birds I couldn't see, but could hear, and, over all, the mountains brooded in the heat of the afternoon and a few little white clouds were foils to the cerulean sky.

Ten miles to the south I could see the break of Overland Pass and at the end of the afternoon I left the marsh and came to a campground. The fee was $2 and there were no showers. My hair was matted again so I came away after filling the water container but shortly I arrived at a collection of decrepit frame cottages with a sign, 'Shantytown'. On an off-chance I approached a man who was watering some saplings with a hose and asked if this place boasted a public shower. It didn't but he said he'd gladly let me use his bathroom except that his water system was fouled up. He'd turn the hose on me if I liked. He was very jolly but I thought that standing on his lawn in a swim suit shampooing my hair might damage his relations with the neighbours so I drove on, past the end of the marsh, looking for the road that crossed the pass.

The shadows were lengthening, the sun slanting across piney hills so that they sloped in velvet folds against the light. The trail was marked 'Pony Express'. It was rough and sinuous, rising gently through the pinyon pines until, after several miles, it levelled on the divide and we came bumpily over little braes to a narrow track running at right angles through sage as tall as the truck. I followed it until it ended in a glade where there was just room to turn, and there I camped.

No one else would have camped here; the wagons pushed on across the divide and down to the next valley. The stagecoaches that used the pass would have done the same. Lienhard had lunch here because, he said, there were several springs nearby. I found one next morning but only by continuing up the path on foot. It was the Cracker Johnson Spring No. 2. No. 1 was a little way to the west. Lienhard must have been told of the springs by Hastings, but who told *him*?

The sun went down at eight o'clock and I sat with notes and maps around me trying to find Antelope Springs, which was a station on the Pony Express route in the vicinity of Ruby Valley.

One night the men at Antelope Springs heard someone among the horses. Elijah Wilson, a rider who'd stopped for the night, thought of the horses before himself and, running outside, was hit by an arrow that pierced his skull just above one eye. His companions broke off the shaft but they couldn't remove the head.

Wilson appeared to have died so they galloped to the next station. Either they thought better of their action or they collected reinforcements; they returned to bury Wilson before he was scalped – but had the Paiutes been after his scalp, they had all night to lift it. In fact, he was found outside the cabin where he'd been left, and alive.

They took him in and rode for a doctor, a day's journey away in Ruby Valley. He came, removed the arrow head (how?), and left. Wilson was delirious for six days and, visiting and finding him in this state, the division superintendent sent for the doctor again. What he did, or could have done in those days, is conjectural, and Wilson lay in a stupor for twelve more days, when he started to recover. Soon he was carrying the mail again, and he died of natural causes at the age of seventy-one.

It was a month after the Pony Express was started that the Paiutes destroyed all the stations across Nevada, but they were rebuilt and strengthened. After the Paiute War the mail came through twice-weekly and the runs were extended, sometimes to 100 miles. Over that distance a man might have as many as seven mounts.

I sat in the glade and calculated that seven horses in 100 miles averaged out at just over 14 miles for each horse.

And why (imagining the hoofbeats coming up the divide, pounding the baked earth), why was it so still this evening? Above my head there was a rush of mighty wings. I looked up sharply. Nothing was there. The sky was quite clear and still light. The pinyons were set back from the sage, hiding nothing, but there was nothing to hide.

I took my bag and, a short distance from Old Crump, now closed against the little opportunists of the night, I lay on my back and watched the stars come out.

In the dawn I walked up past the spring to a knoll from where I could see the next valley, and beyond it the Diamond Mountains: modest sage-green slopes – until you remembered that Diamond Peak was over 10,000 feet high. There were finches with long tails in the marsh about the spring, and the turquoise flash of a bluebird. It was a pleasant place. I wondered who Cracker Johnson was.

We eased down the west side of the pass to a valley totally devoid of habitation. At the bottom of the slope stood a tall cylinder beside a cattle trough. Thinking that I might top up the water container I turned off the track, craning my head to see into the trough. There was a terrible jolt and we stopped, canted.

I climbed down. The near front wheel was in a hole with vertical sides where it fitted like a glove. I got underneath and saw that the track rods appeared unharmed and the shock absorber was clear.

I considered using the jack but decided in favour of some manual labour first. I fetched the shovel and, starting about six feet from the front of the truck, dug a sloping channel back to the base of the wheel. The ground was hard and I used the pick of the ice axe to break the surface. Then I locked the hubs, engaged four-wheel low – and we came out so effortlessly I nearly forgot that the rear wheel must follow.

Our luck held. In the bottom of the empty trough were large rocks which I manhandled to the side and dropped over. Outside was a slab which I couldn't lift but could topple. I filled the hole, plugged the cracks with earth, capped the lot with the slab and eased Old Crump across. I realised I was drenched with sweat.

I unlocked the hubs, returned to two-wheel drive and started. Ghastly clanking noises came from the wheels. I stopped and considered the situation. Eureka was 50 miles to the south, Elko rather farther to the north. It was Sunday morning and not a car nor a house in sight: a valley of desolation and the sun like a furnace. Well, if he'd gone so smoothly in four-wheel drive, why not? Four-wheel high?

Far away, on the other side of the valley, I saw a dust trail. I crawled towards it at five miles an hour, dipping like a lame ox into the dry stream beds, creeping out of them, knowing now the difference between 'dirt' and 'improved' roads: dirt roads are made by the passage of vehicles, improved means a layer of gravel on top, perhaps even a grader. Once I detoured into the sage to avoid a long pool. The sweat streamed off me and soaked my cushion.

I met the vehicle, a mini-bus, and we stopped. It was full of young men. Was this the road to Ruby Valley? I said it was and explained why I was crawling. They were askance; was the road as bad as that? I reassured them and continued, crossing the valley until I reached a gravel road.

For 100 yards I crawled towards Elko and then thought, illogically, that progress might have ironed out the problem – and that 50 miles at five miles an hour meant ten hours of boredom. I stopped, unlocked the hubs, engaged normal drive and, consumed by wonder, felt him work up through the gears with all his sweet familiar panache. Earlier, I must have failed to unlock one hub and I'd tried to drive with one wheel locked and the other free.

It was 29 miles to the first house, and one car passed me. That made two in two hours.

I was still concerned that I might have done some damage not immediately apparent, so I was preoccupied with the need to reach Elko, and by the necessity of clamping down on self-recrimination because that sapped energy. I had forgotten about the trail, that I was following it, until suddenly we were crossing a bridge over a shallow river and I knew exactly where I was. We had reached the South Fork of the Humboldt, the river that we were to follow for 365 miles, until we reached the Sierras.

12

DOWN THE HUMBOLDT

BY THE MID-FORTIES the Paiutes on the lower Humboldt were fiercely hostile but at the headwaters of the river Lienhard found a happy childlike people, generous and intelligent, with a simple sense of humour, and of etiquette. At a spring in the Ruby Valley a band of them came into the emigrant camp and one, approaching 'a surly Englishman', indicated that he would like to smoke the emigrant's pipe. The white man pushed the other away and said that no dirty Indian was going to smoke his pipe. The whites were heavily outnumbered and the tension was acute when an elderly American woman filled her own pipe, lit it and handed it to one of the older Indians, and so it was passed round. The Paiutes showed their appreciation with gracious smiles, 'while they continued to cast poisonous, revengeful glances at the impolite Englishman.'

Two or three days later Lienhard came on an Indian sitting on the bank of a stream and indicated that the man might like to find him some edible roots. The Indian ran off and within a few minutes came back with something that tasted like parsnips. Lienhard was pleased, the Indian was overjoyed and trotted away to find more. This time he brought back some grasshoppers as well, which Lienhard declined.

That evening the Indian invited himself to supper in the Swiss boys' tent. Next morning he came along with his arms full of roots and accompanied by companions. But Lienhard and another white man had been prostrated with diarrhoea and, needing to explain their inability to eat more roots, Lienhard embarked on a graphic mime and 'groaned as if I had severe stomach pains. Then I imitated a certain sound with my lips that could come only from another part of the anatomy, and at the same time I made a quick gesture to my behind. The Indians understood completely, and they all burst out in a storm of laughter. My friend [the Paiute] laughed loudest of all, and threw his roots at my back. We naturally joined in the laughter and parted as good friends in spite of all.'*

These Indians lived in more hospitable country than did those farther down the Humboldt. The Ruby Mountains were in the middle of the Great Basin but they were no desert range. In most years there was snow

* From St Louis to Sutter's Fort 1846 by Heinrich Lienhard, University of Oklahoma Press.

on their crests throughout the summer; this supplied the springs and the
Ruby Marshes on the east, while on the west, streams came down long
canyons to the desolate valley where Old Crump had fallen in the hole.
The longest of these canyons, Lamoille, went back for 18 miles into the
heart of the range, and was followed by a road. There was a good stream,
with pines and flowers and little alps which, from a distance, looked like
meadows. Certainly there was some grazing because I saw a sheepherder
saddling up beside his wagon.

The country was like the Slovenian Alps. The north wall of the main
canyon was continuous, buttressed by steep rock ridges, but on the
south there were subsidiary glens with hanging corries under fine
headwalls. At the top of the canyon I left the truck and walked up a path
that wound through hedges of purple monkshood, through coniferous
woods, past a lake where shooting stars like long-stemmed cyclamen
fringed the lush banks, to come out on a pass at around 10,000 feet. A
breeze that had blown across hundreds of miles of desert felt deliciously
cool. Below the pass was a lake of inky water. Beyond it the mountain
wall rose to a conical peak, dark and symmetrical. Over the wall frail
ghosts of a real desert range shimmered through the humid air that rose
from the Ruby Marshes. To the right of the conical peak the summits of
the Rubies showed one behind the other all the way to Overland Pass.

I came down from the Rubies in the heat of the afternoon and started
along the familiarly dusty tracks. Old Crump had been given a clean bill
of health by a garage in Elko but I drove more carefully now, watching
for holes. I was looking for the Humboldt Canyon. I could see a gash in
the distance but the road leading to it was gated and it looked as if the
only vehicles that had passed that way had been tracked. The surface was
a dry churned bog. I retreated to the last habitation: a mobile home in
the middle of nowhere.

A big powerful woman opened the door to me. Had I seen a red setter?
It had escaped, dragging its chain. I offered to help her search but she'd
looked everywhere and now she would wait for her husband and send
him out with the other dog. He came home soon afterwards: a small
wiry man who drove a truck for a mine.

Until recently this couple had worked as a team, driving long-
distance. Their loads were usually explosives, sometimes radioactive
and not always waste; occasionally it was the raw material. There were
no extra security precautions; they were given a radio telephone only if
they were carrying gold. In the case of explosives and radioactive loads,
they had to use a public call box in the event of emergency.

Husband-and-wife teams were preferred for dangerous loads; they
were more reliable – although one couple had disappeared completely
with their truck and load. It had been suggested that they'd sold the

load. Or been murdered, I said, and then had to explain myself. They were delighted to find I wrote crime stories and invited me to share their supper. They were as ingenuous as children, and they were nomads. They'd spent their honeymoon hauling a load. They laughed a great deal, and every location I mentioned cued them for a story. Omaha was the place Milly drove into by mistake. She didn't like driving in cities so she had to wake Forest and ask him to take over.

Donner Pass. Forest was driving explosives down the slope of the Sierras and was picking up speed. When Milly protested he told her that they had two wheels on fire. They had to pull into a scenic view-point to cool off. It was illegal, when hauling explosives, to stop in car parks, lay-bys, or outside cafés. They were very unpopular, they assured me solemnly. And there was always the risk of hijack; one person had to remain in the cab all the time. I thought about weapons, and Forest saw the thought. Everyone packed a gun in Nevada, he said, but Milly hushed him.

They would, by virtue of their job, be more alert to the risk of radioactivity than most people. Milly was unhappy about underground nuclear tests; she thought the ground water might be contaminated. They drew their water from a well. Forest, accustomed to earthquakes, wasn't bothered about underground tests. He'd been driving along a level plain when suddenly there was a rise in the road where there hadn't been one a moment before. Movement continued but it was the hill that moved, not his vehicle; rolling towards him like an ocean wave until he was going down the other side.

Neither was native to Nevada; Milly was from Seattle, Forest from the east. I asked which of all the states they liked the best. Virginia, they said instantly.

They talked about the missing dog. Forest reckoned the bull would have killed her if she'd snagged the chain. The bull had been roaring all evening. There was the animal that was killing cattle too; people said it was a puma but Forest thought it was wild dogs. He said he'd take the heeler and go out to look for the setter. Their second dog was a blue heeler: a pretty, nervous animal, like a lurcher.

They asked me to stay the night but I assured them I'd be more comfortable on the ground. I drove down to the fence at the end of the dirt road and bedded down in the sage. The bull was moaning still but he was in the creek bed and if he left it I'd hear him coming.

In the small hours I was wakened by coyotes, very close. They surrounded me. I'd seen coyotes now and they were big animals, almost as big as wolves. They came closer. I couldn't see them but the din was harrowing. Reluctantly, telling myself I needed a good night's sleep, I got up. I'd never sleep on the ground wondering all the time if a coyote, sneaking up out of curiosity and taking a nip by mistake, would be followed by the pack coming in like sharks after blood. I put on my boots and dragged the bed to the truck. At three o'clock in the morning, I moved all the boxes to the front seat and lay down in the back. The coyotes drifted away, their calls mocking me.

I was parked near a canyon but it was the wrong one. This was Ten Mile Creek. Next morning I went back to Elko, and the Forest Service sent me out on the old Bullion Road which brought me, after 12 dusty switchbacking miles, to the South Fork of the Humboldt. Below me was a sage flat with the cabins of an abandoned homestead. The river flowed down the other side of this basin to the canyon which lay at right angles to the stream so that I could see no more of the defile than the high red walls of the entrance.

There was a gate, a real one, leading to the old homestead. It was open but a chain and padlock hung on a post. If I drove through that gate and someone locked it I'd be stuck on the inside. On the other hand I didn't want to leave Old Crump outside because there were two doubtful-looking men in the vicinity whom I'd made the mistake of approaching. One was sharp, the other overtly hostile. Now Old Crump's tailboard didn't fit properly and could be levered open with a serviceable tool. Everything in the wagon was insured except my notes – and they were the very thing I couldn't afford to lose. I retreated a few miles towards Elko, found some shade and had lunch.

I wasn't cast down. There were so many places I wanted to see that it was impossible to see half of them in the time available. As one approached the Humboldt Sink the trail would split into numerous variations as people went over different passes or round the extremities of the Sierras that stretched for 400 miles. The length of the Sierras was in my brief, so the Humboldt Canyon was one of the places I'd miss – and I wasn't sorry. At lunch time I heard a weather report and even the Nevada weather man said it was hot. There was a high pressure system off the coast of California.

I propped myself against a wheel in the shade that was warm but not dangerous and read about Lienhard in the Humboldt Canyon.

They camped 200 paces from its mouth, which would be close to the old homestead. Next day Lienhard crossed the river thirteen times, and then came the worst place. The water was deep on the left, shallow on the right, but if they went right the wagon would ride up the bank and tip. So they decided to go left. However, a stubborn old lead ox called Ben insisted on going right. Lienhard had a rope on the right horn and was trying to turn the beast's head to the left but the animal wouldn't come and the wagon was tilting. Lienhard nipped to the other side and with both hands on the horn tried to push the beast to the left. Ben lifted him out of the way as if he were a child. The wagon tipped and fell, the bows underneath, the wheels in the air.

There was a heavy silence. Then Lienhard started to issue grave orders while one man thundered curses and the other roared with laughter. (The remaining two had gone ahead.)

They did what Lienhard suggested: unhitched the oxen, dragged all their belongings out of the water, righted the wagon, pulled it to an island where they'd put the oxen, loaded and hitched up again – 'there were a few little *"Donnerwetters"* as Thomen and I dragged his bedding from the water, a little stream of water flowing from it. . . . The loss we sustained wasn't great. The bows, to be sure, were broken, the cover torn, and almost everything was soaked, but the gun-powder suffered· hardly any damage.'*

They emerged from the canyon and spent the next day drying out. Behind them two wagons turned over at the same place, one of which had capsized at an earlier crossing in the same canyon. Three weeks later the Donners took two days for this section.

Below the canyon the South Fork enters the Humboldt River and the Hastings Cut-off comes back to the main California Trail. While Lienhard and the others were drying their possessions a small train passed which had left Fort Bridger twelve or fourteen days after the Swiss boys but had taken the northern route by way of the Snake and the City of Rocks. Lienhard's comment on this heart-breaking meeting was merely that there was no profit in the cut-off. There was no time for recrimination; all their resources must be concentrated on getting over the Sierras before the winter came.

For a few days the Swiss boys travelled down the river with their company but then, encamped below a small sandy hill, the five bachelors held a consultation among themselves. For all their high spirits and their nervousness (they had suddenly quarrelled about the scale of their separate contributions to the expedition), they were fairly integrated when it came to survival, and they were of one accord in the need for speed. The family wagons were slow in starting in the mornings. The Swiss decided to push ahead.

It was thought that teams would have to be doubled to get over the sand hill but, rising before anyone else next morning, the Lienhard wagon got over unaided, one man turning the spokes of each wheel, the fifth driving. Then they rattled ahead, only to be brought up short by a note in a shrub saying that Indians had attacked a train and injured several men. It was thought that ten Indians had been killed.

They decided that it would be a mark of cowardice to wait for the company, and certainly imprudent so far as time was concerned, but

*Ibid.

shortly after they found the note they were overtaken by a man called
Kyburz, his wife, and father-in-law, in two wagons. The old man didn't
want to be so far out ahead with hostile Indians around so he gave up his
position as driver to one of the Swiss boys and hurried back to the safety
of the larger train.

Beyond the big bend of the Humboldt the Paiutes were hostile,
numerous and cunning. They had been stealing since the thirties, which
was the only way they could survive when the white men killed the game,
trapped the streams and polluted the springs. At first they'd pilfered,
had been mown down by guns, and had learned a lesson. Now they stole
by stealth, and they had learned to murder, and to shoot arrows into the
cattle which might not kill but weakened the animals to such an extent
that they had to be abandoned.

In the nineteenth century the natural world was an hierarchy with the
white man at the top and Indians, human but savage, somewhere
between the lower animals and whites. Mark Twain admired the eastern
tribes but the Paiutes or Diggers nauseated him; he found them
'treacherous, filthy and repulsive'. Like the Australian aborigines, he
said, they must be descended from the same gorilla, kangaroo or
Norway rat. Twain doesn't appear to have been a monster; it is more
likely that his denunciation was a spontaneous reaction to some
dreadful story told to him where it happened. In 1857, for instance, a
small party of emigrants was attacked on the Humboldt and eight
people were killed including a man who lay sick in a wagon. One
wounded man managed to crawl away but the Indians caught a woman
trying to escape with her baby and dashed the child against a wagon
wheel. They shot the woman full of arrows, pulled them out and thrust
them in again, then scalped her. At that moment another train arrived
and they fled, dropping the woman's scalp. She survived to have a wig
made of her own hair, but she never fully recovered and later went mad.
Her husband was among the dead as well as her child.

This was only one in a series of atrocities on both sides that started
when Walker had thirty or forty Paiutes massacred because they were
pilfering from his camp near the Humboldt Sink in 1833. There is a
picture of Walker by Miller in DeVoto's *Across the Wide Missouri*: rough,
tough and romantic, riding some distance in front of his squaw. It is
captioned, 'Bourgeois Walker and His Wife.' And, from DeVoto,
'Bonneville's great partisan, the exterminator of Diggers, the entrepreneur in California horses, and the discoverer of Yosemite.'

Whereas most people paid lip service to the Indian as human but less
so than the white man, being impoverished and pagan, the treatment
meted out to him was that accorded to pests. But the Indians had a
strange sense of values too. Some trappers in the Yellowstone area were

approached by two Arikaras who came into camp to smoke while their companions made off with the horses. The mountain men tied up the two visitors and offered to trade them for the horses. The Indians countered with a bid of two horses for the two hostages, then decided that horses were more valuable, sang the victims' mourning song and rode away. The mountain men made up a good fire and threw the prisoners on it.

White men could be more treacherous than any Indian. In the late fifties a family wagon straggling in the rear of a train was attacked by twenty Indians. The emigrant cut two mules free but his wife and child were shot down as they tried to escape. The man was wounded but managed to overtake the rest of the train. His wagon was looted. There were $1,500 in English gold coins hidden in it, but this sum was found and taken.

Two days later three armed men joined the train, and the following day each attached a white flag to a wagon. This was thought to be a signal and orders were given for the flags to be taken down. The wounded man was lying in one of the wagons and when he got a look at the white strangers he said that the leader, a man called Tooly, had been among the 'Indians' who killed his wife and child. It was thought that he was delirious, but the three armed men left the train. The following evening they came back, found the emigrants unfriendly so rode away again.

When the train arrived at the Humboldt Sink the emigrants found a shack: Black's Trading Post, where whisky was being sold. Tooly was drinking there and boasting that he had 'done up' some emigrants.

They tried him on the spot, with a jury of twelve men who had not until then been associated with him. He denied the charge, the judge refused to convict, he was searched and $500 in English gold was found on him. He was given a choice of hanging or shooting. He made a break for it and was shot.

Back on the Humboldt Lienhard passed a new grave with a notice saying that a man had been killed by Paiutes, buried, dug up and mutilated, and buried again by the next train to come past. Even so, in this country where every willow thicket was a potential ambush, Lienhard rode back six miles, alone on a fractious mule, to recover an axe he'd mislaid.

The smoke of a signal fire was seen on the mountains, and with one exception they voted to have no fire that night. But one of the Swiss boys, Ripstein, insisted on his coffee and for that he had to have a fire. It was the most uncomfortable night Lienhard spent on the whole trip. A few years later Ripstein was prospecting with other men in the Sierras when they came on a village from which the Indians had just fled. The whites went on for a mile or so, lit a fire and left a man on guard. In the night they were attacked, Ripstein was wounded in the hand and the guard died of his wounds. If this man hadn't thrown a blanket over the fire when the Indians attacked they might all have been killed. When Lienhard heard of the incident he blamed Ripstein for the death of the prospector – which is not surprising. Ripstein must have been an overbearing and dislikeable man if no one could stop him lighting a fire on the Humboldt thus endangering the whole train.

The day after Lienhard passed the grave they found a notice telling them to kill all Indians because they were great thieves. Then an Indian appeared whom no one wanted to kill, but thinking he could be a spy he was persuaded to stay in camp overnight and was given presents in the morning. Two days later the emigrants lost five of their cattle including Lienhard's leading team (one of these would be old Ben, who was a good ox even if he was stubborn). The Swiss boys had to take a chest from Kyburz weighing 100 pounds because he'd lost more oxen than they had – and ahead of them was the Forty Mile Desert and the long haul over the Sierras.

Shooting oxen or running them off was as good a way of destroying the white invaders as murder. The Indians knew very well what they were about. And yet in 1841 when Bidwell's party followed the Humboldt to the sink – a lonely little band of men, with one woman and a baby, packing their goods on their cattle – they *traded* with the Paiutes, and this was only eight years after the Walker Massacre. At the start of the great migration the Indians were selective in their retaliation.

As travellers approached the Humboldt Sink they saw that the water in the river was shrinking, and they became uneasy. They recalled the horror of the deserts and dreaded the one that lay ahead. Certainly there was a river on the other side, but they thought less of its advantages at the end of a dry crossing than of the exigencies of its canyons. And beyond the canyons was the pass: the highest and roughest yet, and autumn already. Speed was essential, not only to get over that last pass before the snow but to escape this dangerous river valley where the water was obviously going to give out any day and where the Indians followed them like wolves.

Fear is infectious and takes strange forms. The Swiss boys, who had the least trouble on the Hastings Cut-off, even in the Great Salt Lake Desert, quarrelled as soon as they reached the comparative security of the main trail. Farther down the Humboldt, in hostile country, Ripstein invited attack with his fire. And far behind came the Donners. Already demoralised in the Wasatch, their consequent lack of integration, of concerted decision and movement, contributed to the final tragedy. They were aware of their danger; before they reached the Ruby Mountains they sent two mounted men ahead to bring back provisions from

Sutter's Fort. They had acknowledged the danger publicly, and did so again when they reached the Humboldt where the train split; the first half, which included the two Donner families, forged ahead so fast that they were soon a day's travel in advance. At the big bend of the river they came on the hostile Paiutes and began to lose their cattle. The rear half of the train started to drive hard to catch up.

This party came to a sand hill, which could well have been the one which the Swiss boys surmounted with a man to each wheel. They doubled teams, and then the lead yoke of a man called Snyder tangled with those driven by Reed's teamster. Snyder, suddenly beside himself with rage, started to beat the oxen over the head. Reed rushed forward and Snyder turned on him, reversing the whip and striking with the butt. He laid Reed's head open but the other had drawn his knife. Snyder continued to strike, hitting both Reed and Mrs Reed who had intervened. Then Snyder collapsed. A few minutes later he died of a knife wound.

The train camped. A man called Keseberg, who hated Reed, put up his wagon tongue for the hanging. The Donners were ahead, and Reed had only two men to support him, but that was enough. The three were heavily armed. A compromise was reached and Reed was banished without firearms. His enemies had it both ways for now he would ride to Sutter's and bring back help because he had left his family behind. There was the possibility that the two men who had already been sent ahead had not got through to the fort.

Attitudes hardened further, particularly among the family men. Everyone who could do so was walking now to spare the weakened oxen. An old bachelor called Hardkoop did not come into camp at the end of the day and people who would have ridden back for him had no horses, and those who had horses wouldn't lend them. The old man was abandoned.

They quarrelled over the death of Snyder and the abandoning of Hardkoop. A mare became mired in a water-hole and when the owner asked for help it was refused because he'd refused the loan of her when they wanted to ride back for Hardkoop. The mare smothered in the mud.

Indians stole the cattle and horses, and those they didn't run off they maimed with their arrows. Altogether the Donner train lost 100 head of cattle in the Great Basin. With depleted teams they had to abandon more wagons, and they were perilously short of food. At the Humboldt Sink a family called Eddy with two small children had nothing more than the clothes they were wearing and three pounds of lump sugar. The man's gun had been broken some days before, so he couldn't hunt for game, and they had 240 miles to go before they reached Sutter's Fort.

On October 13 the Donner train left the Humboldt Sink and started across the Forty Mile Desert. It was an extremely hot day.

The year before, on November 24, Walker started across the same desert, joined Frémont on the other side, and crossed what was to become the Donner Pass on December 5 without seeing any snow. The party that would have had little trouble with early snowfalls had a phenomenally late season; those least able to cope were to have the worst conditions possible.

13

THE LAST DESERTS

DONNER PASS WAS only one gateway to the rich valleys of California. The first split in the trail at its western end occurred 110 miles short of the Humboldt Sink, at Lassen's Meadows. In 1846 Jesse Applegate had left southern Oregon and, with a party of hard young men, he came east, living off the land, and established a new route that came out at the meadows that were to take Lassen's name.

Two years later Peter Lassen decided to utilise much of this Applegate Road in order to bring emigrants to his ranch in the upper Sacramento Valley, where he proposed to build a city. As with Hastings, Lassen's resources didn't match his ambitions. Although one party of mounted men had travelled the Applegate Road, there were 200 miles of unexplored country between it and the Sacramento Valley. Through this Lassen was proposing to take wagons.

He left his ranch and went east in the spring. It seems likely that he took the regular trail by way of Donner Pass and the City of Rocks as far as Fort Hall. There he started to tout for custom. By the time he returned to the meadows below the big bend in the Humboldt he was leading ten wagons.

They left the main trail and struck west across low ranges of mountains, the Antelopes and the Kammas, leaving the latter by way of a shallow ravine where small pinnacles like sharks' teeth were set in gentle slopes of scree. Everything is dry and bleached as old bones. I came slowly down the defile watching for the holes (remembering that for the emigrants a broken axle could mean an abandoned wagon) to roll out on the Black Rock Desert that stretches for 20 or 30 miles, quite flat and surrounded by ranges, jagged to north and west – but the nearer peaks are bare and wrinkled and brown. Twenty miles away, across salt flats shimmering in the light, is the Black Rock, a small tower on a plinth at the end of a spur.

There was a muddy piece of road where we had to weave between the holes and where the water was evaporating leaving big sheets of fawn silt. In one place, where the mud had been dry for some time, there were the tracks of a large cat. (One evening in the desert a jackrabbit had raced down the road towards me, swerving at the last moment. Behind it I had a glimpse of a tall shape that watched me for a moment before it turned and stalked without haste into the sage. It was a bobcat.)

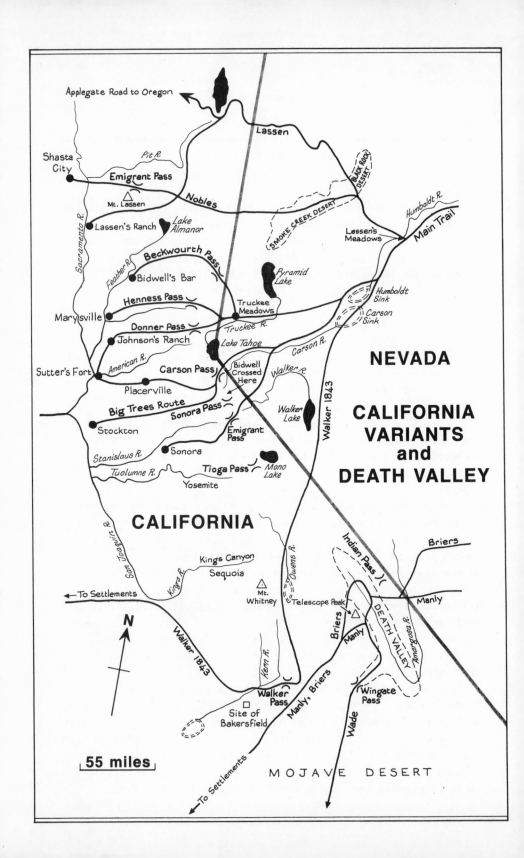

Applegate Road to Oregon

Lassen

Shasta City

Pit R.

Emigrant Pass

Mt. Lassen

Nobles

BLACK ROCK DESERT

Humboldt R.

Main Trail

Sacramento R.

Lassen's Ranch

Lake Almanor

SMOKE CREEK DESERT

Lassen's Meadows

Beckwourth Pass

Feather R.

Bidwell's Bar

Pyramid Lake

Humboldt Sink

Henness Pass

Truckee Meadows

Carson Sink

Marysville

Donner Pass

Truckee R.

Johnson's Ranch

Lake Tahoe

Carson R.

NEVADA

Sutter's Fort

American R.

Carson Pass

Bidwell Crossed Here

Walker R.

CALIFORNIA VARIANTS and DEATH VALLEY

Placerville

Big Trees Route

Sonora Pass

Walker Lake

Walker 1843

Stockton

Emigrant Pass

Stanislaus R.

Sonora

Tuolumne R.

Tioga Pass

Mono Lake

Yosemite

CALIFORNIA

Kings Canyon

Sequoia

Briers

Owens R.

Indian Pass

Kings R.

← To Settlements

Mt. Whitney

Telescope Peak

DEATH VALLEY

Manly

N

San Joaquin R.

Briers

Manly

Amargosa R.

Walker 1843

Kern R.

Briers

Manly

Wingate Pass

Walker Pass

Site of Bakersfield

Manly, Briers

Wade

55 miles

To Settlements

M O J A V E   D E S E R T

I camped in the desert and, eating my supper, was suddenly overwhelmed by an intense and unbearable feeling of depression. I walked out into the sage because I couldn't remain still. I was unable to think, to reason, even to feel frightened. Without any warning I vomited, and when I'd recovered the depression had disappeared completely.

The air was close and very warm. There were no clouds and the sun went down in a burnished glow. As the darkness deepened a light came on in what I'd thought was an abandoned mine about six miles away but there was no sound. I stared at the mine morosely. I didn't like the Black Rock Desert.

Lassen and his party had a bad time of the crossing. They must have felt uneasy when they started towards the Black Rock. There would be no water until they reached it and the going was soft for the animals. Lassen's ranch was due west of the defile in the Kammas Mountains but no one was to take that road for three years; Lassen kept to the Applegate Trail and went way out to the north before coming round in a great loop to the headwaters of the Sacramento River. It was a laborious and labyrinthine route to California, yet in the following year 8,000 people took it, virtually by mistake.

In 1849 the endless trains rolled out into the desert and only when they saw the Black Rock 20 miles ahead did they start to wonder if something was wrong. What had happened was that a man called Milton McGee had guided eleven wagons across the Great Basin with the intention of taking the Lassen road. When he turned off, hundreds of wagons followed him, thinking it was the main trail. Wagons continued to take the turn-off throughout the season so that even the stragglers at the end of that migration turned right at Lassen's Meadows and took the long way round to California. Fortunately that year the military governor in California, General Persifor F. Smith, alive to the possibility of another Donner disaster, sent relief columns out to all the passes. Hearing of wagons strung out along the Lassen route, a column under an indefatigable journalist called Peoples and, later, a Major Rucker – who worked himself until he fell ill – travelled along this section of the trail in reverse, feeding the emigrants as they went.

Three years later William Nobles rode due west from the place where I camped, skirting the Black Rock Desert on the south, the Smoke Creek Desert on the north, to reach the mining town of Shasta City by a route through what is now Lassen Volcanic National Park.

On the ground Nobles' route looked far superior to Lassen's. People had been remarkably gullible in the nineteenth century, although I remembered that only a few wagons had followed Lassen. Presumably the majority hadn't been satisfied with his answers; but why hadn't the people who did go with him asked if he knew the country? His self-confidence was limitless and misplaced. Eleven years after he took his tiny party round the northern Sierras (and must have escaped lynching by his clients only because he represented the slimmest chance of escaping from that wilderness) he was killed when prospecting for silver near the Black Rock, but whether by Indians or whites is unknown. In the fifties there were many shady characters in California who found it easier to let others do the mining until sufficient gold or silver was accumulated to make it worthwhile to move in and appropriate it. There were so many ways that a man could die in the wilderness that a fractured skull – if the body were ever found – stood a fair chance of being diagnosed as accidental. And if it weren't, the authorities, such as they were, had enough lawlessness on their hands without instigating a search for a murderer who could be hundreds of miles away, or quietly going about his business in a teeming tent town close by where any man could be a murderer and undoubtedly some were.

Nasty things would have happened in the Black Rock Desert. When, about midnight, I was roused by the clamorous noise of machinery, I lay quaking and, half-awake, could only postulate aliens. It was as loud as a helicopter landing beside me but it wasn't a helicopter.

I sat up and saw a powerful light crawling across the desert. Following Nobles' route, I thought, with cold despair. It wouldn't have worried me if the light had emanated from the ghosts of a whole wagon train providing they'd progressed quietly; it's the unknown that terrifies, and I couldn't come to terms with that terrible noise. I focused the binoculars on the light and although I could see what was ahead of it even to individual clumps of sage, I could see nothing of the source. I had to conclude there was a road – although I could see no surface ahead of the light – and that this slow-moving object was some enormous piece of mining equipment. In the morning I saw that it was a railroad. A freight train was parked in the middle of the desert.

I drove to Sulphur, marked on the map as a location, but a dismal place: derelict cabins, old cars, twisted machinery, a line of plastic bunting. Its *raison d'être* was presumably as a link between railroad and mine. The railroad was the Western Pacific. People rode through here in Pullman cars, eating smoked salmon, drinking chilled hock; the best of them voicing a tribute to Frémont perhaps, others wondering about calories or blackheads or (being in Nevada) whether silver was safe. . . . I was being insufferable. I had not recovered from my fright.

Frémont camped at the Black Rock in January. He was lucky. There was no snow yet it was cool. Snow on the desert could be as dangerous as heat; the surface became a mire and even a pack train could make no progress. Loads had to be abandoned, and men and beasts were fortunate to escape with their lives. At such times the fiery heat of July would seem preferable. People forgot that it was possible to have heat and a bad surface.

I went out to look at the Smoke Creek Desert, using a compass and working from bearings. There were more roads on the ground than there were on the map, and the only signposts were to the mines. I followed a road for 20 miles, came to an impassable gully and retreated rather than run the risk of getting bogged down in the sand.

The mountains looked quite barren and yet there was the odd cow about and once, on the other side of a draw, I saw three feral burros and a heifer, all fat but wary as deer. The heifer recalled a highway sign south of Battle Mountain: 'Cattle on Road for next 85 miles'.

I started to drift off to sleep – the occupational hazard of driving slowly in the desert. I stopped for a brew.

That afternoon I reached the Humboldt Sink. The river had continued to shrink and now it died in a bed of baked clay. At this point Bidwell, Walker and Frémont all turned south and followed Walker's original route down the east side of the Sierras. They went south because, although a pass over the central mass was suspected, no white man had crossed by it. Frémont could have been the man to discover it, but although he had a pack train when he was here in 1844, since it was January he was too prudent to risk traversing mountains where it was rumoured that the snow could reach unprecedented depths.

Nine months after Frémont passed, 40 wagons came to the Humboldt Sink. This was the train led by Elisha Stevens. He was accompanied by another old trapper, Caleb Greenwood, with two half-breed sons. At the sink someone came in with an old Indian called Truckee with whom Caleb Greenwood communicated in sign language. Truckee told of a river 50 or 60 miles to the west that flowed out of the mountains. Greenwood and two others scouted ahead with Truckee as hostage and returned with confirmation that the Indian was speaking the truth, but still there was no certainty of a pass. They decided to risk it and to move quickly, a decision hastened by the attitude of the Indians. The Paiutes were friendly but young John Greenwood, who was half Crow, hated them. Ironically he wasn't involved when violence came close to eruption just as they were leaving.

A lad called Moses Schallenberger missed a halter, saw it half concealed below an Indian's blanket and grabbed at it. The Indian drew his bow, Schallenberger raised his rifle, but it was struck up by an older man. The elders in this expedition kept control, which could have been one reason for its success. On this occasion the Indians were fobbed off with lavish gifts. Only fools insisted on their rights when the other side had numerical superiority and all the advantages of their home ground.

It is 55 miles from the Humboldt Sink to the Truckee River. There is a dry stretch of 15 miles and then some brackish water at the start of the Forty Mile Desert. In the twentieth century there is no other road but the interstate; there was no road then, even after the passage of many wagons, because the trail was covered intermittently by the drifting sand. Sometimes the wind would expose a stretch of ruts and some of these show still on brows where grooves were worn in the bedrock.

There was no feed for the animals. At the sink the people cut all the grass they could carry; they filled their receptacles with water but that was only for themselves; the animals couldn't drink until they reached the boiling springs, halfway across. They travelled all day and into the night, resting the oxen on the way but not turning them loose. If mounted men could be spared they rode ahead and dammed the overflow from the springs so that by the time the wagons arrived the water would be cool enough for the animals to drink. It tasted salty and some of them wouldn't touch it.

The geysers at the springs have been tamed since the nineteenth century, when there were many, and some ten feet high. Now there is one tall plume. The ground smokes gently. Nor are the boiling sulphurous pools visible: in the early days a spaniel jumped into one, to be killed instantly.

After the hot springs there is a broad ridge of sand rippled by the wind. Many people lost oxen here. The sand continued for six miles and the route was marked by dead and dying animals. When Lienhard reached the sand he found two Americans with a light cart and a yoke of mules waiting for assistance. They doubled teams and Lienhard, Ripstein and one of the Americans stayed to guard the wagons until the teams should return. Lienhard had contracted diarrhoea again, this time from bad water. The American told terrible tales about Indians, and the coyotes closed in, howling fearfully. He said these were Indians imitating coyotes. Poor Lienhard had to keep leaving the safety of the wagons but he always took his loaded rifle and peered in all directions. He observes lugubriously and probably without facetiousness, that his position was highly dangerous. In the morning he examined the tracks of the nocturnal prowlers and found only those of coyotes.

The Stevens train had no trouble in this last desert. Two years later the Donners, terribly weakened, their oxen all hide and bone, only just managed to flounder across. The Eddy family had to walk because they had no transport and no one would take their babies into a wagon. Owners of wagons were trying to spare the oxen. Many people carried loads as they walked. The Eddy children, carried by their parents, suffered critically from thirst. One man, Breen, who had a cask of water, refused to let them drink so Eddy, threatening to kill him, took the water by force.

At the boiling springs George Donner abandoned several heavy cases of books. At the sand ridge six oxen were lost.

Beyond the sand the mountains rise. There have been ranges all the way across the Great Basin; for hundreds of miles I had been surrounded by them, set in grey and unremitting wastes, isolated one from the other by seas of salt. These that stand on the other side of the Forty Mile Desert are neither spiky, nor bare nor isolated. Their proportions are those of hills, not mountains; they are not the climax, just the start of it. They are foothills, but still high enough to have old snow-drifts on their unsensational crests. And the eye travels down the slopes to the foot of them deep in a belt of cottonwoods.

The oxen smelled the water and started to shamble. The drivers stopped and unyoked, for otherwise irreparable damage would be done to the wagons as the cattle plunged down the banks of the beautiful river that came pouring out of the first canyon of the high Sierras.

14

DONNER PASS

I FELT NO excitement when I saw the cottonwoods, only relief so cool it was merely acceptance, as if I'd known all along that we would get through. And, going a little farther in my mind, I saw that excitement would have been extravagant because, while we'd escaped from the deserts, we hadn't yet started on the mountains. But as we plodded up the first canyon and, instead of dust and baking rock, I fancied I could smell resin and even wet moss, I knew a familiar serenity; I had come home. I realised I was split: one half, the mountaineer, relaxed and rejoiced at the escape from an alien environment and the return to the security of country it understood; the involved-emigrant half was cool and tense and watchful, knowing far better than they had ever known, all the dangers that lay ahead.

Like most rivers breaking out from mountains in the west, the Truckee flowed through successive canyons. After the desert came a gorge some 20 miles long and it was the first of its kind encountered by the people who had travelled by way of Fort Hall. It was a shock to them because it was unfamiliar; those who had taken the Hastings Cut-off must have viewed it with a dreadful resignation.

The Truckee canyons were even worse than those of the Wasatch and the Humboldt. It was autumn now, sometimes freezing at night, and the water by day bitterly cold. Most people, including Lienhard, took three or four days to get through the first canyon. The trail emerged on the beautiful Truckee Meadows – but I came out at Reno which stands on the same site. The emigrants camped at the meadows. I stayed on the interstate, driving carefully for there were many exits and a lot of merging traffic. A few miles farther I slid out of the stream that was heading towards the Pacific for the weekend, and looked for the town called Verdi that was the next mail drop.

There was a straggle of hamlets along the interstate wherever the valley broadened to leave room for a few houses and a dusty road, and somewhere west of Reno I found an old frame building with antiques for sale.

When I opened the screen door the interior appeared to be deserted: dark and cluttered with bric-à-brac. A television set mumbled inanely. I edged through the furniture to a back room, similarly cluttered, and came back, seeing that the television set stood on a counter. Behind the counter a man was slumped in a chair. I asked him where I might find the Post Office and he told me. I didn't see his lips move and certainly no other part of him did. I thanked him and walked out, my back feeling as vulnerable as Philip Marlowe's. Chandler was good – but he had priceless material to work with.

'Welcome to Verdi' a sign said. It was pronounced 'Vurd-eye' and was just inside the Nevada state line. At this moment I was unaware of the significance, not of Verdi, but of its location, except that it came after a second canyon which started west of Truckee Meadows.

This was formidable. Constant immersion softened the oxen's feet which were then cut by sharp rocks to the extent that they could hardly pull for the pain. In one place the river was crossed ten times in one mile, the men working waist-deep in the water. Stevens, blazing the trail, had twelve inches of snow in this canyon and the oxen could find no grazing. They offered the animals pine needles which were refused. The cattle were saved when some rushes were found poking through the snow, and after that they always camped where there were rushes because after that there was always snow.

Stevens followed the Truckee upstream through a third canyon, but before they entered it, at the point where Verdi stands, old Caleb Greenwood looked around at the country with the eye of a mountaineer. I had read this somewhere but as I drove down the main street of Verdi at about five o'clock on that August afternoon, I wasn't thinking of Greenwood nor indeed of the trail; I had picked up several boxes of slides and I was concerned only with finding a place to camp so that I might enjoy looking at them.

I saw a sign for the Old Dog Valley Road and followed it. We passed comfortable wooden houses set in the pines, and then the road started to climb forested slopes quite steeply. The surface deteriorated but Old Crump had been bought with mountains in mind as much as deserts and we were, in one sense, home. I drove with confidence and he responded like a good ox.

We came to a pleasant valley of pine-fringed meadows and turned aside on a wagon track. After a while we found ourselves among huge trees so widely spaced that we could drive between the trunks. I juggled until we were level – essential for cooking on the tailboard – and stopped.

I had passed one family encampment since the pleasant valley, one car passed my site during the evening; once I heard children a long way off. Apart from the children and some kind of bird that whooped like a crane, there was no sound but the soughing of the breeze in the tops of the pines.

That night I lay in my bag and, safe, considered the deserts. They had been gruelling, Black Rock frightening. My chief concern had been the possibility of the wagon breaking down. I thought I could have walked only at night. I would have carried a pack and water. I wouldn't have known how far I was from an inhabited house, and that might have been more than the distance I could travel in one night. If I couldn't have reached any kind of habitation by sunrise where would I have found shade to get through the second day? There was no shade: no boulders, no shrubs, nothing. I had tried to keep my travels to roads where habitations were no more than 50 miles apart so that in an emergency I would never have to walk more than 25 miles but inevitably there were occasions when that 50 miles stretched, particularly when places marked on the map were nothing more than a ranch and that abandoned. Of course I would have found shade in such a place but the desert was so alien, the sun so hostile that it was like fighting a madman. I might reason that all the enemy's movements had been anticipated but out there, beyond the fringe, there were unpredictable factors. They were, of course, not out there, but in here, in the mind. I was not sure of my own reactions. And *they*, many of them, walked all the way, and in the daytime. The deserts, for me, had been mightily productive.

Next morning, with plenty of shade in which to sprawl, I wrote letters, and when I left the camp-site it was with the intention of following the wagon track until it gave out and then seeing what presented itself. I felt like having a day of rest.

We crept up the track for a few yards and there was a sign: Donner Trail. I stopped, pulled out the notes, studied the maps – and realised that again, and without conscious volition, I had gravitated. I had been on the trail since Verdi. If I hadn't carried my own water, had pushed on last night to the next spring, I would have camped where they'd camped.

When Caleb Greenwood looked at the country before they entered the third canyon, he'd looked in the direction of Dog Valley but he went with the rest of the train, following the Truckee to a few miles short of the pass. But the following year he decided that he knew the route well enough to bring people into California himself so in the spring he travelled east with his sons and after they'd crossed the pass (Truckee Pass then, Donner Pass later), instead of reversing the Stevens route, he went north from Donner Lake, thus turning the third canyon and coming down to Dog Valley by the route which I was travelling over a century later.

On his eastward journey Greenwood may have ridden almost as far as South Pass, trying to persuade emigrants to follow him to California rather than go to Oregon. By the time he left the Snake and headed south-west across the Great Basin he had picked up 50 wagons. The old man doesn't seem to have been a very good wagon master, for the wagons straggled badly. One reason may have been that they had little fear of the Indians. The Greenwood boys, half Crow (plains Indians), held the Paiutes in contempt. It isn't surprising that this attitude should have had some effect on the worst of the emigrants.

Somewhere distant from old Greenwood's eye a big overbearing Texan called Kinney, who boasted of having killed 'niggers', caught a Paiute and handcuffed him to the back of a carriage. While his wife drove the vehicle, Kinney whipped the Indian until he would walk quietly. After several days of this Kinney said that the man's spirit was broken, and he turned him over to his hired man who was driving the loose cattle. The Indian promptly escaped during the night, taking with him a blanket, ammunition, three hams and Kinney's rifle which was worth $100. Kinney raved and tried to track him with a dog in order to kill him but the Indian had vanished as neatly as if he'd evaporated.

Although people had protested at this behaviour, they had no way of coping with Kinney other than shooting him. Old Greenwood would have dealt with the situation for, even if he shared his sons' opinion of Paiutes, he didn't show it, and in this respect he was prudent.

He wasn't present when a Paiute startled John Greenwood's horse, and the half-breed was so incensed that he shot the man although the other made a sign of peace. The emigrants put the wounded Indian on a quilt and rode on, frightened and miserable. Caleb Greenwood, discovering the dying man, shot him to put him out of his suffering, and rode into camp demanding the death of the person responsible. He thought it was the monstrous Kinney but when they told him it was his son, he made careful inquiries and then reiterated his judgement. It wasn't put to the test; John Greenwood had disappeared and wasn't seen again, at least by the emigrants.

Almost overnight the Paiutes turned hostile, and by the time the Greenwood train reached the foot of the pass a man called Pierce had died, a victim of their arrows.

Greenwood came to his variation and retraced his route of the spring, through Dog Valley. This became the established trail and was a great improvement. That third canyon had almost finished the Stevens train. The first two were bad enough; by the time Lienhard reached the turn-off to Dog Valley, the Swiss boys had crossed the Truckee 27 times.

Beyond my camp-site then was the damp meadow where they'd camped and after that came a rise and a stretch of loose red flints up which we lurched in four-wheel drive. We emerged on a brow, and a valley opened out in front with a lake, except that it wasn't a natural lake but a reservoir that had flooded the bottom of Stampede Valley and drowned a section of the trail.

This section, although gently undulating, was comparatively easy and no diarists had complaints about the terrain. In fact it was generally dismissed. They were pushing ahead as fast as they could go in order to reach the pass before it was blocked. So long as the ground wasn't conspicuously hazardous it was ignored so far as the journals went, and perhaps the drivers weren't all that careful, at least those in thè Donner train.

On October 28 the Donners were still on the wrong slope of the Sierras. They had started up the Truckee nearly two weeks before, a weak and unhappy party. The Eddy family had eaten their three pounds of sugar and the babies were starving. Everyone refused to give them food so Eddy, borrowing a gun, went out and shot nine geese which he shared with the other members of the train. Then they met Stanton and it seemed that their troubles were over.

Stanton was one of the two men who had ridden ahead from Pilot Peak. He had reached Sutter's Fort and Captain Sutter had lent him two Indians, three horses, seven mules, and all the food they could carry. The man who had ridden with Stanton was safe at the fort but sick, which was why he hadn't returned. Reed, with a teamster who had accompanied him when he was banished, had made it to the settlements but only after much hardship. Starving, they had found one bean on the trail and that kept them going in the hope of more. They found five. And when they came up with some abandoned wagons there was old tallow in the bottom of a tar bucket. It wasn't easily digested but it put some substance in their stomachs.

Stanton said that the pass was five days' travel ahead. With the weather threatening, with snow creeping down from the summits, the Donner train rested at Truckee Meadows for five days. The cattle gathered strength, and so did the winter.

While in camp a man died from the accidental discharge of a pistol. Misfortune dogged this train. They had lost five men: one from disease (the consumptive, south of the Great Salt Lake), one – now – from accident, the homicide in the desert – Hardkoop – which might come under the category of negligence, and at the Humboldt Sink something too mysterious for its category to be determined. A man called Wolfinger, having lost all his oxen, was forced to abandon his wagon, and he stayed behind to cache his property. Two Germans remained to help him. When this pair overtook the train they said that Indians had attacked them and killed Wolfinger. Mrs Wolfinger collapsed on hearing the news and the other emigrants made no overt comment on the story out of regard for her, but not all of them believed it – and Wolfinger had been rich.

After they had rested at Truckee Meadows the Donner train continued through the second canyon, then followed Greenwood's route through Dog Valley, Stampede Valley, past Prosser Creek to Alder

Creek. At Alder Creek they were straggling again, the two Donner families in the rear and the others well ahead. On October 28 the last wagons were coming down a steep grade with six inches of snow on the ground, and the sky was leaden. Near the bottom of the slope an axle broke on one of George Donner's wagons.

They stopped and cut down a tree but as they finished shaping it Jacob Donner's chisel slipped and gashed his brother's hand. They went into camp. In the night it snowed to a depth of three feet and they were stranded.

The George Donners built a shelter against a huge forked pine, roofing it with quilts and buffalo robes; the Jacob Donners built a similar structure 200 yards away. The four teamsters erected a wigwam. The widow Wolfinger was also in this camp; she moved in with the George Donners. Altogether there were nine adults and twelve children at Alder Creek.

The site of the last Donner camp is a moody place on a dull warm afternoon. The forked pine towers above younger trees that look curiously ornamental; in the background the marsh is yellow with withered sedges. Five miles away the Donner Pass has the same appearance of anti-climax. The distance from Donner Lake to the summit is a little over two miles as the crow flies, probably nearer three as the wagons went. You could walk it in an hour, if there were a path, and in summer.

For wagons the difficulties were concentrated in the last mile below the pass where the trail, such as it was, left the scrubby bottom to surmount humps of bedrock where the worst problems were short rises of no more than ten feet, but vertical. At one of these the only passage for the unyoked oxen was by way of a shallow gully just wide enough for an ox.

Stevens, two years before the Donners, was the first white person to see the pass and he didn't like it. At the place where the main valley makes a right-angled bend (the Truckee coming north from Lake Tahoe) and a creek comes in from the direction of the pass, his party held a consultation to decide which way to go: south, following the river upstream, or west to the pass.

They compromised, sending a mounted party of six men and women with two pack horses up the river while the wagons followed the little creek that turned out to be the outlet from the lake afterwards called Donner.

They spent several days 'prospecting the route' which would mean that they cleared snow, cut down the scrub and moved what boulders they could; higher, they would have been working out the best line through the bedrock.

They left six wagons by the lake and continued with five. When they came to the little walls they unyoked the oxen, drove them round to the top of the obstacle and then, doubling the teams, fastened long chains to the wagons. In the meantime these would have been unloaded and their contents carried to the top of the pass. Babies and small children had to be carried too. The wagons were eased up the walls with the help of ramps of timber.

The Stevens party reached the top in one day and hurried down the other side. On the crest three young men turned back to the lake, having volunteered to stay with the abandoned wagons through the winter to guard the contents against the Indians. In this party was Moses Schallenberger, the youth who nearly shot the Indian who stole the halter. He was just seventeen.

These three built a small cabin as soon as they reached the lake – and only just in time, for it snowed as they completed it and continued to snow heavily for a week. They couldn't hunt, and there was nothing to hunt anyway; the deer had moved down to lower altitudes and the bear were hibernating. If they stayed there they would starve, so they slaughtered their two starving cows and, taking some of the meat, they tried to get over the pass. They reached the top but Schallenberger was exhausted. They camped there in the open, and in the morning Schallenberger retreated to the cabin by the lake. The others were certain he wouldn't make it and for months it was thought that he was dead, but the snow consolidated the night they camped on the pass, and he made it back to the cabin. He survived the winter living on foxes which he caught in traps that were being carried in one of the wagons. There was also a large store of books which he read avidly by firelight. Even by day he had no light because there was no window in the cabin. He had enough coffee for one cup, and he saved that for Christmas. He was rescued at the end of February having been alone since the middle of December. He was haggard but in good heart.

When the storm came the five wagons that had crossed the pass were about 15 miles down the other side. A baby was born there: Elizabeth Yuba Murphy. Yuba from the creek nearby, although creek and baby must have received that name later. After the week's snowstorm the wagons couldn't move. It was decided that the women and children and two men should be left while all the other men, seventeen of them, pushed ahead on foot for assistance.

When this party reached Sutter's Fort they found that the mounted group had come in a few days before, but there was a revolution in progress in California and all the men of the Stevens party were pressed to fight in it. No one returned to relieve the wagons.

Back at the women's camp, Schallenberger's two companions had come in from the lake and they pressed on to the fort. In the camp the snow fell and the people ate the cattle and then they ate the hides. They boiled the bones and made a soup like glue, and they discovered that if bones were boiled for long enough they broke down to a brittle porous substance that could be chewed.

A man called Martin 'deserted' from the revolution and returned alone through the snow. He reached the women's camp, continued to the lake and brought Schallenberger back with him, having made the lad a pair of snowshoes. Other rescuers followed in Martin's trail, reached the women and children and took them down to the Sacramento Valley.

The Stevens train suffered great hardships but no deaths. Two babies were born, and survived. They had to abandon their wagons but none was lost. In the summer the men brought out even those that had been left by the lake. Their contents had been pilfered by the Indians, but not the firearms. Paiutes were still afraid of guns.

The following year, 1845, the migration went better, profiting from the experience of 1844. Despite the labour of getting the wagons over the pass, the Greenwood train – straggling as it had straggled all the way – came into Sutter's Fort during the second half of October. One of its members reckoned he'd had 'a comparatively pleasant journey of five months'.

About 100 feet below the summit of Donner Pass the trail is visible as a pair of ruts in a little green basin where pools are fringed by willows and Indian paintbrush. The old highway is on one side of this basin, the interstate being out of sight and mind a good two miles to the north. The railway contours the slope on the other side, and across pink granite slabs are the rusty marks of wheels. The rest of the trail has disappeared under the spoil heaps of railroad tunnels and avalanche sheds.

Above the basin are the walls of the pass: crags between 200 and 300 feet high. They are delightful little outcrops and when I had photographed the wheelmarks and worked round until I had the northern crag in the background, I relaxed and wondered if there were any routes on the crag, and traced a line up a wall beside a slab.

I met two men who asked if I would care to climb with them, and they took me up the route I'd played with in my mind, and it wasn't playful but quite fierce at first, and then eased off to the kind of floating beauty implicit in all steep granite: coarse and friendly and firm.

It was a dreamy sensation, performing actions that were most familiar to me: fingers curling round an edge, feet on friction holds that could have been in Cornwall or Chamonix but were above a pass in the Sierras; and in the background was the lake where the Donner train had camped. From here it looked as it must have looked when they saw it although now the water was blue as speedwells; then it was black, and the surroundings were white except for the pines that had shaken clear, and rock below overhangs where the blizzards hadn't reached.

The vanguard of the Donner train, five wagons, reached the lake on the last day of October by which time the pass was blocked. They tried to get over on foot but failed. They remained at the lake and, as the others arrived (with the exception of the Donners themselves who were five miles behind, stranded at Alder Creek), they built cabins. One family moved into Schallenberger's old place. There were 60 people in this camp, of whom 29 were children.

In the almost continuous snowstorms at the onset of winter the cattle strayed, died, and were buried under the snow so that even their carcasses were lost. During the lulls in the storms several attempts were made to get over the pass, and one succeeded with the help of snowshoes made from ox bows. Stanton and the two Indians from Sutter's Fort were with this party but the conditions – of deep new snow and stultifying cold, of sleeping without tents for over thirty nights – were fatal for men who were weak when they started. Stanton failed first. Sitting by the camp-fire, smoking his pipe as they left in the morning, he replied to the question of fifteen-year-old Mary Graves: 'Yes, I am coming soon,' and spared them the decision to abandon him.

The men died quickly then, five of them, one after the other, and their bodies were eaten. The two Indians, warned by Eddy of what was in some minds, escaped but were too weak to get far. They collapsed on the trail and, when the others came up, were shot by a man called Foster, with the tacit approval of the others, who walked on. They ate the Indians' bodies too.

Of the ten men who set out only two, Eddy and Foster, survived. None of the five women died.

The first rescue party from the settlements was made up of seven men, none of whom was familiar with mountain conditions, who carried 50 to 75 pounds of food each. They reached Donner Lake and brought out seven adults and seventeen children. Then this party started to fail and a man and a child died before they met a second rescue party. Cheered by the news that they were almost out of the snow, the first group struggled on.

The second rescue party was led by Reed. They crossed the pass, reached the lake and started back with the next group of survivors.

Now Eddy and Foster returned with food for their families but Mrs Eddy had died and the widower was met by Keseberg, who confessed to having just finished eating the last Eddy baby. Mrs Foster had gone out with the people on snowshoes but the Foster boy had been left in the care of an old widow, Mrs Murphy. Keseberg had taken the boy to bed one night and in the morning the child was dead. Keseberg hung the carcass inside the cabin, which they didn't do normally although there were coyotes outside. Keseberg was quite mad, at least at this time, which may have been why neither of the fathers killed him, although Eddy considered it.

Tamsen Donner had walked over from Alder Creek and she met Eddy and Foster. Her three small girls, aged seven, five and four, were at the lake already. She had sent them over with two previous rescuers, dressing the little girls in their best clothes to go down to the valley. Tamsen herself would not leave because her husband George was still alive, and so was her small nephew Sammie. Jacob Donner had died months earlier, in December, and three of the teamsters shortly afterwards. Elizabeth Donner was dead. George Donner had been in great pain throughout the winter from the infection which had set in after his hand was gashed with the chisel.

Tamsen had struggled over from Alder Creek because she had heard about Keseberg's condition from previous rescuers and her daughters were in his cabin. Now she gave them into Eddy's charge and walked back to Alder Creek. At that camp were three able-bodied men: two rescuers and the remaining teamster. On her return they deserted the Donners.

Around April 17 a group of men arrived at the lake to salvage the emigrants' property. They had not expected to find anyone alive, and Keseberg alone had survived by scavenging between the two camps.

At Alder Creek George Donner was dead and although partly butchered had been laid out in a sheet, which argued Tamsen's having survived him. For some reason the men thought George had been dead only four days but there was no trace of Tamsen. The child Sammie disappears into oblivion. Certainly he didn't survive.

At the outset Keseberg gloated on the details of his diet, became contrite, finally recanted. A few years later, after working in the mines, he opened a restaurant in Sacramento, then a hotel, and prospered.

The disappearance of Tamsen Donner need have no sinister application. With no one else at Alder Creek, and with Keseberg at the lake, a woman of her calibre would have tried to get out. Whatever Keseberg was, he would not have been a comfortable companion with whom to wait for rescue. It is possible that, making her way to the pass and trying to avoid the camp on Donner Lake, she was lost in the forests. Once she collapsed she would have died quickly and the coyotes would have disposed of the body.

Of the original 87 in the Donner train, only 47 survived.

15

NORTHERN SIERRAS

SOME TWO MONTHS before the Donner party reached the divide a new pass had been found two miles to the south. Although longer and involving a crossing 700 feet higher than Donner, the approach was easier and the new way was to become the established trail. Conversely, in the twentieth century, it was the Donner Pass that was celebrated; the other was unnamed, unmarked on the map, and only the term, Emigrant Canyon, gave an indication of where the route went.

It started up the Coldstream Valley with a steep stony hill where we used four-wheel drive, but at the top there was a stretch so level it was utilised by the Southern Pacific railroad that went up one side of the glen and down the other. The absence of commercialism after Donner Lake was refreshing. I passed a dark little encampment that would have been a tinker's camp in Scotland: a peeling caravan, a heavy old tent, a dirty towel on a line. It looked abandoned, dead, sinister, and although I was in the area for two days that towel never changed its position. Had something happened to the owner?

The trail left the Coldstream Valley and, with a second steep hill involving four-wheel drive, climbed into Emigrant Canyon. There came another level stretch but this one only the width of the track and with a drop of hundreds of feet below. It may have been here that a wagon went over the edge in 1846 or it might have been at the next hill, where I left Old Crump at the bottom and continued on foot.

A band of granite slabs stretched across the canyon, the trail squeezing up a loose stony rake at the side to emerge once again on level ground where the walking was delightful but the outlook restricted by the timber. The trail gave out and I spent hours here, climbing to vantage points, zigzagging up tongues of forest between rock outcrops, finding a stretch of ruts which would be lost again in undergrowth; once, coming on the trail only because a mule deer faded away so quickly and quietly I knew that she was on cleared ground.

It was August and the rioting flowers were gone but animals were all around: not only those with which I'd become familiar, like squirrels and deer, but also the exquisite California quail: a plump little bird carrying a head-plume that curved *forward* – and the cocks had harlequin faces.

I weaved back and forth across that canyon all one afternoon and the following morning, and at last broke clear of the forest to find myself in a high meadow below the headwall. There was a short stretch of ruts under the foliage of mules' ears but these gave no indication as to which of two wooded depressions the trail had taken to reach the crest. I chose the wrong one.

The pines ran out against crags of steep puddingstone which I climbed by clawing my way up gullies under crumbling brown spires where the holds were round stones that rolled under my weight and plopped out of their sockets as I passed. It was amusing, it was different, but it was not the way the emigrants came – and there was no view from the top because trees covered the other side up to the crest. So I went up the mountain on my left, Mount Lincoln, which had a ski terminal on the summit.

I turned my back on the buildings and looked south over mile after hazy mile of timbered hills and valleys, where Stevens' mounted party rode after they left the Truckee River. Down there, between me and the Walker Pass, there were nearly 300 miles of wilderness. Northwards there was more of it, where balding heights rose above the forests and were crowned with small red crags like tors. Near at hand Donner Lake showed over Schallenberger Ridge, the water as I always saw it: a bright unshadowed blue. I could see the pass, could even trace the line of the climb I'd done with the two young men.

Close under Mount Lincoln was a deep scoop of a corrie called the Sugar Bowl: obviously a snow-trap in winter. It was ironical to think that the element which had been the setting for so much suffering in the last century should provide so many delights in this. A track came up the side of the bowl; that would be the way the wagons went down. It was steep – Lienhard got terribly worried about their speed down there. Below, the corrie ran into Summit Valley west of Donner Pass, and the two trails merged. I looked farther west, trying to see the line of the ridge they followed, the lakes they passed. I saw lakes but couldn't tell if they were the right ones. I would be there tomorrow anyway. I turned to look for the place where they had climbed out of Emigrant Canyon.

It was where the second wooded depression came up to the ridge, except that the trees stopped about 300 feet short of the top. Those few hundred feet were the crux. There were more puddingstone spires, one with a hole through it, one standing right in the centre of the steep and terribly loose gully up which the wagons had to come because there was no other way. They used various methods but all involved many oxen and men. Probably they camped in the meadow at the bottom, where now I could see their ruts like crop markings, and brought the empty wagons up one at a time. As many as 24 oxen might be used, half at the top pulling on a long chain or rope, the other half pulling *down*, with the rope round a roller acting as a pulley. It bore some similarity to raising a stretcher up steep but not vertical ground. There would be a lot of belaying: taking turns round a tree trunk with rope or chain. One trunk still bore the scars.

I found it difficult to keep my balance even in cleated soles, and yet when the last wagon came to this point in 1846 it was snowing hard and a woman with a new baby insisted on walking. She may have seen the wagon go over the edge in the canyon. So she walked, or rather climbed. Would she have worn boys' nailed boots or smooth soles? The surface was nasty at the best of times; with a skin of snow it would be as slippery as ice. She needed one hand to grab at the rocks, the other to hold her baby. The other women might have helped her had they not been engaged in loading up their wagons at the top, or pushing down the other side. Everyone would be frantic to reach lower altitudes, knowing that two years ago Stevens had been trapped after he'd crossed the divide. All the time it snowed, and kept on snowing, but the woman crossed the pass and the baby survived. There were no tragedies on this route.

So the two trails merged below the Sugar Bowl in Summit Valley which was now occupied by the railroad, the interstate and a rash of structural excrescences mostly dependent on the skiers who, by the look of things, were dependent on the state of the economy – for some of the buildings were not merely closed up but collapsing into decrepitude. Summit Valley didn't have a prosperous appearance.

I followed the trail down the Pacific slope and it was dark before a track showed in my headlights and I crept into the pines to camp. I was only a few yards from the interstate, the ground was damp and there were mosquitoes. There were 7,000 miles of rough living and wild camping behind me but despite the traffic, the grinding of locomotives, the whine of mosquitoes, I slept like a cat.

Next morning I encountered a feature of the trail that was to prevail throughout the Sierras: whenever they could, the pioneers followed ridges down to the main valleys. This led to some hair-raising situations, not only for them but for us, for those ridges ended abruptly, and then we had to plunge down the sides, go off the end, or go back.

The first of them appeared innocuous: a broad granite way strewn with rocks and fringed with pines, and after several miles we came to a lake on the other side of which rose a mountain with a great cock's comb of a crest – but this was only backdrop; I was concerned with the ground immediately to the north.

According to the map the wagons went down the left bank of the outlet from the lake. I found no trace there but on the right bank there was a wide swathe ending in a path that descended to the railroad. Below the tracks the ground dropped steeply but with faint indications of the trail.

The wagons were belayed down drops like these, the strain taken by a turn of the rope round a tree. If they had to contour, men walked on the slope above holding ropes that were fastened to the tops of the wagons. It would be reasonable to think that once they'd reached a valley all they had to do was to push down it westwards, but the bottoms must have been choked by timber and debris and where they would camp on a river for one night, next day that river wandered northwards and they would get up on another east–west ridge only to be forced off it when it came to an abrupt end.

This laborious mode of progress was borne in on me as I turned back from gradients where I dare not take Old Crump, and we would return to the start of a ridge and take the modern road to a point where I could look at their descent from the bottom. I became exhausted merely from looking. This was a hot day, a Saturday, and in the afternoon I turned off the interstate and took a quiet road to Bear Valley. There was a dead porcupine on the grass verge: a big animal with small black feet, neat as a hedgehog's – one for whom the road wasn't quiet enough.

Bear Valley was a place of level meadows set in magnificent trees in the shade of which pinedrops displayed their toffee-coloured bells – and the girth of those trees emphasised the work the emigrants had to do before they could lower the wagons into the valley.

They crossed this bottom land and up they went again: to the crest of Lowell Hill Ridge. We followed for miles along a rough track where the ground dropped breathtakingly on either side and forestry roads forked in all directions, but I kept to the crest and came to a pond which was the reservoir for the Liberty Hill Diggings in 1850. There were ripe blackberries round the pool and, like the Lienhard contingent whenever they found fresh fruit, I got down and browsed.

Farther on I came to a flock of geese in the road, a cluster of old buildings and two men in chairs on a porch who waved as I crept through the farmyard, trying not to raise dust. An ancient notice on a barn equally old said 'Peace Progress Prosperity'.

I took a turn to the left and dived down a hill so steep I knew we'd never get back without four-wheel drive. The lane was cut out of the mountain and below was an abyss; the first tree grew on the verge, the next had its crest level with the road.

At the bottom an enormous pipe angled down a precipice and there was just room to turn. A brook dropped through the woods, deep in shade. I did my washing and bathed, cringing from the cold, then, smug and smooth as ever, Old Crump went back up the hill.

We allowed the trail to lead us towards the sun until a narrow cart-track meandered through bushes that were hung with dull red berries and led to a tiny clearing before one of those monstrous drops.

On the other side of Bear Valley a short scar marked the railroad. I could hear the trains when they passed but I could see nothing other than the dense timber that filled the valley and clothed the slopes seemingly without a break. One saw why the emigrants chose the ridges.

I spent the night there and next morning found our ridge ended within a mile, but whereas we had a graded road to descend Steep Hollow *they* dragged logs behind the wagons. At the bottom there was merely a shallow creek but it was here that the first party to go to the rescue of the Donners had to fell a tree to bridge the spring flood, and a horse was swept 100 yards downstream.

After Steep Hollow their problems were over. It was a little more than 30 miles to the first ranch and by now they were out of reach of the snow. When I came down to the interstate the first elevation sign read 2,000 feet; in a short time I was at 1,000.

We came out of the foothills and turned north through rolling country that would have been beautiful but for the poor parched grass. It was bleached yellow, and chocolate weeds stood on the verges like tall docks. The hardwoods had the dull green foliage of late summer, but on the slopes of quaint and unexpected orchards fat milch cows grazed, their hides wet and gleaming under the sprinklers.

I came to Wheatland, a village on the site of the Johnson Ranch, which was the first the emigrants came to, and the altitude was 85 feet. I stopped at the house next to the church and knocked at the door. An elderly neighbour accosted me, bristling with suspicion, and directed me to a bar. A *bar?* I repeated, bewildered, wondering whether I'd find the minister there, whether I looked like an alcoholic or whether my informant was psychic. He was merely rational; the bar was one of the social centres for the village.

It was cold and dark and crowded. They told me Johnson's Ranch no longer existed. Deflated, I sat on a stool and answered questions and watched the beers arrive. They treated me as if I'd just struggled down from the divide through five feet of snow. The landlady, a Belgian, was upset when I declined her offer of a bed for the night, but the beer and the heavy heat were already affecting me (the air conditioner was turned off when someone complained that he was cold as a frog and then the heat crept in as if we were in a tin box on top of a furnace). I pushed on to Yuba City where I lost my way in the Sunday evening traffic and two girls who were looking for an apartment insisted on leading me out of town and putting me on the right road, making sure that I had enough petrol before I drove away because it might be difficult to find on Sunday evening.

Fleeing from the heavy, almost inert air of the Sacramento Valley I drove north-west, returning to the hills, and came to the western end of the long ridge that carried the Henness Pass Road. This was established in 1852, leaving the main trail near Dog Valley and crossing the divide by way of unspectacular but thickly forested country north of Donner Pass. I was travelling in the wrong direction of course – west to east – but that was inevitable for half of the Sierra passes I must traverse and, apart from sentiment, it was immaterial: I was seeing the country even if I saw it the wrong way round.

I camped on the crest of the ridge in a little depression beside the road, surrounded by trees except for the way I'd entered. A notice said 'Mining Claim Keep Out', and there were two shallow pits in the ground. A body might remain hidden indefinitely in the Sierras.

The moon rose, three days from the full, and I ate my supper by its light. Afterwards I walked up the road through a world that, once I turned my back on the trail, was primaeval.

The slope was so steep that no trees grew on the outside edge and below me there was a gulf of velvet shadow. No empty chasm, it exuded neither warmth nor the breath of air that rises from water or cooling rock and yet it had presence, and all the more because it was inaccessible: a tangled teeming world that one might hope would never be touched by man. On the other side, where clear-felling had left glades that glowed in the moonlight, sheep grazed unseen, the sound of their bells coming faintly across space. No light showed other than the moon; I looked south over an infinity of forest.

As I strolled back something moved above me on the slope. I remembered I'd left the tailboard down, and all the food temptingly displayed. I wondered about bears. The previous night something had *gnawed* at the metal of the car. Thinking of skunks, porcupines, and animals with formidable jaws, I'd declined to risk a confrontation and without leaving my bag had suggested sternly that the visitor go and gnaw a tree, which it did. Now I looked for humped shapes at the back of the car but there was none. I slept happily under the brilliant moon.

Next morning I drove on, turned down Lucky Dog Creek and came out in Forest City: a handful of old houses with a population of 25. On a porch gay with petunias, a pottery rooster and ducks, an old man was scraping down a chest of drawers. In the hot silence a little mobile swung and tinkled from a beam. Forest City dozed through the August morning at the foot of its canyon where, for all I could see, there was no soil, no rock; only a gash several hundred feet deep composed of nothing but trees.

The old man's wife owned most of the village, which was a former mining camp. They and a neighbour equally elderly set about putting me on the right road, which was a protracted business. After much discussion, after coffee on the porch, the filling of the water container and the photographing of wild sweet peas in what once might have been an orchard, another neighbour materialised, a husky fellow in his thirties called Handlebars. If I would follow him towards Alleghany he would put me on the right road.

I took formal leave of my hosts and followed Handlebars' truck until he stopped to point out my turning but then a chance remark elicited the fact that I had never been in a gold mine, so I must see his. I followed him to Alleghany (a store, a petrol pump and an inn) where he had business and waited for him in the inevitable cool dark bar where a man who worked a dredge in a mine vied with Handlebars to claim my time, and invited me to Alleghany's Arts Festival the following weekend. A lady told me her husband got $187,000 from one strike in the Kate Hardy mine, which was the one Handlebars was to show me. I drank my beer in a state of continual astonishment.

Handlebars lived with a Yorkshire terrier called Little Handlebars in a ramshackle hovel in the forest. It was the kind of place where I would choose to live. He had electricity and running water, some nice but neglected pieces of furniture in the living room, an old wall telephone, some good plain chairs. In the hot and dusty attics I found a straw hat by Berg of Fifth Avenue. Some 50 years ago it had been a rakish panama but now, sporting the odd rat-nibbled hole and a few unravelled straws, it had great character. Handlebars gave it to me graciously.

Originally from Massachusetts he had found his niche and had taken on the job of renovating both house and mine. The house looked like a life's work but he was more interested in the mine anyway. He'd been an aircraft engineer but couldn't live in a city. Next year, he said, he'd have the mine running. Obviously he was far more concerned with the work involved in this than in the production of gold.

I had no interest in gold either, but the means of obtaining it, the violent and poignant stories associated with it, were fascinating – and the Kate Hardy mine was a museum-piece.

The little ore trucks squatted heavily on a rickety track built out over Oregon Creek. The bridge from the offices to the mine was equally fragile. There was a pool with trout in it and orange lilies with recurved petals under rocky banks overhung by strange hardwoods. Above these and the dwarfed buildings the conifers climbed to a rift of sky.

The tool shop was fascinating – from the anvil strapped to a tree-stump to rusted nuts that looked as if they'd started life with the mine. On the other side of the creek were the crushing and separating plants, the crusher working with steel balls from mere marbles to specimens four to five inches in diameter and weighing like lead. There were tables that shivered horizontally, sifting gold from gravel, and one table so sophisticated that Handlebars couldn't explain its system. An old-timer was coming in to rebuild it.

The mine itself was approached by way of a flimsy door in the side of the canyon, secured by an equally flimsy padlock. The passage inside was lit by electricity, and the air struck cold.

The passage was cut out of quartz with a lot of iron ore – and serpentine, said my guide. He'd brought his can of soda pop along as if it were a talisman. I remarked that the passage wasn't shored up. There was no need, he told me, through rock. We passed a rickety section, propped with timber; that was where a shaft had collapsed. He was laconic.

We came to the main shaft where he was replacing the winding gear. Yellow girders lay on the ground. He pointed upwards to the holes he'd made to take them. He used dynamite to make the holes. I stared at him in the dim light. He worked down here, all alone except for the little dog, using dynamite. He was a strange fellow, ingenuous, unselfconscious, talking without restraint, falling into a companionable silence. He had no trouble attracting girls, he told me, but privately I doubted if he could keep them. He'd have to wait a while before another of his species gravitated to this strange sanctuary.

He dragged chairs outside the office and we sat above the trout pool discussing Steinbeck. He looked sad when I shook hands and left, and for once I hoped that someone would not be influenced by my life-style, because I thought he might have found his here, deep in the Sierra forests, but the wistfulness suggested that he might not realise it.

I took the road he'd indicated where the dust lay in drifts a foot deep and rose like an atomic cloud behind me, and I grieved for the cameras. After ten miles I came to a level area that had been clear-felled and, following two ruts, reached the shade at the edge of the forest.

As I ate my supper I was aware that I was being watched. Twigs snapped quite close at hand. The forest watches you all the time and after a while you find this comforting. Frightened animals make different sounds from animals that are merely curious. I didn't mind being an object of curiosity; although I had no illusions. They came because they smelled food.

The Henness Pass Road was between 60 and 70 miles long and in the main it kept to the high ground but when it had to switch from one ridge to another it would plunge straight down one slope and up the next in a swoop that for excitement was surpassed only by the occasional horizontal sweep into a ravine and the tremendous exposure as it climbed out the other side.

Next morning the road was wet, a water wagon having gone in front of me spraying the dust. I had come to the commercial part of the forest and gigantic timber-trucks were on the road. As if it wasn't hazardous enough to have twelve inches of slime instead of twelve inches of dust I never knew when I might meet one of these juggernauts as I came crawling out of a ravine, right on the corner, and ourselves on the outside edge. I approached every bend as if we were about to be confronted but we never were; instead we always met on the straight stretches and with one exception all the juggernauts reversed for me, even downhill, their luscious young drivers waving as they passed. The exception was middle-aged and sour.

I came to a still lake where a merganser left a lazy arrow across reflections of pink rock, pines and light, and I listened to Haydn from Sacramento. After days of radio silence – silence because, when looking for a weather forecast, every station would be playing pop – I might be in a glade at sunset or looking over a lake in the cool of the morning, and I would turn a knob and hear a Haydn symphony and would wonder how the scene could have seemed complete before when this made it perfect.

Henness Pass was so flat that its crest was imperceptible, but despite the general angle this road was never popular, possibly because of those tight hairpins and exposed corners which would have been highly hazardous for a long outfit (the road would have been improved for the twentieth-century juggernauts). Besides, by the time the Henness Pass Road was made, there was a better route 20 miles to the north, discovered by the mulatto mountain man, Jim Beckwourth. It was the easiest of all the Sierra passes.

At this point the great range is losing cohesion as it approaches its northern termination, and a confusion of spurs is broken by the enclave of a plain, rendered lush and fertile by the headwaters of the Feather River. In the north-east corner of this basin the ground rises gently to just over 5,000 feet at Beckwourth Pass, a height which, as innocuous on the eastern slope as on the west, does little to shield the Sierra Valley from the heat of the deserts. Heat and water have provided prosperity for cattlemen for over a century and this is reflected in magnificent barns, the walls of which may be ten feet high while all the rest, perhaps a further 50 feet, is a simple, steeply-pitched roof of silver shakes. Wooden ramps lead up to the doorways and a raised wooden floor, windows are unglazed but closed by shutters that still slide as easily – more easily – than the day they were made, polished by 100 years of use. In the cavernous interior a central manger runs for most of the length and the great beams and rafters are in proportion, the whole being considerably larger than a tithe barn. I was entranced; I had been brought up with tithe barns but I had discovered these beauties of the Sierra Valley for myself.

I drove east over Beckwourth Pass and turned left at Hallelujah Junction where one road went right for Reno and I went north to Susanville and intersected Nobles' Emigrant Trail. This was the one that skirted the Black Rock and Smoke Creek Deserts to reach Shasta City by way of Mount Lassen. I was to encounter it several times in the next week, that and Lassen's Cut-off, and to be amazed at the roughness of the terrain which they, and particularly Peter Lassen, had to traverse. The land was thickly forested, strewn with lakes and seamed with water-courses and now, working northwards, I was suddenly confronted with signs of recent volcanic activity. Trying to reach a lake in order to swim I found myself driving for miles over sage and scrub only to lose the way in lava beds like big brown breadcrumbs. I never reached the lake and had to content myself with lunch on the fringe of a wood where osprey wheeled against a hot sky and bluebirds went flashing over the lava.

Baulked of a swim (it would have meant trespassing on the ospreys' territory) I settled for a visit to a fire look-out on Antelope Mountain which, I was delighted to find, was powered by solar energy. It was in the charge of a woman, Virginia, whose husband worked at the marina on the lake and passed only the nights at the look-out.

Virginia had spent most of her working life with the Forest Service in various look-outs, taking time out to raise a family, all of whom were now married. Her work lasted from May to October, the exact dates depending on the precipitation. When the autumn rains damped down the forest she left; when it started to dry out, she arrived. They had a house in Susanville but they found it difficult to sleep down there for the noise of traffic and the barking of dogs. I was reminded of Daniel Boone, who said it was time to move on when he could hear his neighbour's dog bark.

They could see fourteen look-outs from this summit. All around stretched the low timbered hills with, close to the foot of the mountain, islands of yellow meadows. Mount Lassen was the most obvious feature, an isolated bulk against the sun; Shasta was just visible over 80 miles away. Eastward were the desert ranges, and there the sky had that hard white look that is the reflection off salt flats.

Red-tailed hawks were in the air, hunting for the sage grouse which, they said, had young and was keeping her head down. A doe with two fawns visited the look-out. One year the coyotes hung around so Virginia's husband went out with his rifle to scare them off and ever since the doe had brought each year's fawns to browse within sight of the windows. The couple looked at the sun and decided it wasn't time for her yet; she'd be up presently.

The job, of course, was fires. A 'sleeper' was one that smouldered. Virginia had reported one that hadn't burst into flame for 21 days. Every part of this great and ranging wilderness where the Forest Service managed the land was covered by their look-outs. Big Brother, I thought, but conceded correction, thinking of the deer, of the sage grouse, of the limitless acres potentially at risk from fire.

They pointed out Papoose Meadow where the settlers came out from Susanville and killed all the Indians, but people went up and found a baby and took it back to town and raised it. She'd died only recently. The Modocs in the north were very warlike; they went raiding in 1927 and killed a doctor on his ranch. The army needed 5,000 men to flush 30 Modocs out of the lava beds. I looked at Virginia, strong but homely in her apron, who had raised a family, who spent six months of every year on the curving arc of the earth, and I saw a link between two centuries. This was the kind of woman who took the road west.

I left, they waved until I was out of sight – and here, walking up the road to feed within view of the man with the rifle, came the doe and her two fawns.

I went down the mountain and through the meadows westward where nothing moved but Old Crump and our long dust trail and, just before I crossed a paved road, I intercepted both Lassen's and Nobles' routes and camped in the forest, probably at one of their sites. Probably, because by now I was looking at the land through their eyes and there weren't all that many camp-sites to choose from. Lassen's train was going south at this point making for his ranch in the upper Sacramento Valley, and the roughest part of their journey was about to begin.

Their wagons were drawn by three yokes of mules and each outfit was 40 feet long. Few wagons could turn at an angle of more than 30 degrees because few had front wheels small enough to swing under the wagon bed. Small wheels made wagons harder to pull. They forced their way into canyons which ended blindly and from which they had to retreat. The only way they could have done this was to unhitch the teams and turn the wagons manually. They came to dense forest where a passage between the trees was impossible. So they sawed the wagons in half, making two-wheeled carts of them which could be drawn by one pair of mules, at the most two, but even then their progress was only two or three miles a day. They slaughtered the cattle for food but by October they were exhausted by road-making, demoralised, and close to starvation.

They were saved by a large band of settlers going south from Oregon to California after gold: a wagon train with 70 fit men. The settlers overtook Lassen's party south of the mountain that was to bear his name, fed them and escorted them down to the ranch in the Sacramento Valley.

I walked in the Caribou Wilderness which I had looked across from Antelope Mountain: a gentle wooded country where the forest was filigree set with lakes like jewels with sweet peasant names, Gem, Beauty,

Posey. I travelled on bearings, lining up trees at a hundred yards to prevent drifting. The wildlife was abundant and exciting: a red-shafted flicker (a woodpecker with a scarlet moustache), golden-mantled ground squirrels with stripes that looked as if they'd been put on with grease-paint, baby chipmunks, and lizards so large that when an elongated streak crossed the path, I had to look twice to determine whether it was mammal or reptile. The trunks of the huge 100-foot pines were bright with lime moss. At this time of year the forests were all in shades of green, the tarns a dusty emerald and fringed by vegetation the colour of spring grass.

I came to Lassen and walked a trail that skirted the forest above a petrified lava-flow. Between forest and lava a few trees stood like scarecrows ankle-deep in ashes and above this bleak waste stood the volcano, Cinder Cone. Treating the cinders as scree I spiralled up the shifting slope to emerge on the rim of the crater: reddish, funnel-shaped, with the odd pine growing inside and the bottom plugged by its own clinkers. Sulphur flowers bloomed in the stones, and a plant with flowers like bistort and crooked stems looked as if someone had stuck it there for a lark. Below me was Nobles' route, the familiar ruts running with deceptive ease across acres of ash towards the pale pile of Mount Lassen. On the lower side of the volcano was the main lava-flow: mile upon mile of rotten stone fading into the Painted Dunes, equally sterile but strangely beautiful, beige and red and cream where the iron ore in the cinders had oxidised on the red-hot lava.

I ran down the cone and took a trail with trees on one side, tottering crimson crags on the other, that led me to a sparkling lake. My day was made by a garter snake which, unaware of my arrival (I was moving as if on broken glass on the loose lava blocks), was exploring the lake margin. Brilliant yellow lines ran from head to tail and when I stooped I could see dull red splotches on the dark flanks. It saw me then but made no overt sign, only the head turned and the body slid out of sight very carefully over the rough wet rock.

Each night I camped outside the national park, sometimes wild, sometimes in Forest camps. The latter were free because they were 'primitive', which meant doubtful stream water and lavatories that were pits. I preferred my lonely clearings where shadows slipped like benign ghosts through the trees and no one was there to have hysterics when the coyotes burst into song as the sunset flamed across the sky.

Nobles' trail ran through the northern section of the park, skirting Mount Lassen by way of Emigrant Pass. From here Lassen looked too large and too raw: a big scree mountain with the odd craggy excrescence on its flanks. Lassen's only feature is bulk and has to be seen from a distance to appreciate its dominance in relation to its frame; at close quarters it is overwhelming and ugly. At Emigrant Pass I ignored the mountain and idled up the bank of the exquisite little Hat Creek. I found some faded gentians and, because it was hot and there was no reason why I shouldn't, I stepped into the water in boots and jeans and waded up the creek looking for more. As I walked through deep pools and across sandy shallows with thickets of willow on either side I remembered those others, waist-deep in the Weber, the Humboldt, the Truckee, and saw the association – even to the cameras round my neck. They would have been holding firearms, not when they were coping with the wagons of course, but the scouts in the van, leading their horses through the canyons, watching for ambush.

I splashed back to the car park, changed and drove on to Bumpass Hell.

Kendall Vanhook Bumpass didn't only discover this thermal basin, he stepped into a pool and lost his leg. The temperature in places reaches 240°F. One concludes that Bumpass, like the spaniel in the Forty Mile Desert, was not all that bright.

Bumpass Hell had a nature trail. It started conventionally, given that we were in the California Cascades. The beaten path was a high level traverse past little outcrops, patches of chunky scree and beds of mauve and silver lupins, a species with hairy leaves. A thousand feet below, the little Sulphur Creek sparkled in the bottom of its glen while across space stood a crenellated ridge ending with the scarp of a peak called Brokeoff. I had observed the continuous riband of people plodding the cinder path to the top of Lassen and decided that Lassen was not for me. Now I looked at Brokeoff and thought it would make a pleasant substitute.

I came to the rim of the thermal basin and all hell was in plain view: yellow, red, ivory, poison green, steaming here and there, with a few figures moving along the boardwalks; images without sound until you realised that the silence was merely an absence of human sound. There was an undercurrent of noise as if diabolical factories were at work, a conglomeration of evil sounds. One descended into this place hesitantly, looking aghast at what lay far too close to the boardwalks. Bumpass must have been a madman; surely the only people who need to be warned of danger here are idiots?

The mud pots were black and horrible, and plopped lasciviously. The Steam Engine was a grotto in colours like jewelled chalk. A breeze carried steam away so that intermittently there were holes that bore no relationship to windows in hill cloud through which a cool reality is seen; through these rents I glimpsed colours and heard sounds that shouldn't have been there. A clean, clear shallow pool had a grey bottom, all boiling. A small patch of dry red clinker hissed softly, exhaling faint wisps of steam. The colours came out of a laboratory, a laboratory inside the earth. It was the earth turned inside-out.

I crawled back to the rim. A fat man came bouncing down the trail in shorts trimmed with red and blue braid. He wore a pork pie hat and a yellow sweat shirt stamped with edelweiss. His socks were long and white with red and blue cuffs. He remarked that it was all very pretty.

On the trail above Sulphur Creek two boys started heaving rocks down the slope. I turned on them so viciously that I frightened them. The thin crust, I thought, it's catching.

Brokeoff was refreshing, with a summit crest of red and black crags and a tumbling escarpment where gully walls made a good foil for Lassen, now correctly proportioned at the end of a ridge studded with old volcanoes. Under the ridge, scree slopes in sorbet shades of orange and cream looked like steep parks dotted with pines.

On the descent I met two fawns, spotted, with black muzzles. We stopped and regarded each other gravely, then they separated, one to each side of the path. The doe stepped out and watched me. I waited, looking at the view. I was aware of movement smooth as mercury as they came together and drifted away. I went on, realising, and accepting with pleasure, that in this country I had learned to move more quietly than I did at home.

On the way south from Lassen I looked at the Feather Canyon, which was large and long and dull except when a train, the colour and size of a toy, crossed a rock face. In the river people panned for gold and it was very hot. A woman in a helmet of curlers allowed me to use her shower for two dollars. There was nothing to the canyon except the road, the river and the trees and yet in dark bars, at petrol pumps, in campgrounds, I found people who had perched here like birds, who assured me that they had discovered paradise in these baking depths at the bottom of a gash like a sword-cut.

I came south again: down the crumbling edge of the Sierras, through Sierra Valley where flax and lupins made a mauve mist in the meadows, past the great barns with their silver roofs, past the Little Truckee River and Truckee Summit to Prosser Reservoir under Donner where I would spend one more night before Lake Tahoe.

Suddenly it was cold. I slept with my feet in the rucksack and in the night pulled the squaw blanket from under my head to spread it over my shoulders where the bag was losing its down. Before sunrise I looked out and saw that we were in cloud. I put on my survival gear and sat on the tailboard drinking my sheepherder's coffee, black and scalding and sweet. The sun came up and burned the mist off the water. Pale ghosts swayed against the trunks of pines still and quiet as statues. I packed up and left this place of cold and noble memories and came to Tahoe.

16

TAHOE TO SONORA

STEINBECK WINTERED once at Tahoe and although he had dogs with him he found it lonely. Doubtless there are still places where, if the man-zanita grows steep and thick enough to discourage skiers, one may find Steinbeck's solitude, but not in summer, not on the shore of the lake.

Tahoe was suburbia rampant. A large sheet of water is nothing without its frame of rocks, trees, distant mountains. Tahoe had these but it also had a rash of urban development that had destroyed the beauty it was promoting. Like the Riviera, Tahoe is a memorable name where the memory lingers only in the odd corner at the odd time: before dawn for instance, or at twilight when for a moment the traffic thins and the power boats are silent and the pink granite broods above Emerald Bay as it did before the white man came. I passed through Tahoe without stopping and, turning west again, crossed the divide at Echo Summit.

The central mass of the Sierras that defeated the emigrants until 1844 is now crossed by roads that take passes of varying heights and grades of difficulty. Between Tahoe and the southern termination of the range there are 250 mountain miles and six main passes. From here onwards I proposed to travel in great zigzags as far as Walker Pass. I had thought of this as a pleasant meander but after Tahoe I was appalled. Was the rest of the time to be crowded with people?

Preoccupied by this dread I had only a glimpse in passing of a granite cliff in the canyon west of Echo. If this was Lover's Leap I had promised to telephone one of the men with whom I'd climbed at Donner. To telephone him now would mean waiting a day for his arrival – waiting in the canyon of the American River where two streams of traffic were in constant motion between Tahoe and Sacramento. I passed, raging at fumes and people and the lost opportunity to climb and, watching for an escape, took the first likely turning, drove over a ridge through the Eldorado forest and came to the Silver Fork of the American.

It was some time since I had left the desert but it still made me happy to see abundant fresh water. I had never taken water for granted and after weeks of being dependent on what I could carry with me I had found that I could achieve serenity merely by sitting in contemplation on a river bank. The Silver Fork was green and ran between shapely boulders of bone-white granite. I camped beside one of its creeks where my only visitor was a belled cow. Her presence suggested a house in the vicinity but no dog barked, I smelled no smoke. Twelve hours by the creek restored my equilibrium.

The following day I lost myself in the forest, probably not without an element of deliberation. It was late in the afternoon when we came out on Iron Mountain Ridge – another of those lofty lateral spines where people had established a route in the mid-nineteenth century.

This time it was men of the Mormon Battalion who, having served their enlistment at Sutter's Fort, were looking for a way home to Salt Lake City that would avoid the 27 crossings of the Truckee River.

In 1848 they assembled at the western end of the ridge and sent out three scouts to see if a way could be found for their wagons. When after ten days these men hadn't returned, ten more were dispatched. These last returned having followed their predecessors' tracks to a point where they stopped and then, aware of their main purpose, pressed on and found a pass which they reported practicable providing some road-building were done. Working parties started along the ridge and within two days they were able to move the wagons forward 20 miles. It was a broad regular ridge but, to judge from its appearance today, they must have needed to cut down a lot of timber, and the trees were huge. A Ponderosa pine stands beside the road in the full flush of its maturity. It is over 200 feet tall.

At one of the springs where they camped they found evidence of the missing scouts. All the way along the ridge they would have been looking eagerly about them for signs of these men and now they found a place where the ground had been disturbed. So they dug, and found the corpses, naked and full of arrow wounds. They called the place Tragedy Springs.

Another grave on Iron Mountain Ridge is that of Rachall Millton, a native of Iowa who died on October 4 1850. No age is given, no elucidation. The grave is about twelve feet long and strewn with wax flowers.

I came to a hill above Silver Lake with a craggy red peak on the other side. The trail takes a wide loop to the south here and I needed a full tank of petrol to follow it so I stayed at Silver Lake over night. In the morning I had to wait until the gas stations opened – stations in the plural because at this time and in this part of California, only five dollars' worth of petrol could be bought at any one garage.

The southern loop of the Mormon Trail (which came to be called the Carson Route, not through any connection with the man but because it came over Carson Pass) was one of the roughest sections of my journey. It wasn't just the angle. Erosion had washed away the soil since the pioneers were here to leave boulders and bedrock standing proud, waiting to catch an axle or a sump.

After three miles of this we came down to a glen with meadows and old ranch buildings where I had lunch in the shade and then we climbed to a ridge by amazing hairpins. The trail levelled, collecting itself, and then lunged at the final slope. I had to wait for a convoy of powerful trucks descending. They eased down a few inches at a time but with vehicles that were shire horses compared with my ox. For all that Old Crump fought his way up gamely and then, as the gradient eased, we came on a stretch of rocks so broken and spiky that the trail gave out and one took one's own line, trying to avoid the worst of the fangs – which were like a *chevaux-de-frise*.

Once on the ridge the going was splendid, over clear and swelling land: a superb and photogenic line of ruts where trees stood as if in a timberline park. As we ambled along the spine I listened to *The Magic Flute* which Sacramento was relaying from Salzburg. I had long passed the stage where I might find Mozart incongruous on a Sunday afternoon at 8,000 feet in the Sierras.

And then the brakes failed.

One cylinder had very little fluid in it. Apparently we had sprung a leak. With the trail ahead an unknown quantity it seemed imprudent to follow it; at least I knew the devilish road in the rear. So we turned back (*The Magic Flute* had finished and Beethoven's *Fifth* was so sombre in the circumstances that I was forced to switch it off) and when we came to the rough hill I was literally standing on the brake pedal, my body a straight line from the foot to shoulders braced against the back of the seat. There was some response but in our lowest gear we were still going too fast and the bumps were shattering, but this was nothing compared with the horror of descending those hairpins when the trees obscured any glimpse of traffic coming up, and it was all I could do to turn the wheel fast enough to get round the excruciating bends. Without power steering I couldn't have done it and had it not been the end of the afternoon and all traffic sensibly gone home, someone would have taken a header off Squaw Ridge, for only at long intervals was there room to pass.

I reached the bottom of the worst hill with one leg so weak that I had to stop to let the muscles relax. I looked at the cylinders. The fluid in the one that was nearly empty was frothing, presumably from the effects of my pumping the brakes. I had a rope with me and considered dragging a log behind but it was late in the day for that; the steepest descent was behind us. Also belatedly I ladled fluid from one cylinder to the other, but it was to make no difference.

I climbed out of the valley where the old homestead was, aware that if I met a vehicle descending, Old Crump couldn't hold his position and would run backwards, most horribly out of control – but we made the top without meeting anything, rolled on for a mile or two as far as a little

Formations in the defile approaching the Black Rock Desert

Reefs on the main trail through the City of Rocks

Emigrant Canyon's forests from its headwall: the route that avoided Donner Pass

Granite in the City of Rocks

King's Canyon

Lover's Leap

Barn in the Sierra Valley

Mount Lassen from Brokeoff

Right: The author in Carson Canyon

Below: Old Crump on the Carson or Mormon Route

Little towers on Boulder Peak with Disaster Peak behind

Sand dunes in Death Valley

Tower on the Dardanelles. I came down its left side.
To the right and below is the ground the Bidwell party traversed

Erosion, Death Valley

Death Valley

Red Rock Canyon at the start of the Mojave Desert

lake and stopped. In the short term we'd won; I was alive, Old Crump not even dented. The problem of the brakes could be shelved until morning.

There was no problem. With night-cold drums we dropped down to Silver Lake and climbed to Carson Pass. Timber was thin at this altitude and there were glimpses of jagged ridges under short squat towers. Below the road the granite rolled and dipped and swelled, freckled with pines. Frémont came through this bleak country in winter, working his way north to the American and west to Sutter's Fort. Fitzpatrick and Carson were with him but they hadn't come over the pass although they'd crossed the divide at a point that was near enough to make no difference. It would be four years before the Mormons crossed, with wagons and in the opposite direction. Frémont came through in February and by the time they reached the Pacific slope they were eating their mules and dogs. Preuss, the map-maker, was lost for five days farther west, and lived on wild onions, ants and frogs' legs.

The granite made for dull scenery (granite more than any other rock depends on angle for sensation) but it was overlaid by the kind of puddingstone that relieves the ridges around Donner, and it was this, loose and rotten but scenic, that formed the dramatic crests to the peaks around the Carson Pass.

The Emigrant Trail returned from its southern loop a few miles west of the pass. The Mormons had an easy descent on the east side and even the Carson Canyon needed only three crossings compared with the 27 in the Truckee. They built bridges in these places and were never forced to take to the water.

Out in the Great Basin the Mormons met Chiles leading one of his trains to California. He must have been delighted to hear that there was a new pass that would eliminate the Truckee canyons and when he came to the Humboldt Sink he went south, crossed a desert that, like the one before the Truckee, was 40 miles long and equally formidable, came to the Carson Sink and followed the river and its west fork to the pass. He didn't have an easy time crossing the divide, for he was going up when the Mormons had been descending, his draught animals were nearing the end of a 2,000-mile journey where the Mormons had merely come along Iron Mountain Ridge, but he had the bridges across the river. Taken all round it was a better way than that by the Truckee and the following year many companies took the Carson Route. In the rear of these was the solitary wagon containing the Royces: Josiah, Sarah, and their two-year-old daughter, Mary whom we last saw plodding west from the Great Salt Lake.

The Royces reached the Humboldt Sink on October 2, which was far too late for safety, but their only chance of survival lay in plugging ahead. They knew of the Carson Route and they took it, first taking 'a side road' where they might cut grass and fill up with water. In the dark they made a mistake and, without fodder or water, found themselves at daylight miles out on the desert trail. They had no chance of crossing without sustenance and they turned back, passing a small company who sympathised with them but could offer no practical assistance because everyone needed all he could carry for his own use and that of his oxen. The Royces returned to the Humboldt Sink with exhausted cattle, rested them, cut their grass, filled their receptacles, and tried again.

Two of the oxen died as they crossed the desert. On October 12 they started up the Carson River with a weak team and full of foreboding. Two days previously such a storm had ravaged the divide that one train lost all its animals except two mules which had come in close to the fire. The Royces didn't suffer from this blizzard but they would have seen the signs of it ahead and been afraid.

As the remaining oxen laboured through the sand beside the river Sarah prayed for help. It was midday, and she was moving into the sun when she looked up and saw winged beings riding down the mountain in a cloud of light. What she saw was men in loose-sleeved blouses leading pack mules. They were part of the relief columns sent out by General Smith in 1849. The rescuers had been told of the Royces by a woman in the little train which had passed them in the desert.

It was November 1 before the last party came over Carson Pass that year, and they survived only because the rescuers persuaded them to abandon their wagons. That there wasn't a string of disasters right down the Sierras, from Lassen to Carson, was due to these men who distributed food, mounted women and children on fresh saddle horses, and argued with the husbands who put the value of their property before the lives of their families.

The traveller going east down Carson Canyon debouches dramatically into low waves of hillocks where the road runs between high banks of sage. Then comes one of those plains that look as if they've been laid out with a spirit level, with cattle belly-deep in grass, flowers in gardens, and white houses, here colonnaded, under tall shade trees.

At Minden we put ourselves in the hands of a garage where the pipes were bled, the cylinders filled, the master cylinder inspected and a new kit fitted, and we came away the poorer by $68 while no one, least of all the garage, was certain that the trouble was remedied. They thought I'd put undue strain on my brakes.

A storm was threatening as I returned up the valley, pale green poplars bowed against black mountains and a purple sky. The aspen leaves shivered and turned up to reveal their silver sides, the white frame houses shone in the dazzling light, roofs were startlingly red, and coloured cattle, Hereford and Friesian, looked painted, like Noah's Ark animals. The desert air, invisible except in its effect, raged against the mountain barrier; it blew hot then cool, dry then steamy as a cold front fought the stored heat from the inland basin.

I camped primly at a campground in Carson Canyon. In the morning people came and talked. A very old Jewess stopped and, in a thick middle European accent, asked the kind of questions one accepts from the old, then: 'And you are all alone?' She shook her head with a sweet conspiratorial smile and answered her own question, 'But of course you are not alone.'

In order to see how the land lay and to get a good view of the trails I went up a peak called Roundtop – an inept name for a ridge with a fine northern escarpment and with enough sound rock on it to give something of a scramble if one looked around for the difficulties. There were two summits with a fierce gully framing a dark lake between walls that were brilliant with lime and orange lichen. The lake was Winnemucca, and beyond it was a tarn called Frog. I reckoned that Frémont crossed the divide by a line that took him between Winnemucca and Frog. The expanse of country visible from this peak, which was over 10,000 feet high, was bewildering. One needed to find points of reference to feel comfortable: Squaw Ridge where the brakes had failed, Tahoe beyond the divide that fell to the headwaters of the Truckee, Carson Pass . . . but east were hazy desert ranges I didn't know, and west a brown band lay above the great valley. The day after they crossed the divide Frémont saw the setting sun reflected from San Francisco Bay; no one would see that again while motors ran on fossil fuels.

As I climbed down from the eastern summit a shadow, about the size that an eagle would make, crossed the scree. I looked up but the sky was quite clear.

South of Roundtop was a wilderness called Mokelumne. A man was on the western summit with his son, the boy quiet, the father shivering with the cold. I asked if there were much wildlife in Mokelumne. There would be, the father said grimly, if people left it alone. There had been grizzlies once; there were still lion and black bears. This man's forebears were Welsh; one had been burned at the stake for publishing the Matthews bible.

People were even more friendly in California than elsewhere. That evening a solitary back-packer had coffee with me and then, because I said I might go to the Desolation Wilderness and he'd just walked through it, gave me his map. Next day a woman gave me tea in a store in Carson Canyon on a table that was a slice of redwood 1,100 years old.

I went back to Tahoe, not because I'd changed my mind about it but because it was the best access point for the Desolation Wilderness. I spent the night in a glade a few yards from the road where, of all the most unlikely places, a pileated woodpecker was in residence – black as a crow and the same size, with an ornate crimson crest.

In brilliant sun and a cold wind I went up Mount Tallac and looked down on a bare world of granite without puddingstone. A peak called Pyramid stood to the south, quite steep at the top, then less so: a concave slope of around 2,000 feet, all of granite, and the trough in the bottom filled by a lake in which were innumerable islets like a school of basking whales.

From this height Lake Tahoe looked as it might have looked when Frémont and the mounted Stevens party saw it, providing I ignored the south shore where there were some offensively neat and geometrical lines that must be of concrete.

Although these peaks were approached by such gently graded paths that nowhere was so much labour needed as on a Scottish or Welsh peak, if the trail were missed the only option was a kind of jungle. On the lower slopes of Tallac I came to a place directly above the truck but with 900 feet of manzanita scrub between us, and the gradient was what might be ironically described as at its angle of rest. I went straight down, grasping those bushes which I hoped weren't thorny, forgetting all about poison ivy, allowing gravity, impetus and the weight of my body to carry me down. There was no question of walking. I'd plant a foot and lean forward, dragging the rear leg clear of obstruction, falling but never falling over for the shrubs held me up – most of the time I was treading on branches, not ground.

I emerged in the yard of a cabin and, going up to the balcony to apologise for the intrusion, walked in on two small children and their sleeping mother. She woke and although she must have been startled, she revived me with iced ginger ale and said that her family had descended that slope in the dark, having sent the strongest man ahead to switch a light on in the cabin to serve as a beacon. She told me how Tahoe used to be, with deer and bears, and waterfowl nesting in Truckee Marshes which now were a holiday complex called Tahoe Keys, the monstrosity I'd seen from the top of Tallac.

That night I camped in the forest below the cliff of Lover's Leap and next day did a route with a couple from the east, Al and Lauren. It was a steep cliff but the rock was striated by thin dikes which looked as if they'd been extruded through the bedrock. Where these were continuous they formed airy traverses across the walls and where they came to vertical cracks, they broke to form little juggy holds on the edges.

We started up a steep crack with a long run-out of 140 feet. I got a crick in my neck watching Al and I was glad I was wearing boots; the holds were small and sharp and my feet were tender from much walking on granite. But when I came to follow I found that the holds weren't all that small and there were plenty of them, so that one could rest with four points of contact on the rock. With three points and a forlorn hope the body, and in particular the leg muscles, can become hard to control.

I found the first pitch delightful, not least because I knew it was the hardest and if I could get up this, then the more exposed pitches ahead held no terrors. I think it was at the first stance, rather small, where Lauren had led through, that Al told me there were rattlesnakes on the cliff, that they crawled up the cracks. Now rattlesnakes are one thing on *terra firma* where one may choose one's ground; on a ledge several hundred feet above space they are a different animal. One might be forgiven in thinking them malignant. I looked around me carefully. Al had his moment of triumph.

The best pitch was a delicate traverse that started with a few feet of descent, the kind of move at which the mind jibs a little because of the necessity to take the ground into consideration, and the ground is a long way below. But all the holds were there: those delectable little dikes. I kept exclaiming: 'Is Yosemite like this?' 'Yes,' Al said, 'without the dikes.'

The sun came round but we could withstand the heat for we were near the top. A buzzard called. A few people were on the cliff, just enough to be companionable, their cries soft and clear in the golden afternoon. Somewhere down there hidden behind the floodlight of the sun the American River whispered in the bottom of its canyon. On the opposite side pines climbed a slope to a crest that was the lip of the Desolation Wilderness. Behind us our route ran straight up to some overhangs and broke out along a ledge that fined to a traverse. We followed it, quietly, on rock that was made for worship, along the ledge and the traverse, snaking up to the overhangs at their weakest point and pulling out on the exquisite finishing holds of the dikes.

Next day I went to look at a waterfall, met the local postmistress, was given the guide book to the area signed by its author, 'because you climbed the cliff', and drank beer in the bar beside the Post Office, served by a local woman who told me expressionlessly about arson (a fire was reported while I was there). She had a sprinkler on her roof which was switched on whenever she left the house in the summer. While we talked a string of small children passed through the bar, back and forth, earnestly concerned with some private business, earnestly trailed by a blue point Siamese. I asked about bears. I had found bear traces on

Tallac. There were 'nuisance bears' in Desolation, I was told; they were caught in Yosemite and released here, when they promptly came down and raided the Post Office's garbage bins.

I walked along the track below Lover's Leap. People were staring at the cliff. About 800 feet above, Al was perched on the sunlit face while, at the end of a very long run-out, Lauren was moving up to a bulge. When she reached it she extended a slim arm (from here she looked all limbs) and, without a pause, with no break in the lovely rhythm, stepped up and over the bulge as if it were an interruption in a slab. She had told me that her forte was steep walls.

That evening I crossed Luther Pass where the sun slanted through the top of the forest to gild old sedges about a sapphire lake. I slept in Carson Canyon. Next day I called at Grover Hot Springs for no other reason than its name and because Frémont placed a base camp there while he went forward to reconnoitre the divide.

The springs fed a pool in which a few people were splashing about. A ranger invited me into his trailer where he gave me black cherry yoghurt and told me what he proposed to do over the next few years. He was twenty-nine and had been travelling for ten years. He'd studied Marxism, poetry and sociology at Bordeaux and in the States, had worked with children, written a child's history of California and was about to do one of Israel. Then he thought he'd write a play. He knew what he would do two years hence. He wrote best when he was settled and happy. 'If anyone asked me to write about that stove, I'd do it.' He had interest in my job but no envy. He knew where I was going and that he was on his way: a good man.

The road to Ebbett's Pass rose interminably, becoming ever narrower but never quite deteriorating to dirt although I expected it to at every turn. At first the Carson River, then one of its creeks called Silver brawled below. There is a lot of repetition in pioneers' names. This is a different Silver from the Silver Fork of the American, and this is the East Fork of the Carson River. It was the West Fork below Carson Pass.

The peaks were hidden behind the skirts of their foothills and the contrast between those arid slopes and the dashing water was delightful. I stopped several times to appreciate it properly, and to look at strange flowers. On the verges there were large white poppies, their crumpled petals having the texture of dragon-flies' new wings, but the honour went to blazingstar: exactly as its name, a Christmas decoration four inches across, growing like a tall weed in the roadside wastes. It was bright and hot and people were floating down the river on inner tubes, their skin wet and brown as hazel nuts.

The road climbed to a frieze of reefs and pinnacles, snaking round corners above huge drops. Vehicles crept up and down in low gear and we reached the summit at 8,731 feet where an historical marker informed us that this was never an emigrant trail but that one, Ebbett, had recommended the pass as a route for the railroad. One does not hear of Ebbett again.

It is thought that Jedediah Smith in 1827 may have been the first white man to cross the pass as he travelled east after entering California by way of the Old Spanish Trail south of the Great Basin. He was certainly the first white man to cross the Sierras but could have done so by a line that was followed 29 years later by the Big Trees Route built by businessmen of Stockton to divert emigrants from Sacramento. This trail branched south from the Carson Route some five miles west of that pass and continued through the Mokelumne Wilderness (where the bear and lion were, and which I had looked down on from the summit of Roundtop) to emerge about five miles west of Ebbett's Pass in Hermit Valley. I camped there that Sunday night.

The big trees of the Stockton route are sequoias. They stand at Calaveras, some 40 miles west of Ebbett's, in a state park and are concentrated in two groves. On arrival at the picnic site, a cool and pillared place among these trees, I allowed the car door to slam. After five minutes I found myself closing a door gently as if afraid of disturbing something. To say that they are massive is misleading; underneath them, beside the trunks, their height is lost because the eye cannot encompass it. A trunk disappears, receding into the dark and fretted gloom of its own canopy. The base of the trunk cannot be connected with a tree; it is the base of a trunk only.

The senses are aware of silence. If the topmost branches whisper (and the needles are very small) the sound is so distant as to be inaudible. There are birds and squirrels of course; jays are intrusive, but natural. The sound of an engine is alien but unobtrusive, puny.

They have a quietening effect on people. A party of Japanese were scampering up and down the enormous paws where the base of the trunk clasps the earth, photographing each other with Nikons and zoom lenses but they did it silently, like industrious ants.

The place is beyond understanding; like death it is overwhelming. There is no joy, only wonder. I welcomed as familiar and comprehensible a pair of nuthatches, and a squirrel stripping a cone. Here only the little animals can go about their business without awe.

Next morning I went to the other grove very early, ahead of the people. These were the largest trees, over 300 feet tall: pillars sculpted in apricot stone – and yet the bark is fibrous, which is what gives that impression of paws, and a hint of the Sphinx.

One stood on its own in a glade, like a deity revealing itself for the first time, surrounded at a decent distance by satellites 100 feet tall. Birds played in the canopy. I could hear them but see no movement. The trunk rose to a softly humming, twittering world of sound: the last unattainable refuge.

Some, stricken by fire, point mutely at the sky. They are wonderful even when they are dead. All are marked by fire. When one fell in the sixties, people thought it was an earthquake. They are brittle, and break into sections when they fall so that they lie up a slope, jointed, like wounded gods.

I drove down the valley to a town called Murphys where the hotel had been listed as an historic monument and was being restored. Byron had stayed there, and Mark Twain – they had come to look at the big trees. In the bar there were posters, one for the Pony Express:

> RIDERS WANTED
> Young, skinny, wiry fellows. Anxious
> for adventure and chance to see our
> great WEST. Must be expert riders,
> willing to risk death daily. Orphans
> preferred. $60 PER MONTH and keep.

A second bill referred to the head of Joaquin, a bandit, being exhibited for one day only on August 19 1853, along with the hand of the notorious robber and murderer, Three Fingered Jack.

The third poster announced $1,000 reward in gold coin for the arrest and conviction of the robber Black Bart. It was put out by the Sonora Stagecoach Company.

The manager of the hotel gave me coffee and told me he was the nephew of Lydia Pinkham who had bottled an elixir that was 80 per cent alcohol and sold it to women as a tonic for cramps and other mysterious feminine ailments. Eventually she sold out to a pharmaceutical firm for half a million dollars and put all her children through college.

I was shown the bedroom that General Grant slept in, with its original bed and washstand and a piano that had been shipped round the Horn. In the hall there was a glass-fronted cabinet with gold-bearing rock specimens, rattlesnakes' rattles and little pickled snakes in jars.

I had to see the jail: a tiny pill box with barred windows, its size implying that Murphys never contained more than two criminals under restraint at one time, or that this was another Black Hole.

On the river bank was a pocket-handkerchief park with flower beds, and a bandstand where 20 of the townsfolk gave concerts on Thursday evenings.

We turned south-east, skirting the foothills of the mountains, making back towards the next pass to the south. We were crossing the grain of the country now and suddenly I found myself on a tall and airy bridge spanning a canyon with a bird's-eye view of water and sand flats over 200 feet below. There had been signs in advance: Scenic Viewpoint presumably, but 'Viewpoint' obliterated and 'Drowning' substituted. On the inside of the bridge environmentalists had written their message. This was Melones Canyon, shortly to be flooded for power, or water. Americans use 200 gallons of water per head per day and treat it as if it were self-perpetuating, as do the British.

Sonora continued a theme which had been apparent at Murphys (where the hotel's façade was spoiled by litter bins), conspicuous at Melones; Sonora had fine buildings but, to judge by the evidence, not much weight behind its town planners.

I laid in a good stock of food and drove on towards Sonora Pass. Looking for a certain forestry track I took the wrong turning and found myself in an exclusive rural housing development. The streets had names like Bambi Lane, Snow White Drive, Tinker Bell Lane.

I found my road and realised that it was getting dark too quickly. There had been pregnant clouds at Melones, now they had sunk to hide the Sierras. I turned and twisted through the forest and finally, wilting after a very long day, stopped where the track widened, and cut the engine. It was still and dim and cool. As I was trimming beans for supper a weird call came from the forest. I was not myself that evening, and unfamiliar sounds had to be classified quickly when I was that tired, so I decided it was a strange owl and continued with the cooking. Then the old dry leaves of the mules' ears started to rustle when there was no breeze and although I was used to that, it was always disturbing. The only other sounds were the soft hiss of the cooker flame, the bubbling of the saucepan. I found myself licking my lips like a nervous cat and I thought of a great paw on my shoulder. We were too close to Yosemite . . . but there were no grizzlies left down here . . . and surely I could cope with a black bear. But I wasn't thinking of bears, not really; I was exhausted, I was excited, I had reached Sonora.

17

STANISLAUS TO DEATH VALLEY JUNCTION

SONORA IS THE name of a town and a pass. The country between the two is the Stanislaus forest and it is the area through which the very first California emigrants came in 1841. This was the Bidwell group, no longer to be termed a train when they reached here because their wagons were strung out across the Great Basin, abandoned, and their remaining goods were on the backs of mules and horses. History says that they were lost. Bartleson got lost certainly, but not Bidwell and the main party. They followed the right stream to the correct pass; they came down the other side and emerged quite close to Marsh's Ranch in the San Joaquin Valley for which they'd been making all along. They wandered for twelve days in the Stanislaus forest after crossing the divide, but the distance is 45 miles as the crow flies. Had there been a trail that distance could be increased to 60 to make allowance for some of the roughest ground in the Sierras, but there was no trail and across these timbered corrugations they averaged five miles a day, presumably steering by the sun. They were, as one of them said in his diary, smelling out the way, and they did it well.

This is sometimes referred to as the Bartleson party but Bartleson was only the titular leader, having been elected because he was one of a faction of eight or nine men and the party was so small when they assembled on the Missouri that they couldn't afford to lose such a large proportion.

Chiles was also in the party, making his first journey west, as they all were. Besides the Kelsey family there were Benjamin Kelsey's brother and two frontier school teachers, both of whom kept diaries. Bidwell was one of these, the other was called Dawson.

When they reached the Humboldt Sink, Bartleson and his faction left and headed south. They got lost in mountains near Walker Lake, looped round and – amazingly in this vast and untravelled country – were reunited with the others where they had halted to reconnoitre the eastern slope of the Sierras.

The mountain barrier was breached by timbered canyons about the headwaters of the Carson River. They chose to follow the East Fork almost to its source, ignoring Silver Creek which led to the pass that would be called Ebbett's eventually. They crossed the divide and descended the Pacific slope to an 'impassable canyon'. They turned north-west, and that was where they spent twelve days working through timber and granite to the San Joaquin Valley.

Naturally I was attracted by the impassable canyon but this had been flooded to form Donnell's Reservoir. It was on the Middle Fork of the Stanislaus River and the lake might have been beautiful had I not known that it had drowned a magnificent canyon, had it not been for the tide-line left by the water level sinking in the drought. That the canyon had been a fine one was obvious from the angle of the rock walls which would continue at that angle to the bed of the lake.

The Bidwell party turned this obstacle on the north and, across the line they must have taken, I looked at a prominent peak called the Dardanelles. From that one might see the whole of their route. I filed it for future reference and went off to find the Forest Service to see if they had further information.

Stanislaus was a place of enchantment. The valleys were populated but not crowded, the mountains were empty, and so were the hidden corners of the forest to which residents slippped away before the summer's visitors. I was directed to a woman called Bashford York: a fresh, powerful person in middle age who took charge of a ranger station in the season and spent the winters teaching music and cooking gourmet dishes for a restaurant. She lent me books and an unpublished thesis on Bidwell which arrived in her mail the day after we met. I worked on these at the ranger station through a curious day of harsh facts and vicarious passion while the young rangers went about their business and I could hear the drone and sometimes the words of the tourists (always American, I was way off the international routes) asking for information at the counter. As I reeled with fatigue Bashford carried me off to her cabin, planted me at a table and went away to pick elderberries. Sighing, I took one look at the fascinating furniture of a new life-style, opened a beer, a book and a note-pad and resumed work. I had ground myself to a standstill by the time she returned. She put the dinner in the oven, filled a carafe with velvety red wine and settled to talk.

I was exhausted by the images, events and reactions of four months' wandering, and the intense concentration of the last few hours had been the final straw. The good food, lovingly prepared, pleased me, the wine unlocked a series of doors, the fatigue and all the clutter seeped away and, long after darkness fell and the lamps were lit, we were still talking. We were discussing curiosity when Bashford suggested that some questions should not be answered – or asked, it was immaterial. There had been times, particularly when tired, that I had wondered what I was doing in America, following the California Trail. The short answer was that I had signed a contract – and suddenly the pattern clicked. I was here therefore I was.

From 9,000 feet I could view the East Carson Valley objectively. At that distance it had no beauty; it was merely a steep-sided glen fretted with pines that climbed out of the dense forest in the bottom. The slopes would be sandy; so much could be deduced from the ground on the divide itself, where the granite had weathered to a deep coarse sand that, away from the trail, was like wading through dunes. That would have been hard on men and animals as they came up Golden Canyon from the last camp in a meadow on the Carson. Nicholas Dawson looked back 'and saw Mrs Kelsey a little way behind me, with her child in her arms, barefoot, and leading her horse. . . .'

They crossed about October 18 so it would have been cool for the climb, but to balance that they had had the fear of snow. No wonder Nancy carried her daughter; her husband would have been taking his turn at the front, scouting the way to a crest which they would have hoped was the last one. They would have been fooled by false crests many times in the past 2,000 miles.

I came up the west side of the divide and emerged some four or five miles south of Golden Canyon so that I might have an airy ramble before I intercepted their trail. All the way along the top I had their line in sight as they came up the Carson River. There was never any more to learn than that it was timber and granite, granite and timber – and they had no trail. Always one had to remember this: that they came first. There were Indian trails, of course, but these, like game trails, would seldom go the way the emigrants wanted to go. They forged their way west.

I went over Boulder Peak where stunted pines grew on the summit among little stumpy towers of yellow sand, I contoured below a point that was a pile of loose lava, rose up the long grain of a ridge to Disaster Peak and there at 10,000 feet, I stopped. Their pass was 500 feet below me with timber climbing both sides to meet, if thinly, on the crest. They would have known by the angle when they'd crossed, but they'd have had to find a clearing to reconnoitre the line of descent. They would have looked down Clark Fork as I did and seen that this was the obvious way west, and perhaps they saw the sea. There was no way of seeing it now; the smog of humidity and pollution and the smoke of fires ensured that visibility was scarcely 50 miles.

I had better visibility to the south where shapely peaks above Sonora Pass claimed my attention before the eye slid on to Yosemite. These were not high mountains but they had an air of expansiveness about them that was sweet and welcoming, unlike the hard bright challenge of the Alps.

A thousand feet below me was a hanging valley called Paradise. I came down to it as they must have done, and then came a gentle decline where gravity did the work and the body was a separate entity carrying a dozing mind. I registered the big pines that Bidwell saw and I smelled their resin, I saw deer as large ears and lustrous eyes, and I heard the quail as they ran. I was in a state of bliss after a good day, perhaps 20 miles of walking.

This day the Bidwell group did about 15, coming down to Clark Fork. Next day they followed the creek for six miles until it ran into the Middle Fork of the Stanislaus. In 1851 a pack bridge was to be built across a chasm where Bidwell had been too prudent to approach the edge but could hear the water roaring in the bottom. That suggests they were having rain or that new snow was melting; certainly there was more water in the river than when I saw it at the end of August. From here three people scouted separately down the right bank: a young man who probably didn't get far, Bartleson who exhausted his horse and had to rest a day before he could return, finally Bidwell, almost certainly on foot.

The impassable canyon, now drowned, was some four miles downstream. I made an attempt to reach the reservoir but although I found game trails the undergrowth was so tangled that I gave up after a mile. I admired Bidwell for trying, and he was weak and tense, for the snow would be visible by then and creeping down. I was fit and fresh and unencumbered; I had time to look for the deer paths.

They turned north-west then and travelled for some miles until they came to grass and water where they killed an ox. This would have put them on the granite plateau under the Dardanelles which is now approached by a climbing forest road. I camped under Ponderosa pines and started for my peak early one morning.

As I came up the path I heard twigs breaking and realised that I was approaching a hunter. He carried a bow with the arrow strung, ready to fire. When I was close I spoke to him, not wanting to be shot. He showed me his bow with great pride; it weighed five and a half pounds and involved a pulley system which made it easy to draw, and lethal for the victim provided the right spot was hit. Hunting was getting into its stride. I'd spoken to a couple of polite men at the road-end who had stuck an advertisement for coon shooting on their truck, or it could have been a slogan. I was reminded of a picture in a coffee-table book of Bashford's: of a trapper stamping to death a trapped raccoon. It is the custom. The pelt remains undamaged. Presumably it is the head that is stamped on.

The hunter told me there was no deer about. This was true of his own vicinity. Either because they didn't like to feel alone or because they didn't want to be shot, he and his companions whistled incessantly to each other. Moreover, they had clumsy feet. The deer had gone high.

The Dardanelles were volcanic. I came up against their escarpment and worked along it until I found a formation of fine basaltic columns which appeared to be locked at their base and where, by using them with the utmost delicacy, I managed to evolve a climb of at least 100 feet which brought me classically to the summit ridge.

I swung off my pack and . . . no shadow, but substance came floating by on wings that looked like a ten-foot span. The cool eyes surveyed me as it passed, and then it sailed slowly away. I watched it until I could no longer see it and never thought of the binoculars in my sack. If I saw nothing else in the hours ahead a golden eagle so close that I could hear the air through its pinions was all I needed to make me happy.

The Dardanelles was a ridge without spurs: a day of great simplicity when I went up one end, came down the other, and in the middle were knife-edges, gendarmes, chimneys, and even slabs in rock that was chunky or blunt or spiky and just sound enough to be trusted provided I didn't venture on delicate traverses above the impressive scarp on the left that had now increased its height to several hundred feet. This crown of cliff was echoed on the other side of a sloping basin where a ridge came swinging down from Dardanelles Cone to end in a funny little rock-girt mesa which must be a volcanic plug. For old volcanoes, not yet eroded to their granite base, these peaks made interesting and amusing shapes. I trod my own ridge gaily – to be brought up short by a sensation of space through which I peered to the continuation of my line on a saddle a good hundred feet below, bland, wide and gravelly. Something nasty was underneath me.

I retreated, descended, contoured the foot of the obstacle, crossed the gravel and looked back. Straddling the ridge was a splendid tower made of a strange brown lava. On my side of the saddle the rock was basaltic again, the columns running into rock so steep and crumbling that I wouldn't have touched it had I been roped. I turned it by something a little more sound, a little less steep, and came to the summit.

The ridge continued to a timbered pass. South and west I looked over the country where Bidwell travelled. It was all granite, with little black lakes that hardly showed as water among the cloud shadows and the dark conifers. They had started north-west from Clark Fork and then, finding that the drainage was south-west, they would have turned and gone with the grain of the country. Perhaps that made travel a little easier. But they were hungry. Four days into that wilderness they killed their last ox, then they started to eat the mules. The Indians were not overtly hostile, but if the old man who led them into a dead-end and then disappeared did it deliberately, then the Indians didn't intend that the whites should survive – and they coveted the horses. A man called Cook was suspicious and when they came to a place strewn with horses' bones, and they threw away some old clothes, he stayed behind when the others went on. As the Indians came in to scavenge, Cook, in hiding, saw that they were led by the old fellow who had left them in the dead-end. Cook shot him. Later the Indians stole two horses.

The emigrants' position was desperate; they'd lost a number of animals that had fallen down precipices and they were so hungry that some didn't wait for fire but ate their mule meat raw. Once Bidwell was glad to eat the windpipe and lights of a coyote. But the same day that they saw the snow creeping down the Sierras behind them, they came out of the wilderness near the present site of Sonora.

For some their lives continued to be remarkable. One of the Kelsey brothers became a grazier but treated his Indian neighbours so badly that they murdered him. Cook, who had shot the Indian, made money in '49 but lost it and died three years later. He had been involved with Talbot Green, another member of the party. Green carried a lump of lead all the way to California but cached it, with Cook's help, before they reached the settlements. Subsequently they retrieved it and became rich. Green was popular and ten years later, standing as candidate for mayor of San Francisco, was recognised as Paul Geddes who had robbed a bank in Philadelphia. The lead was supposed to have encased bullion.

Bidwell became a successful politician and a rich rancher. Nancy and her husband continued wandering, from California to Oregon, to Texas and back to California. Nothing appears to be known about the baby who was carried across the divide although they lost another little girl in Texas, scalped by Comanches.

No one else followed Bidwell through the Stanislaus forest and when the next emigrants crossed the divide to Sonora they didn't come by the route the present highway takes over Sonora Pass but by Emigrant Pass, nine miles to the south and 10,000 feet high. A man called Joseph C. Morehead was responsible for that; flamboyant and ineffectual, he syphoned off sixteen wagons from the Carson Route and somehow got them across the pass, but ran into difficulties in a wilderness which he had ridden through on the outward journey. Like Hastings and Lassen, he made no road, and formed the erroneous and familiar assumption that where a horse could go a wagon could follow. Nevertheless, leaving the wagons and people, he went to Sonora and returned with a pack train that saved their lives. The adventure is commemorated in names such as Emigrant Meadow, Relief Valley, Starvation Lake.

The area looked interesting for a pack trip but I could spare only one more day. I compromised and set out for Leavitt Peak which might overlook Emigrant Pass. It was a high mountain for the area, over 11,000 feet, but then Sonora Pass was over 9,000, so one had only 2,000 feet of height to gain: a short day, a day for fun.

A ridge ran south from the pass to the summit with fine crags, even cliffs on it as it approached the peak and where, gilding the lily, it threw out a grand and jagged spur to the east. So the path ran through varied country, starting conventionally in hairpins to gain the first ridge and with the views little different from what I had been seeing for some days from the pass: east to the pale Sweetwater Range, west down the mighty gash of the Stanislaus to the smog that hung above the great valley.

Slowly as I drew closer to the heart of the mountain, the silence increased, marked rather than broken by the whisper of water in the long glens below. Heading for the cliff under the summit, I'd just caught the gleam of Deadman Lake below the screes when the path turned, climbed the ridge and swooped to contour a new basin with a new vista.

I walked round a stony bowl to a col on the east ridge and looked through a gateway of pink granite to the Yosemite peaks. It was a world of mountains, two worlds really: the far confusion of grey and white ranks, and the closer one, of crimson and black ridges, screes in heliotrope and crushed rose, of little lakes in peacock colours sparkling in the sun with splashes of yellow mimulus on their banks. And a third world, closest of all, in which colonies of alpine gentians grew about my feet with ivory trumpets and stripes that were almost black.

I turned to the summit and trod the soft red clinker above deserts of brown stone and came to the top where there was a tin box containing tinted photographs of a new baby, a child on a pony, and an admonition to me to stop watching television and climb mountains.

Across from me the elegant black triangle of Kennedy Peak stood above its lake, one of a group of mountains dominated by a tower on a ridge called Relief which effectively hid the whole of Morehead's route through the Emigrant Wilderness.

The shadows were lengthening as I came down and the mountain bloomed with colour: puce and purple, magenta and mauve, with threads of green from copper, and rusty lichen among the gold. And when I crossed Sonora Pass for the last time (having gone down to the station to say goodbye to Bashford) all the arêtes were catching the sunlight above the shadowy canyon, but Leavitt stood immute, an animal carved in stone, a noble peak.

I dropped down through the eastern canyons and came too soon to fenced land and so was forced to camp properly, in a campground. Another solitary camper was a woman of eighty-five who had rafted down the Colorado two years before and had made her first attempt at water-skiing in her seventies.

I drove south parallel with the eastern front of the Sierras, reversing Frémont's route as he came up to cross near Carson Pass. I stopped to take a picture of a gash called Devil's Gate but found access to the best viewpoint barred by a notice warning me of trespassing and rattlesnakes. Some distance away stood a fine wooden house where a man was ostensibly examining the soil in his yard.

He was a retired builder who came here first as a youth, fell in love with the area and returned for 20 years until plots were put up for sale when he bought 40 acres and built this house. He liked exploring in the hills and showed me a trail that led to what they called the Gold Mine but where in fact cinnabar or mercury was extracted. I asked him for the name of those papery Chinese poppies growing in his yard but he didn't know; he'd worked the soil over and the flowers just came.

They had only four inches of snow in the winter. The highway was cleared and he reached it with his own blower. I was welcome to take a picture from his land, the sign was a deterrent only; they would be over-run with hunters shortly. I drove away with a last glance at the mysterious hills behind his house and feeling suddenly blissful. There was no reason to account for it other than that I had met a happy man.

We ran across a well-watered plain covered with cattle towards our highest pass. Plain and pass were the last concessions to conformity; after this the land went wild.

Mono Lake was of an incredible blue, but then it wasn't real water; it was alkaline with a wide fringe of salt. Beyond it stood mountains of white stone speckled with bristlecone pines 4,000 years old. To have halted to contemplate such phenomena might, one felt, entail losing oneself in time and space – to have more than glanced at them as I drove carried familiar dangers. It was not a driver's road.

I climbed the long gradients to Tioga Pass, the summit crowded by dark towers. I dropped to the 35 m.p.h. demanded by a national park and drifted down through the meadows of Tuolumne. A leviathan of rock rose above the pines, pale, smooth and alien, then the trees closed in but I caught glimpses of its hide in the depths and was uneasy.

We ran into the clear again and on our left was a tilted grey sheet of stone with an overhang, like icing that has oozed to the lip of a cake, drooped and petrified in a rounded eave. Three insect-men on rock like glass were stationary at wide intervals, connected by a rope of green gossamer.

I came to the Yosemite Valley with the sun behind me, with my road dark and empty in the trees. I came round a bend and the world was filled with a white and floodlit mass reaching to the sky: El Capitan.

They debate who saw it first, grizzly hunters in '49 or Walker's scouts in '33, but Indians had lived under El Capitan for centuries before the white man came. (They were removed to reservations in the San Joaquin Valley when they became a threat to the advancing gold miners.)

Joseph Walker traversed the northern part of Yosemite leading an exploratory expedition sent out by the entrepreneur, Captain Bonneville. Zenas Leonard, clerk to the expedition, said that they started to encounter streams which would 'precipitate themselves from one lofty precipice to another, until they were exhausted in rain below. Some of these precipices appeared to be more than a mile high.'

They saw the falls in the middle of October; I saw them a month earlier, in the drought. Yosemite was a black stain on the rock, Bridal Veil had less water than a Highland burn in September; only Nevada and Vernal came pouring out of the high country with enough force that the boulders grinding at midday were audible over a mile away.

I spent most of my time working in the park headquarters and the library: studying Walker's route, listening to the administrators. They were dedicated and genial; I learned a lot and felt the cool familiarity of the working journalist. I might have been in Blackpool or Windermere, except that here, loaded with books and hand-outs, scrabbling in a pocket for the car keys, I would look up and see the pinnacle of the Lost Arrow above the supermarket and the stinking streets. For stink they did; the fumes enclosed by the mighty walls were as overpowering as those in the canyons of New York. And yet amongst the smells, the heat and the glitter those walls could still disturb the mind, and sometimes soothe. The climbers' Camp Four, renamed Sunnyside by the authorities, was crowded, noisy, smoky with fires, at night erupting with hysteria as men thought they saw bears, but even here in the dark where the street lights couldn't reach, one might look up at rock awash with moonlight and weep for the beauty of it all.

One morning I drove up to Wawona for the sunrise. The shadowed side of El Capitan was towards me and while I was still in darkness the sun came up and struck its eastern face, but all I saw was a line of light that ran down the vertical edge of the cliff, and that almost imperceptible flare at the base, 3,000 feet of laser beam.

I went on to Glacier Point and saw the sleek cowl of Half Dome, its curved back full in the sun, the north face black; and all around rose the satellite domes, silent and shining in the dawn.

I spent the day up there, thousands of feet above the valley, doing little more than look. Near Taft Point a weasel came along below my perch, flicked an eye at a startled lizard but ignored me completely. At

Glacier, as the crowds thickened, I met a young man who was sitting at a picnic table, writing an opera based on *The Masque of the Red Death*, with Half Dome in front, and behind him the stall selling Coca Cola and lemonade for 35 cents.

The shadows deepened under the Royal Arches and I came down late to eat my supper on a shingle bank by the river as the moon rose and a fox called from the woods below Cathedral Spires.

The climbs were hard and high, and so hot that no one was doing the great routes on El Capitan. They told me that for a five-day climb one must take five gallons of water, and this apart from all the ironmongery, the ropes and sleeping gear, the food. As for the exposure, they said you didn't notice it after the first hundred feet. That could be true; when you're climbing well, exhilaration increases with the drop. El Capitan, I chided myself, was just another Dolomite. It wasn't. The Dolomites are horizontally striated. El Cap was sheer.

I went back to Tuolumne where it was cool and quiet and I strolled among little granite peaks where the deer were unafraid and the only threat came from a red squirrel which rushed at my feet mewing like an angry kitten. Late as it was, such a display implied young in the vicinity.

I went up Mount Hoffman from which I'd calculated I'd see the pass by which Walker crossed the divide. I could see it; the problem was its identification. Away to the east stretched the high Sierras and I could take my pick of Burro, Virginia, or even Rock Island Pass, any one of which he could have come over to the headwaters of the Tuolumne River. The country was like that of the Stanislaus forest, rock, timber, canyons. The passes were a little higher, the rock a little looser (I could see huge chunks of it lying on the bottom of a lake 1,000 feet below) but it was all the same kind of terrain, never level, never clear – and the pioneers always had the threat of winter coming down behind.

Walker crossed the Grand Canyon of the Tuolumne and worked his way south and west down the ridges, sending scouts out all the time and it was those on the southern flank who rode down a glen and came out on a lip above space with Half Dome across the way. It is obvious how they made the mistake in thinking that the precipices were a mile high. If they saw Half Dome with the sun behind it, the north face in shadow, the plinth might appear to continue the vertical angle, and the summit of Half Dome is nearly 5,000 feet above the valley.

By the time the Walker expedition reached the Pacific slope they were subject to the same kind of hardships that the Bidwell party were to suffer eight years later and 30 miles to the north. Walker had the added hazard of lying snow. He was eating his horses by the time he came through Yosemite. But he got through and was able to winter among the rich farms and the vineyards of the Franciscan friars at San Juan Bautista.

Beyond Tioga there is no way of getting back east of the Sierras until their end is reached, not with a vehicle. So we came down the western side, crossing the long ridges of the foothills which were covered with that yellow grass that looked like hay which has been dried too long. Wild oats swayed on the verges and the rivers were no more than lines of stagnant pools. There were houses on these uplands but they were closed against the heat and for all the people I saw it could have been an un-inhabited country.

I came out of the foothills into the San Joaquin Valley. The road ran through vineyards and groves of fruit trees. It was terribly hot but the temperature was only 106 degrees. This was my introduction to humidity and I didn't like it although, once I'd got used to streams of liquid pouring down my body, I found that copious sweating was a relief.

Humidity was explained to me that evening by an evangelist in a pink trouser-suit who approached me in a campground. She had lived in Minnesota where her husband worked on the roads, driving a snow plough in winter. When it took him 24 hours to get to work, with the thermometer at 60 below, they moved to Oregon. After three years they were grumbling at 40 inches of rain and they came to California. This they found more suitable. I was fascinated to hear that senior citizens were allowed to glean once the crops were in. When she found that I hadn't tasted nectarines she insisted on my accepting some, with plums and peaches, all from her own trees.

I took the road for King's Canyon. 'Hill for 12 miles' said the sign. There were views of a stupendous hanging glen as we descended through a stark but hazy light until we were looking up a rift that was indecent in its exposure except for the thrill of knowing that in that place there wasn't even a walkers' trail.

King's Canyon was the next one we came to and that was magnificent. It had no rim but was bounded by towers and superb, hanging, timbered ravines. The big coloured cliffs were sometimes in the back of the ravines, being the walls of amphitheatres, or they formed dark portals 1,000 feet high, or culminated in fangs above long slopes of tawny grass. There were reefs and faces, spires and pinnacles and, oc-casionally, an expanse of pale grey rock that looked as if it would make good climbing. Yucca grew in the most inaccessible places, sprouting from bouquets of spears. On the cliffs, the dead stalks looked like fallen trees.

Upstream of the narrows the canyon widened until there was room for a strip of woodland. This teemed with wildlife and in particular woodpeckers. There were hairy woodpeckers with scarlet napes, red-shafted flickers with their bright red whiskers, white-headed woodpeckers. There were the little garter snakes with yellow stripes – and small silent flies which would try with the most obscene determination to crawl into my eyes.

South of King's Canyon were more foothills, gradated in a bright grey haze of smoke against the sun. I could feel myself growing bad-tempered. I had strained my back lifting the heavy tailboard, I was very dirty and now the smoke of forest fires got in my eyes and lungs, and photography was impossible. I was petulent, paranoid and silent until one night I lost my temper with some drunks who were playing a radio at full blast. The safety valve had blown. One man mended the tailboard, others invited me to visit; next day I limped, then walked up a little peak and the stiff strained muscles relaxed – but the fires I saw from the top were worse than those I'd seen before.

I came down and protested to a ranger who agreed with everything I said and told me that they were prescribed burns and out of control. Another ranger, fat and merry, gave a slide show one night in Sequoia National Park, leading the audience in community singing first then showing pictures of the big trees in winter, without smoke, without smog. The people loved it; they brought their children and their dogs. A large Airedale and a Samoyed sat beside me, intent and immobile. Above us one of the trees towered like an indifferent god and when I went to find Old Crump, just the first hundred feet of the trunks showed in the arc lights about the car park; the rest was lost to the night.

Their great height constituted a peculiar danger, at least where Ponderosas were concerned, for they bore large cones. One morning I was having breakfast in a campground when a cone came down like a bomb. I grabbed my crash helmet and moved Old Crump to the next space. Cones continued to crash down. After an hour a squirrel descended, picked up one as big as himself and made off with it.

Sequoia bark feels like the hairy pelt of a large animal; the sapwood exposed after they have been burned is like fibrous muscle. The burns themselves, as much as 100 feet long, are ghastly wounds. They resemble charred corpses in Glaister's *Medical Jurisprudence*. When these trees fall, they roar down. One of them, measuring over 250 feet, had fallen uphill, fitting into the troughs and crests of the ground, not spanning them as a fir would, and the cracked, disjointed cadaver looked less than ever like a tree, and yet more animate.

Sequoia National Park is high and to reach the Kaweah Canyon to the south there is a drop of 4,000 feet through innumerable hairpins; and in the cool of evening I came to an exquisite campground. Across the valley were high hills, their pleasing shapes softened but not hidden by thick timber, while on our side were slopes of scrub, with grass showing like a glimpse of a lion's hide. Two old men discussed me grumpily: 'That's a widow over there. . . .' 'Not getting enough to eat. . . .'

One came over in the dark, and asked me what kind of gun I carried. He accused me of imprudence when I said I didn't carry one, and he apologised when I said I carried a knife. I didn't tell him it was a Swiss army knife. He went away but returned to show me his guns and to persuade me to buy a Derringer. I couldn't reach so far with a knife, he said.

I left Sequoia, came to my mail drop at a town called Three Rivers and found the mail hadn't arrived. I looked at the map, saw another road, another canyon, and went back into the mountains, climbing 8,000 feet in 25 miles to Mineral King. The sound of shattered silencers thundered back from the rock, even from the forests, and fumes filled the car.

The road was narrow, the drops abysmal; there were no parapets. Here and there were houses perched on platforms like eyries. It became cooler as we gained height and when we reached the campground at the head of the canyon, the air was quite pleasant.

Long after the sun left the valley a high slag-heap of a mountain gleamed gold, then carmine and was suddenly colourless and hard. One tiny fang on its summit ridge had earned it the name of Sawtooth.

The timber line was high and the last thousand feet of Sawtooth was a tedious grind between granite boulders and reefs of bedrock where I turned aside to scramble. It took no longer than walking and it was rock under the hands.

I saw Mount Whitney from the top, a mountain higher than any of the Oberland peaks, yet bare of snow. I was a long way south, and Whitney stood above the deserts. The mountains were big and stony; across from me a trail rose in graceful *lacets* to Black Rock Pass. In the basin under Sawtooth lakes of jet and indigo filled hollows in the granite troughs.

I had taken an hour to reach the summit from the timber line; I ran down the scree in a few minutes, the deep gravel chips running with me. I was fit again.

In Bakersfield in the San Joaquin Valley I booked a room in a motel and had my first hot bath in two months. I washed all the clothes, meanwhile Old Crump was fitted with two shining new exhaust systems and when we left next morning and drove across the plain to the Walker Pass we purred, and we did not smell.

It was a low pass, not much over 5,000 feet – which was why the pioneers liked it, although it was so much out of the way. It is flat and has little distinction except for the sudden appearance of Joshua trees, about 15 feet tall, with shaggy trunks and limbs, and long spiky leaves. The emigrants used them for fuel and tied their animals to the trunks. That was after they'd abandoned their wagons.

Walker came west over his own pass in 1843, guiding the women and children of Chiles' train. That was when Chiles had ridden round the northern termination of the Sierras as Walker now came round the southern. The wagons had come all the way south from the Humboldt Sink, over 300 miles of sand and lava and gravel, until just short of the pass when the mules were too exhausted to pull them further. They buried the heavy mill machinery in the desert, made pack saddles and burned the wagons. There were six inches of snow on the pass which didn't bother them unduly, and spring had come to the San Joaquin Valley. The people feasted on deer meat before coming down to the settlements in the New Year of 1844. Chiles had reached Sutter's Fort on November 10.

I camped in the desert again, and a soft and sensuous wind from the south was moving the fine sand. With sunset the wind died and the air was cool. In the morning there were tracks of coyotes around the car.

I drove north to the White Mountains and the Bristlecone Forest but I coincided with the first day of hunting. It had been bows and arrows, now it was rifles, and Bristlecone was overrun with armed men. The trees failed to soothe me and, unlike the beautiful sequoias which they surpassed in age (the sequoias being less than 3,000 years old, the bristlecones over 4,000), these trees were grotesque and stunted.

I was happier in the Schulman Grove where the car park held only family cars and a flock of little birds like nuthatches that followed me twittering, while quiet and smiling people walked the shady trails, and somewhere in the depths Pine Alpha, 4,600 years old, stood unmarked and unremarked, and safe from souvenir hunters, although one wondered if it were quite safe.

The road goes to 11,000 feet at Bristlecone. Coming back I saw the wall of the Sierras in front, and the rays of the sun, striking upwards from behind the range, revealed two layers of brown haze that held a hint of red – brick-coloured courses with a blue space between. The smog was spreading east. Mankind was asphyxiating itself. The bristlecones would go first; the soft green needles wrapped round the stalks like foxes' brushes would turn brown and fall. I wondered how long it would take: 50 years? Ten?

Outside Big Pine I took the road east where a sign said 'No Roadside

Services for 109 miles'. That suited me; I was in a savage mood, too. I passed a couple of ranches, Deep Springs and Oasis, and came to the long pale deserts where there were no more houses and dust devils spiralled round the gaunt brown hills.

Since Walker Pass I'd travelled the half of a great circle and now to my west were the backs of the mountains that fronted on Death Valley: the Grapevines and the Funerals. I was approaching, as I should do, from the east. Already I'd passed two roads going down to the valley, but they were the wrong ones.

Outside Beatty I stopped to take a picture of Bare Mountain, striated in reds and pinks and cinnamon. A few yards back from the road was a mound about seven feet long weighted down with large stones. Surely a grave, but unmarked. A new grave?

We came down the northern fringe of the Amargosa Desert to Forty Mile Canyon and intercepted the last of our trails. We turned with it, south towards Death Valley.

18

THE SAND WALKING COMPANY

No one had meant to come to Death Valley; it was discovered by accident. The people concerned had assembled on the site of Provo in Utah. When Manly floated down the Green River, abandoned his boats and walked towards Salt Lake City, he came out at Provo. There he met Bennett, an old friend whom he'd intended to travel with originally but whom he'd missed on the Missouri. The emigrants were assembling to follow the Old Spanish Trail to the gold mines. This trail skirted the Great Basin on the south, running from Santa Fé to the coastal settlements of southern California, and was utilised by those emigrants who arrived late at Salt Lake City and did not want to risk an early winter on the Sierras.

In 1849 a big train was waiting to start. They called themselves the Sand Walking Company, which was a corruption of San Joaquin and, as it transpired, dreadfully appropriate. They were guided by a Mormon called Captain Hunt.

They left Provo in October with 107 wagons, 250 people and 1,000 head of cattle. It was too large a caravan and they were slow. Captain Hunt took a short-cut, abandoned it after two days, and their faith in him weakened. At the southern rim of the Great Basin they were overtaken by nine mounted Mormons led by a Captain Smith who had a map indicating every spring and camp on a new cut-off which would save time and miles and bring them out at the Walker Pass. A clergyman, the Rev. James Brier, was boyishly enthusiastic about the cut-off; Captain Hunt was opposed. The train split: seven wagons continued on the Old Spanish Trail with Hunt, nearly a hundred followed Smith.

They came to a steep escarpment which they named Mount Misery and where Smith was able to descend with his horses but where the wagons couldn't follow. Seventy of them turned back to the original trail while the others sent scouts ahead to look for a way round the escarpment. Meanwhile Smith, well in advance, thought better of the terrain he was encountering and looped back to the Old Spanish Trail. Behind him – and ignorant of his retreat, their scouts having been successful – the 27 wagons that contained the nucleus of the Sand Walking Company started across the deserts towards Death Valley.

There was a large proportion of young single men in this train: one, a group which called itself the Jayhawkers; another, a party from Georgia, and one from Mississippi; also a number of family wagons including those of the Bennetts with whom Manly travelled, and John Rogers, one of the men who had floated down the Green with him. In addition there was the Rev. Brier with his wife Juliet, and three sons aged five, seven and nine.

Their journey across the Utah and Nevada deserts was difficult – dry, rough and hard. That line can no longer be followed because for about 200 miles it goes through Nellis Nuclear Testing Site. This section ends with Forty Mile Canyon that comes down to the Amargosa Desert. By the time they reached here they had mostly split into their original groups and taken different ways. Some of these were better than others.

The Georgians and some Jayhawkers came down Forty Mile Canyon and many of them, including the Briers who were trailing in the rear, left their wagons there. The sand was so deep that the oxen couldn't pull, even downhill. Most of their possessions were abandoned, of course. Forty years later a miner found Juliet's table silver and returned it to her.

When they reached the Amargosa (which is the last desert before Death Valley) they found the water in the Amargosa River so alkaline that it made them ill. The Georgians burned the rest of their wagons, killed the oxen and smoked the meat, then started west for Death Valley on foot, over Indian Pass.

The Briers left the Georgians and went south, joining those Jayhawkers who had taken a route east of Forty Mile Canyon and which was a smoother line. They had come through with all their wagons but they had been without water for five days. They were saved by a snowstorm. It was December and the few inches of snow that fell on this country meant life, not death. It came too late for some of the oxen; they were slaughtered and the wagons burned on the gradient out of the Amargosa Valley.

Coming along behind were the family wagons. Three middle-aged men had joined the families when the young bachelors went their own way because they felt they couldn't keep up. One of them, Captain Culverwell, was an old seaman and not very fit. The Rev. Brier had insisted on tagging along behind the Georgians and the Jayhawkers despite the reluctance of the younger men to have him.

James Brier was unpopular to start with. Far back on the plains a gallows of wagon tongues was set up and he was publicly taken to task: 'You have been conducting yourself in a very cruel, heartless, and shameful manner towards your wife. You compel her to do all the drudgery while you do nothing. Well, we have decided to hang you if you do not do your share of the work, drive the cattle, attend to them, get the wood and such things.' This was said by a man called Abraham Owen. Brier left that train at the first opportunity. Conversely, Juliet

Brier, who weighed 100 pounds and yoked the oxen while her husband prepared his sermons, was adored by the men. They called her Little Mother. She was thirty-six. In her early pictures she looks rather naïve, a little wary, and stubborn as a mule. She decided early on that she was going to carry this family on her shoulders, and that only death could stop her.

The Briers were packing when they reached the Amargosa and now, instead of yoking oxen, they had to be loaded each morning, unloaded at night, and herded in between. The eldest boy, being nine years old, helped with the herding.

The company had lost twelve young men when they first saw Telescope Peak. Apparently, thinking that it was the Sierras, this group abandoned their wagons and taking only enough food for ten days set out on foot. But Telescope Peak is above Death Valley and they had three more deserts and two more ranges to cross before they reached the Sierras, 'and the last we saw of them they were going up the blue mountain'. Years later Manly met two of this group, Pinney and Savage, working in the mines, but when he questioned them they could only weep. In the 1860s miners found nine skeletons huddled behind a windbreak in the Argus Mountains, and there is an Indian tale of a white man who, having broken his leg as he climbed out of Death Valley, was shot by his companions to avoid a slow death.

We must have camped quite close to where the Jayhawkers burned their wagons. That night a new moon hung in the sky and the air blew soft from the west. I went to bed early because I would have to be up before sunrise. Even the Indians shunned the heat of Death Valley and said that no man should go far there who could not sleep in the shade of his arrows. I knew that the temperature could reach 130 degrees in the summer; I didn't know what it would be in September so I would get up early, prepared for the worst.

Next morning wasn't hot at first but then the pass below Pyramid Peak was at 3,000 feet and there was a breeze. The peak was like raw beef in the sunrise: a bare and ragged mountain with tortuous gullies. The pass was merely a dip in a stony plain where even the sage looked dead.

At the boundary of the national monument I found a solitary kiosk – nothing else, only the desert and the bony mountains. I pressed a button and a fruity voice started to impart information. I listened for a while and drove away, leaving it to instruct the desert.

A side road took me to Dante's View. There would be two ways of approaching the valley at this point: as they did, slowly, intimately, unaware of what would be revealed when they broke clear of the hills; and by way of the scenic viewpoint where all was revealed at once. This was one occasion when I might have my cake and eat it. I went to Dante's View.

We climbed. We drove for 13 miles and came out at a point nearly 6,000 feet above a pale valley where the wide salt flats were smeared with cloud shadows and the Panamints stood on the other side. They walked across that valley – although the reality of the crossing didn't strike home to me until I was down there myself, feeling the ground through the soles of my boots. Their shoes had disintegrated long ago, and the moccasins they made from rawhide would have known every pebble in Death Valley. Nancy Kelsey went barefooted, but the Sierras had been sandy. This was a stony desert.

It is a long valley, about 100 miles, and only three or four miles wide at its narrowest. The Black Mountains, where I stood, had a steep escarpment, but below the Panamints great washes of scree fanned from the mouths of their canyons. That wall across the way, culminating in Telescope Peak, was over 11,000 feet high, and stood even higher above the valley where the largest salt pan was 282 feet below sea level.

There was no colour in distant views, a lot in the near mountains, and the immediate foreground could be astonishing. The Panamints were grey, the valley off-white and grisaille, but the Funeral Mountains in the north were red, and in one place a toxic green tip tailed like a spill of icing sugar under a rusty cliff. Death Valley is full of old mines.

I came back to the main road which was much lower, and the wind had died. A few miles towards the valley I stopped in the dry wash of Furnace Creek where its banks were the colour of old teeth. In the wet the flood that poured down here had made a wide channel and the ground had baked like concrete round the stones. Down this dry bed on Christmas Eve Juliet walked in the starlight, carrying the eldest boy on her back because his strength had given out. He must have weighed nearly as much as she. The little ones trailed beside her asking for water. The oxen had gone ahead on their own and she had to get down on her knees and crawl, feeling with her hands for their tracks. Perhaps the ground was soft after the recent snowstorm, otherwise it would have taken no imprint except in chance pockets of gravel and sand. The ground was hard on the knees. I looked up to see the Panamints on the other side of the valley. It was fortunate she came down Furnace Creek in the dark and couldn't see that wall ahead.

At midnight she came round a rock and found her husband sitting by a fire. 'Is this the camp?' she asked. It was six miles farther. They reached it at three o'clock on Christmas morning.

I drove to it under a lowering sky. A thicket of greenery extended down the side of the road, and where it started was a jungle of palms and willow, of grass and golden rod. This was Travertine Springs.

They killed an ox since it was Christmas and that night one of the Jayhawkers asked Juliet if it wouldn't be wiser for her to remain at the spring with the children until he should send back for her, presumably meaning when they reached the settlements and could return with food. It was curiously worded for a man not her husband, but Juliet ignored that and concerned herself with the other implication: 'No. I have never been a hindrance, I have never kept the company waiting, neither have my children, and every step I take will be towards California.'

Manly, scouting ahead of the family wagons, came on the Briers alone at Travertine Springs and was astonished to find the father lecturing his three small boys on the advantages of an early education. Manly spent the night with them, without a blanket, but he was used to that by now. Crossing the other deserts, he had often gone ahead with a spy glass to climb mountains and reconnoitre the land, and he had often been caught by darkness and slept out.

In the morning he let them get away first although no doubt he would have helped them load the oxen. There was nothing lazy about Manly. When they'd gone he scratched around and found and ate the delectable bacon rinds they'd thrown away, then he went on to overtake the Jayhawkers and find out what they were doing.

There were Indians in Death Valley when the white people arrived. They were Shoshonis. They were so terrified of the strangers that they fled to the Panamints but left behind one blind old man. Manly came on him curled up in a depression but didn't disturb him. Others watched him catching beetles. One story says that he was buried, all but his head, so perhaps he was demented and thought thus he might escape attention. When the Indians returned after the emigrants had gone he had died, probably of neglect.

Travertine Springs are little more than a mile from the valley floor and now, as we rolled down the slight gradient and the banks of the wash opened out, I was staring at the Panamints and wondering where the pass was. The modern traveller is side-tracked by the Spanish exuberance of Furnace Creek Inn, by the date palms of the ranch, but when I'd done with these, I could see that some miles up the valley on the other side the mountains fell back, or there was another range. The pass would be in behind there.

I was given every assistance by the monument staff; from a place to work, and food (dates from the palms) to the key of a closed gate. It was the summer season still and parts of the valley were not open to tourists.

I pitched my tent under some tamarisks in a huge dusty campground. The temperature at midday was 107 degrees and the water in the cold taps was hot. They told me the ground temperature had reached 201 degrees once when the air temperature was 128 degrees.

In the afternoon thunder growled round the valley and showers drifted across the face of the Panamints. In places the roads were wet. I saw one or two spots on the windscreen but there was never enough for one to jump out and know the delight of cool rain sluicing down the skin.

In the evening the silent lightning played over the northern hills and the wind sighed in the tamarisks. The night was all sound and flickering light, and through it in the small hours came the song of the coyotes.

The air was cool before the dawn and there were enough clouds to obscure the sun. In the north they trailed black skirts across a sky green as a duck's egg.

I kept a wary eye on the sun. On the mornings that it came up without clouds I would revel in the last few moments of bliss: now the light was on the foot of the Panamints, then on Tucki Mountain but had not yet reached the tamarisks. It didn't appear to move across the valley because I was level with it. In any case, it streaked across the flats. There was no penumbra; its breath and its light came simultaneously – and there was no shade. Tamarisks are very feathery.

I looked at the sights: the maze of golden gullies below Zabriskie Point, rock formations along Artist's Drive, fretted by the wind to a semblance of badly-made lace above screes in pastel shades – and that laboratory tone of verdigris. The colours were best at dawn, not sunset; they needed a stark light, not a golden one. But sunset, I realised, is not reflected in salt, which retains its fish-belly white in all circumstances.

I drove across the valley to the west side. This was the way the family wagons went. Manly had overtaken the Jayhawkers in the north, looked at their proposed route and returned to the families (who were now in camp at Travertine Springs), to tell them that the northern way looked so strenuous that the Jayhawkers were burning the last of their wagons.

Indians had been shooting at the oxen in Furnace Creek Wash and one of the animals had to be slaughtered. Manly said that this was probably retaliation because back along the trail the emigrants had stolen squashes from Indian gardens. Whether Bennett and his friend Arcane were worried about spending another night at the spring, fearing an Indian attack, or whether they took umbrage at Manly, they wouldn't wait for him to scout the route but pressed on, south down the valley.

After a few miles they started to cross to the other side and came to ground like frost-heaved soil. It was salt with a coating of dust. From even a short distance away the expanse looked level and innocuous but, closer, it was fretted with pinnacles and honeycombed underfoot, resounding metallically to the tread. There was a fear of breaking through and lacerating their legs for the shards would be like fractured earthenware. Nothing lived here. There was no vegetation of any kind, not even lichen.

In the middle was the river, which looked like baked salt, not like ice because that gleams. This was matt. Now an earth dike has been thrown across it which carries the road. I stopped, stepped down the bank and on to the salt. I went straight through the soft crust making deep holes in which there was something liquid. I tasted it. Brine. As my boots dried they were encrusted with white crystals.

When the wagons came to the river Manly took off his boots and waded ahead, sounding with a stick. Once across it, and the shattered crystalline crust, they came to the great scree fans at the foot of the Panamint canyons and turned south. Here Bennett, Arcane and Manly made another bad mistake. All the way across the deserts they had been experiencing great vicissitudes while travelling parallel with the Old Spanish Trail but the worst irony came here: they were looking for a way over the Panamints when the main trail was only a few days' journey to the south.

Unaware of this, they camped at a spring below a canyon and six men, Bennett's and Arcane's teamsters and two middle-aged men called Isham and Fish, left to go back up the valley and join the Jayhawkers. The rest of them tried to get the wagons up a canyon, failed, and returned with the oxen exhausted. The bottoms of the canyons are nothing more than rising boulder fields which go on for five miles to their headwalls. The wall at the head of the canyon where they made their attempt was between 5,000 and 6,000 feet high.

They went into camp and sent Manly and Rogers ahead not only to reconnoitre the route but to try to reach the settlements and return with food.

It was early in January that the two men left, probably going up Six Springs Canyon. They took very little food, and an astonishing comment on the condition of the cattle is the fact that they could pack seven-eighths of an ox's flesh into their knapsacks. They took no blanket and slept huddled together with the temperature around freezing. The first night they found water near the head of the canyon; the next day they reached the crest of the Panamints and looked back across all the country they had travelled over during the past two months. Northwards and close at hand was Telescope Peak while to the west range after range stood across their route.

They descended to the Panamint Valley, which is another desert, crossed it to a col between the Slate and Argus Ranges and found a trail. The Jayhawkers had already escaped from Death Valley and looped south. Mr Fish (who had left the family wagons two weeks before) had joined them but been unable to keep up. His body lay unburied on the col.

Manly and Rogers came down to the next desert, the Searles Valley, and, leaving the trail, had a bad 24 hours crossing the Argus Range. They continued to travel by moonlight, sucking pebbles, and in the dawn found a little ice. After sucking it they were able to eat some of their dried meat. Stephens, of the Jayhawkers, said of thirst: 'there is no punishment that has any comparison. It is the most agonising suffering possible and the feeling is indescribable. Our tongues would be swollen, our lips crack, and a crust would form on our tongue and roof of mouth that could not be removed. The body seemed to be dried through and through, and there wouldn't be a drop of moisture in the mouth.'

Manly and Rogers caught up with the Jayhawkers that night, at Indian Wells close to Walker Pass. They learned that the Briers were – as usual – somewhere in the rear (they may have missed the Briers when they left the trail as they climbed out of the Searles Valley). Next day they passed some more Jayhawkers, and then came up with the four teamsters who had left the family wagons. They were starving, so Manly and Rogers gave them some food before striking out into the Mojave Desert.

On the day that they feasted on a crow and a hawk they descended to good water and the Santa Clara River. Manly started to have trouble with his knee but they kept going through jungly undergrowth, past the San Francisquito Rancho, to the settlements. There they bought food, three horses and a one-eyed mule and started back for Death Valley.

The horses gave out in the steep canyons and had to be abandoned but the little mule continued, carrying most of the provisions. In one place she had to traverse a gully wall. They unloaded her and put her on a rope. 'Carefully and steadily she went along, selecting a place before putting down a foot, and when she came to the narrow ledge leaned gently on the rope, never making a sudden start or jump, but cautiously as a cat moved slowly along. There was now no turning back for her. She must cross this narrow place over which I had to creep on hands and knees, or be dashed down fifty feet to a certain death. When the worst place was reached she stopped and hesitated, looking back as well as she could. . . .'

Manly felt the whole journey epitomised by this moment: everything that they'd done and everything that could happen. He and Rogers might do as the teamsters had done, walk down to the settlements, but the fate of the families hung on the load the little mule was carrying, and on her move across a hiatus in a line of holds on a gully wall: 'I could not help bursting in tears. . . . Finally Rogers said, "Come Lewis" and I gently pulled the rope, calling the little animal, to make a trial. She smelled all around and looked over every inch of the strong ledge, then took one careful step after another, over the dangerous place. Looking back I saw Rogers with a very large stone in his hand, ready to "holler" and perhaps kill the poor beast if she stopped. But she crept along trusting to the rope to balance, till she was halfway across, then another step or two, when calculating the distance closely she made a spring and landed on a smooth bit of sloping rock below, that led up to the highest crest of the precipice, and safely climbed to the top.'*

They came down to Death Valley and camped by the spring at the foot of the canyon. They couldn't see the wagons and felt sure that their people had been massacred by the Indians. With their own rich load they were equally vulnerable. They were very wary as they followed a wagon trail up the valley, and after about eight miles they came on the body of the old seaman, Captain Culverwell, with his little canteen beside him. He appeared to have died peacefully.

They sighted the wagons about noon, still a long way off. As they approached they let the mule forage ahead, trusting that she would warn them of danger. They noticed that there were only four wagons where there had been seven when they left.

At 100 yards there was still no sign of life, but nor could they see any marks of disturbance, such as bodies or burned goods. They fired a shot and watched carefully. Nothing happened for a moment and then a man stood up from where he'd been lying in the shade of a wagon, waved his arms above his head and shouted: 'The boys are back! The boys are back!' They had been gone 26 days.

The three missing wagons were those of the Wades, the Earharts and one that belonged to a group of single men. The Wades were a man and wife, four children and one or two teamsters. The Wades were English and throughout the journey had remained aloof and seldom joined in the group discussions. After Manly and Rogers left they started south on their own. They sent scouts ahead to look for water and grass and to put up smoke signals when they found them. So they escaped from Death Valley, reached the Mojave River and the Old Spanish Trail and came down to the settlements about five weeks after they had left the spring under the Panamints. It is thought that they took a route over Wingate Pass which is only 2,000 feet high and attains that altitude gradually over 30 miles. It is the route the twenty-mule teams took in the eighties, each team drawing 36 tons of borax from Furnace Creek to Mojave.

The Wade wagon was followed by the Earharts, who were a family of men unaccompanied by women, by the third wagon and by men on foot. All these people reached the settlements although it is less certain, apart from the Wades, that they got their wagons through. As for

* *Death Valley in '49* by William Lewis Manly. Chalfant Press, California.

Captain Culverwell, he had gone after the Wades but he had no food and they had none to spare. He turned back and collapsed before he could regain Bennett's camp. He had never been in good health.

At the time that Manly and Rogers returned, no one had any idea that the escape route lay to the south, and they started to make preparations to cross the Panamints. Of course the wagons had to be abandoned. They sewed panniers and made all the harness: shoulder straps, hip straps, breast straps and breeching. They had no buckles or rings so straps had to be fastened with knots after pulling them as tight as possible, one man on each side of an animal. The loads were dried beef, blankets, bedding, a light tent and two water kegs.

The doyen of the oxen was Old Crump. He was to carry the four children: the babies in panniers made of hickory shirts, the two oldest on his back, holding to the cinch. There were no bridles. The two women were each to ride an ox.

Mrs Arcane was a city woman and on the morning of departure she dressed in her best clothes and trimmed her finest hat with extra ribbons that streamed behind her. She put her little boy in his good suit and then everyone followed her example, wearing their best and most serviceable clothes, leaving their rags for the Indians.

They moved out on a warm morning in early February. The mule led the way, then came the oxen – about five of them – and the dog Cuff. Most of the dogs were left on the plains where the alkaline dust made their pads so sore that they couldn't walk, but Cuff, although crippled, had refused to be left behind.

Everything went well for the first few miles then a pack slipped, the ox became frightened, then frenzied, and its panic infected the others. Mrs Bennett slipped off her mount and grabbed her baby from one of Old Crump's panniers, Arcane scooped his boy out of the other, the two older children jumped clear. Old Crump stood quite still.

Meanwhile Mrs Arcane's ox was bucking and kicking like a bronco, bawling at the top of its voice, its rider clinging desperately to the cinch, her ribbons flying behind her 'like the streamers from a mast-head'. Eventually she was thrown but wasn't hurt, and it was Mrs Bennett who looked as if she were about to have a stroke and had to be settled on a blanket and comforted. All the time the little mule, who had stepped aside when the circus started, looked on in astonishment.

The loads had to be collected and the harness mended, so they were forced to camp after only four miles. Rogers took a shovel and went to bury Captain Culverwell to prevent the animals panicking a second time.

Old Crump, steady as the mule, continued to carry the children but the women walked, complaining a great deal but hardening a little as time went on. When they came to descend the place where the mule climbed the gully wall, they built up a pile of sand below and pushed the oxen over, Manly pulling on a rope attached to their horns so that their necks should be extended and not broken. The only damage was a few cuts. When she was pushed, the mule jumped and landed on her feet.

They crossed the col where Mr Fish's body lay, and a few miles farther, at the head of the Searles Valley, came on the grave of Mr Isham. They were to learn that Isham, who like Fish was in his fifties, had not been able to keep up with the Jayhawkers, that they had gone back to him with water, but he had died as they raised him to drink.

The Manly–Bennett party continued on the Jayhawkers' trail towards the settlements.

Back in Death Valley I picked up the Jayhawkers at McLean's Spring where Manly had found them burning their wagons before attempting to cross the Panamints north of Telescope Peak. The spring had bad water and thin grass and they were considering their bleak prospects when the Georgians came down from Indian Pass. They had seen snow high on what came to be called Pinto Peak and so the decision was made to cross the mountains just below the snow and thus be sure of water.

The Briers came in to the spring and the Georgians moved off, due west across the valley. Then the Jayhawkers left and finally the Briers with a herd of oxen. People didn't abandon the oxen that were not slaughtered immediately; they gave them to the Briers. This may not have been altruism, for if a man became hungry he could always turn back to Mrs Brier bringing up the rear with her beef on the hoof, such as it was.

I went north up the valley on a stormy afternoon with the dust whirling across the salt pans and funnel-shaped clouds trailing rain that evaporated in the hot wind before it touched the ground. I passed the Sand Dunes, and where the modern road turns south-west at Stovepipe Wells their track went west, sidling away from Pinto Peak – a line taken to avoid the worst of two great scree fans but which meant a dry camp at the foot of the Cottonwood Mountains. However, here they struck an Indian trail that led them along the base of the range in the direction they wanted to go. It was marked with cairns, each with a white stone on top. That meant a trail leading to water and they followed it to Emigrant Springs.

I camped nearby and before the sun rose I went back to the Sand Dunes. I couldn't get the scale of them until a jackrabbit got up and lolloped over a crest about 30 feet above me. The sun came up from behind the Funerals and the dunes were breath-taking: swept by the wind into graceful arcs and whorls, and serpentine ridges that swooped into troughs where there might grow one lonely bush of creosote, its shadow reaching long arms like an animation in the dawn. Apparently empty, the region teemed with life, for everywhere there were the marks of little animals. Sidewinders had left their curiously discrete traces, each imprint unconnected with the next; there were marks of lizards, of something like a huge centipede, of a small cloven hoof. A sidewinder had climbed a dune but been forced to tack twice; there was the deeply indented curve made by the heaviest part of the body, and places where it had slipped in the sand.

Something large and grey and furry melted back into a hole. The sun grew hot. In the lowest depressions there were clay pans jointed like crazy paving, and burrows and slits and crevices, nearly all with tracks leading to them.

I went to Titus Canyon to see the petroglyphs that the Indians have pecked beside a spring. The canyon was an irregular cut with walls 1,000 feet high so that where at one moment the sun would be blinding, at the next I ran into unfathomable gloom. Titus is a deep wound in the earth, the trail squeezed in the bottom like extruded toothpaste, but Mosaic Canyon is wide and shallow and hot, ostensibly gay and innocent, until I realised that I was starting to flag and that where I had felt the heat at the road-end, an hour later in the wide upper reaches of the canyon I no longer noticed it. When this happened I went back to the narrows, sprawled in the shade under the largest overhang and, with the water bottle beside me, watched the whiptail lizards. And so, I thought, a lost emigrant might have watched from the shade, his empty canteen beside him. Had women been lost here? It's said that one train came into Death Valley and never found a way out, that the wind shifted the sand and un-covered a skeleton with a few shreds of calico attached.

The whiptail pauses in its jerking run across the pink marble and stares over your shoulder interminably. You pull yourself to your feet. This place is hypnotic; you could relax too much.

On my last evening I followed a storm up the valley while another came along behind. The Grapevine Range was purple under the clouds that almost, but not quite, touched the tops. The rock was burnished like copper in the sun between the storms. Puddles lay along the roads and without much hope I looked for flash floods.

At the campground of Mesquite Flat the trees were shining, green and wet. The next storm came up the Grapevines and a rainbow stood between the desert and the mountains framing the lightning as it stabbed the crests. In the night I got up and sat in the car to watch the rods gouge and tear, rending the world. Sometimes the lightning struck in several places at once, a mile or so apart; occasionally it flashed upwards from one point while light ran along a crest to streak off the next summit. There were discharges between cloud and cloud, sudden flashes with no rods, and often several flashes at the same time from different points of the compass. Colour was achingly vivid. And all the time the crickets sang. I wondered if the snakes were out, soaking up the sparse rain. In a lull I listened for water in the wash but heard only the crickets and the wind in the mesquite.

Next day I went south and west past the Sand Dunes and Stovepipe Wells and up the modern Towne Pass road to the place where the emigrants came over from the Cottonwoods and crossed the scree to Emigrant Springs. Now they had a choice of two feasible routes, Towne Pass or Emigrant Canyon. They took neither but went up a depression that came to be known as Jayhawker Canyon that brought them out 500 feet below Pinto Peak, where they camped. They had been making for the snow and here, at Summit Camp, snow fell. And it was here that a man came in with enough silver to make a gunsight, and ever since people have been on Pinto Peak searching for the Lost Gunsight Lode.

They split forces; the Georgians descended due west to the Panamint Valley, crossed it and went over the ragged end of the Argus Range to come out north of Walker Pass by which they reached the settlements. The Jayhawkers started after the Georgians but when they reached the Panamint Valley they turned south looking for water under the back of the Panamints. Five men stayed with the Briers. Juliet had chosen a route to the south.

I drove up Emigrant Canyon to Harrisburg Flat under Pinto Peak. It was a lonely road haunted by an old burro stallion. There were many of these on the Panamints, feral burros, descendants of donkeys turned out by the prospectors.

South of the flats vast sage-covered slopes rose to the summit of Wildrose Peak, with Telescope looming behind. The road dives into the big canyon under Wildrose where the Briers didn't go, wisely choosing a shallower depression to the north but missing a lovely spring, now a jungle of tamarisks and cottonwoods, oleanders and palms.

The road comes down the dry Panamint Valley, a gloomy place on a hot evening, shadowed on the west while the sunlit slopes to the east look strangely bleak. Far away at the foot of a canyon are the buildings of the Indian reservation on the site of Horse Bones Camp. When the emigrants reached that place they thought it was the start of civilisation until they noticed that the bits of harness lying among the old huts and the skeletons of horses were all of native make – and Indians could live anywhere.

In the middle of the Panamint Valley a sign said 'Possible Sonic Booms for next 14 Miles'. I was back in civilisation.

At Horse Bones Camp the men who had descended with the Briers left to go over the northern Argus and catch up with the Georgians. The Jayhawkers and the Briers drifted south. We followed through the brilliant evening, stopping to stare up all the canyons that came down from the Panamints, wondering which one Manly descended, and where the place was that they pushed the oxen down the wall. It gave one an odd feeling to look up those ravines flooded with the westering sun and to think that four men, two women and their children had scrambled down one of them, accompanied by a mule, five oxen and a dog.

It was 16 miles from Horse Bones Camp to the exit from the valley. The Jayhawkers and the Briers made several false casts before they decided that the col between the Slate and the Argus Ranges was the way out. They may have been deterred by its steepness. Mr Fish reached the top only by holding to an ox's tail and got no farther than the summit. That was where he died; the others pushed on and a few miles down the other side Mr Isham died.

The view south when they'd crossed the col was appalling: another desert, and a lake some 12 miles distant showing the unmistakable lividity of brine. For a moment when I saw it I knew their utter hopelessness and then I remembered that I'd filled the water container at Emigrant Springs. I turned right at that and bumped along a track towards Argus Peak, camping close to the place where Mr Isham died. They camped at Providence Spring, a mile or two farther on.

I slept lightly but easily, waking often. The clouds were like ice floes, pale round the moon. As it sank an animal called with long, long howls.

All the emigrants who came down into the Searles Valley left it as quickly as possible, crossing the Argus Range by an Indian trail that went up a canyon close to Providence Spring. The area through which they travelled is now restricted and I drove down the Searles Valley, through the borax town of Trona and turned west along the southern boundary of the restricted area. At Inyokern, just short of Walker Pass, I picked up the trail and followed it to Red Rock Canyon.

This was southern California – dry, hot, a place of Joshua trees and that strange and friable rock that is a feature of the southern deserts. At Red Rock it formed mazes of holes and tubes and caves which coalesced for long enough to form depressions that might be termed gullies, and corners that might pass for buttresses. The material was a little too hard for mud and a little too soft for sandstone. There was one tall cliff with a carved façade: grey columns in stages layered by crimson ledges, and the whole fluted face capped by bubbling grey gargoyles. On top there was gravel and a few desert plants and a breeze, below there were Joshua trees and heat.

At the mouth of the canyon was Kane Spring on the edge of the

Mojave Desert. After Kane the emigrants went without water for 48 hours, until they found a muddy pool in a patch of willows. This is a new kind of desert; beyond the stumps of mesas it fades into infinity with no ranges to limit it, only the fag-end of the Sierras to the west, and the San Gabriel Mountains coming up.

After the spring in the willows they plodded on towards the south. Were the Jayhawkers thinking that they should be going west, as the Georgians had done, over the Walker Pass? A man called Robinson became very weak and they put him on a mule. In the evening as he approached the camp he slid to the ground and begged them to leave him. A quarter of an hour later, when they returned with water, he was dead. A Frenchman called Coverly wandered away in search of water and never returned. Fifteen years later he was found, by a party of surveyors, living with Indians.

Soledad was the last canyon. There was water in plenty, and trees. Manly, coming along behind, had been cheering the women on with his descriptions of sylvan charm and now he watched them drinking and staring at the water and drinking again.

On the skyline of the canyon great rocks stand like gritstone edges, and the canyon suddenly becomes grand with steep slopes up which the road climbs to round a corner, and below is the Santa Clara Valley. Manly came round the spur and 'there before us was a beautiful meadow of a thousand acres, green as a thick carpet of grass could make it, and shaded with oaks, wide branching and symmetrical, equal to those of an English park, while all over the low mountains that bordered it on the south and over the broad acres of luxuriant grass was a herd of cattle numbering many hundreds if not thousands.'

The valley is now full of fruit farms. I was driving along when I saw a sign indicating an historic marker. It was on the other side of the road and difficult to get across with the sun in my eyes and the valley having its small rush hour with the workers going home from the farms. But I edged out into the traffic and in a lull slipped across to the far verge.

Under a canopy of shade trees, with a glimpse of sunlit walls in the depths, I stood and stared at a plaque or a sign or an image in my mind over a century old. It was the San Francisquito Rancho. We had reached the settlements.

EPILOGUE

WHAT DID PEOPLE do when a journey like this was over? Prosaically and immediately, they ate too much, but a doctor, warned of their arrival, was on his way, and treated this new form of suffering that could have proved fatal.

The Rev. Brier started a hotel. Manly worked for him for a while, until he recovered his strength. Juliet had three more children, all girls. They inherited their father's straight brows and their mother's rounded chin. In the family portraits Juliet still looks diffident and Brier looks like a pugnacious and ageing boxer. Alone and perhaps at the age of fifty, Juliet loses all wariness, all diffidence, and becomes hauntingly beautiful, with hooded eyes. She lived until she was ninety-nine.

Taking the little one-eyed mule, Manly went prospecting but he never made a fortune and he was always on the move, opening a store, doing a little cattle dealing. He returned east by way of Panama but didn't stay, coming back to California, again by the isthmus. Some years after his epic journey through the deserts he was riding in the San Joaquin Valley when he came on Old Crump feeding with a herd of cattle. Fat and sleek, the ox allowed himself to be petted. His current owner knew the animal's history and would neither sell him nor allow him to be worked, 'for he knew the faithful part he performed in the world, and respected him for it'.

Mrs Bennett died not long after she had her fifth child. Bennett gave the baby to another family and with his remaining children set off overland to Utah, to Idaho, to Nevada. The dog Cuff had disappeared soon after they reached California. He was a good hunting dog and it was thought he had been stolen.

Lienhard, who wrote his book when in his fifties, worked for Sutter, first laying out vegetable gardens at the fort and then conducting his employer's family from Switzerland to California. The experience must have unsettled him for he went back to Europe, bought an estate near Zurich and married a Swiss girl. But the new country called to him and, only ten years after the Swiss boys drove from the Missouri to Sutter's Fort, he took his family to the States and settled in Illinois.

To pick out a few of them is to be partial; there were many less well educated, less articulate, who left no record – although we would have heard of Manly through other people, and all we know of Nancy Kelsey is what other people wrote. One tries to be fair but we all need heroes, and heroes we had: Manly, Lienhard, Nancy Kelsey, Juliet Brier, Tamsen Donner, Stanton, Schallenberger, the Indians. There must have been many heroes among the Indians.

I fell into the trap of thinking that the desert regions were un-inhabited, but every region I travelled through was known before the white man saw it. The high mountains would have been empty of people in winter, Death Valley in summer, but they all had their Indian trails, and even the desert has springs. The wilderness was alive and wonderful; it is so still. It is the greatest asset of any people: inordinately powerful and precious, and equally vulnerable.

So far as the white man was concerned, the American west was dis-covered by the hardest, roughest stoics that ever exploited natural resources in the service of fashion. All that is left of them is the part that matters: vitality. It has been inherited by people who with meticulous care are trying to repay the debt to the land. Between the two, the despoilers and the partisans, came the overlanders who were also extreme, the most extreme of them, but a little less resplendent as they plodded at two miles an hour into the eye of the sun.

They had their sadists too, and their martyrs. There were no saints, but a few saintly fools. There was stupidity, cruelty, and ignorance – but their compassion and their loyalty stopped with their breath. Women had children, their hostages to fortune, and so were forced to survive. Single men endured great discomfort (which can be a harder trial than danger) for the sake of people who had no claim on them other than humanity. Their fortitude was almost incomprehensible; they learned to accept grief and they learned how to cope with fear. Cold and sad but without panic, they took the measure of fear and walked through it, realising in the empty centre that there was nothing to be afraid of except death, and that was an old acquaintance and therefore could be dis-regarded. So they lived, and they survived, with dignity.

INDEX